FINDING WORK OVERSEAS

How To Books on Living & Working Abroad

Applying for a United States Visa
Become an Au Pair
Do Voluntary Work Abroad
Emigrate
Find a Job in Canada
Finding a Job in New Zealand
Finding Work Overseas
Find Temporary Work Abroad
Get a Job Abroad
Get a Job in America
Get a Job in Australia
Get a Job in Europe
Get a Job in France
Get a Job in Germany
Get a Job in Hotels & Catering
Get a Job in Travel & Tourism
Live & Work in America
Live & Work in Australia
Live & Work in France
Live & Work in Germany
Live & Work in the Gulf
Live & Work in Italy
Live & Work in Japan
Live & Work in New Zealand
Live & Work in Portugal
Live & Work in Spain

Living & Working in Britain
Living & Working in Canada
Living & Working in China
Living & Working in Hong Kong
Living & Working in the Netherlands
Living & Working in Saudi Arabia
Master Languages
Migrating to Canada
Obtaining Visas & Work Permits
Rent & Buy Property in France
Rent & Buy Property in Italy
Retire Abroad
Selling into Japan
Setting Up Home in Florida
Spend a Year Abroad
Study Abroad
Teach Abroad
Travel Round the World
Working Abroad
Working as a Holiday Rep
Working in Japan
Working in the Gulf
Working on Contract Worldwide
Working on Cruise Ships
Your Own Business in Europe

Other titles in preparation

The How To series now contains more than 150 titles
in the following categories:

Business Basics
Family Reference
Jobs & Careers
Living & Working Abroad
Student Handbooks
Successful Writing

Please send for a free copy of the latest catalogue for full details
(see back cover for address).

LIVING & WORKING ABROAD

FINDING WORK OVERSEAS

How and where to contact international
recruitment agencies, consultants and employers

Matthew Cunningham

NOW WE'RE HERE-
WHO WANTS TO
WORK ANYWAY

How To Books

Cartoon by Mike Flanagan

British Library Cataloguing in Publication Data
A catalogue record for this book is available from the British Library.

© Copyright 1996 by Matthew Cunningham.

First published in 1996 by How To Books Ltd, Plymbridge House, Estover
Road, Plymouth PL6 7PZ, United Kingdom. Tel: (01752) 202301.
Fax: (01752) 202331.

Note: The material contained in this book is set out in good faith for
general guidance and no liability can be accepted for loss or expense
incurred as a result of relying in particular circumstances on statements
made in the book. The laws and regulations are complex and liable to
change, and readers should check the current position with the relevant
authorities before making personal arrangements.

Produced for How To Books by Deer Park Productions.
Typeset by PDQ Typesetting, Stoke-on-Trent, Staffs.
Printed and bound by The Cromwell Press, Broughton Gifford, Melksham,
Wiltshire.

Contents

Preface

Most of us are excited by the thought of working and living abroad. Perhaps it's because of the prospects of thrilling new experiences, the challenges, a better way of life, the financial benefits of a higher and tax free salary. Whatever the reasons are, the fact is each year more and more people are travelling abroad and opting for the expatriate life style and, as the numbers of international job opportunities increase, so too does the demand for a wider range of skills.

The purpose of this book is to help individuals to find work abroad, by giving them useful guidance in drafting an effective curriculum vitae or CV and providing them with valuable information to accurately target potential employers, agencies and consultancies. To the speculative job seeker, these two activities are important and ultimately they can determine the end result – success or failure.

Part One explains how to write and present a CV and how to plan and manage a successful overseas job search campaign and gives practical advice on related expatriate issues, such as healthcare, finance, travel, dependants, social survival and other matters. Part Two provides information about more than 1,500 firms and offices offering job opportunities overseas.

Part Two is sub-divided into two sections, the first for those firms offering consultancy services and the second a mixture of recruitment agencies and non-agency employers. This is done so that the reader can easily locate specific consultancy and/or recruitment based services. Where possible, I have included telephone and facsimile numbers for firms based outside the United Kingdom. I have included the full international dialling code.

Matthew Cunningham

Part One
The Recruitment Process

HOW THE PROCESS WORKS

People are recruited for work overseas in two ways – directly by an employer or indirectly through an intermediary, that is, an agency or consultancy. The process varies depending on the urgency and administrative procedures of the employer and the host country. However, as a general rule the time-scale is measured in months rather than weeks, so be prepared!

Creating a target list

Once your CV is ready you can then identify companies to contact and create your target list. Think carefully about this, as proper selection guarantees a better response. Always send CVs to a specific person and if you are not sure, telephone each company on your target list and find out. The person you need to speak to may be a Human Resources or Personnel Manager/Officer, Recruitment Manager/Officer, Department Head, Recruitment Consultant etc.

If you get an opportunity to talk, gather as much information as possible. Try to form a clear picture of the job opportunities available now or of those planned for the future. Send your CV immediately after your conversation and without fail follow up by telephone three or four days afterwards.

Following up

The follow up gives you an excellent opportunity to gain more in-depth information. A vacancy may not exist now but you can gain useful advice or alternatively, your details may be retained for future possibilities. If you are talking to a recruitment agency or consultancy, another option is to ask the recruitment consultant to make a speculative approach to a client company on your behalf. Recruitment firms do this frequently, and are good at this type of approach. Often they successfully draw attention to candidates. In many cases, this type of initiative proves to be much more effective than a speculative approach made directly by the candidate.

In doing this, the recruiter simply takes the initiative, contacts a client by telephone or merely forwards your details, hoping to generate an interest in your application. It's a gamble, but recruiters know it is an excellent method of generating vacancies and it does work. Recruitment organisations like any other businesses are stimulated by profit. They earn fees from their clients when individuals are placed in work. Sometimes, and like most of us, recruiters need prompting, so never hesitate to offer suggestions. It will be appreciated.

Keeping in touch

A good recruitment organisation is a valuable asset and once you register your details with them, always keep in regular touch with them. Keep them informed of any relevant changes in your situation, new address and other contact details, newly acquired skills and qualifications. Research those companies which might potentially offer you employment and pass on the information to them. Think creatively, too. If you are a chef, don't limit your choices to hotels; there are many options, hospitals, large companies especially those in the oil and petrochemical industries, government ministries – the list of potential employers can be extensive.

THE CURRICULUM VITAE (CV)

Creating your Curriculum Vitae or CV is your next step and probably it is the most common starting point for every expatriate. If your application for work is in response to a specific vacancy, then the procedure is straightforward. However, if you are speculatively searching for opportunities, then a different approach is called for and success will depend on a number of factors. These will be discussed in detail throughout this section of the book.

A well written CV is crucial: it is your marketing brochure and, from the reader's point of view, it represents the main source of information about you. Your CV is likely to be the stepping stone to a new life and its role in obtaining that all important interview is beyond doubt.

Laying out your CV
Keep to a simple and uncomplicated layout and bear in mind all of the following points:

- Use good easily understood language.
- Maintain a logical and interesting pattern.

- Use only adequate technical terminology.
- Include all relevant career details.
- Keep pages to a minimum, three maximum but two preferable.
- Maintain a consistent presentation and use only black print on plain white paper.

And remember, for work overseas it is likely that the most influential reader of your CV speaks English as a second language!

The key headings and details

We all have difficulty deciding what information to include and exclude, but generally your CV should include the following headings and details:

Full contact and personal details
- name
- telephone and fax numbers – home and work
- full address
- date of birth
- marital status and dependants
- nationality.

Educational results and training courses completed

A full employment history
- List the most recent employment period first and subsequent periods in sequence.

List hobbies and interests

List two referees, but only if required

Where to start

Start with the difficult part, the employment history, listing each period of employment in sequence. Your current or most recent job should be described first. Highlight details of your job, the duties and responsibilities. Convey a sense of achievement, describe your role clearly, mention any improvements you successfully introduced to your area of responsibility, any significant challenge you met and any other significant contributions made to the company and its success.

A well thought out CV will have a positive impact on the reader. You will be judged by what is written, so keeping the reader's attention is

```
1. CONTACT & PERSONAL DETAILS

                    Curriculum Vitae
Name:                               Tel/Fax Nos:
Address:

Date of Birth:                      Nationality:

Marital Status
& Dependants:
```

A quarter of the front page is sufficient using this layout. When your work telephone number is given, be sure to stress that calls must be made confidentially.

```
CV – J. TUCKER                      Page 2 of 2
```

At the top of each additional page insert your name and page number, indicating the total number of pages, as shown above.

2. A BRIEF SUMMARY

I seek a position as Chief Facilities Engineer or similar. I am a professional mechanical engineer, with 15 years industry experience, specialising in facility maintenance.

Mention the type of job you seek and add a brief supporting statement, as shown above. This section must be the briefest mention of you, four or five lines is adequate.

3. EDUCATIONAL, TRAINING AND ADDITIONAL SKILLS

List all your relevant educational qualifications, starting with the most recent and listing others in sequence. List O/A Levels, GCEs, further & higher education, degrees, training courses and all other relevant skills.

4. EMPLOYMENT HISTORY

1 January 199X – 1 February 199X   *ABCDEF LTD*
Accountant   *London, UK*

List all the relevant details as described above. Try to keep the dates of employment in line with the name of your employer and your job title in line with the address. Limit the address to the name of the city or town and the abbreviated form of the relevant country if possible. Position the text immediately below without a gap and separate each employment period.

5. HOBBIES AND INTERESTS

List the most important first especially those which show a recreational interest in your work. For example, an accountant might be a treasurer of a local club or a carpenter might enjoy restoring antique furniture.

6. REFEREES

List two, but only if necessary or simply mention references can be supplied on request.

the key. To do this effectively, keep the information brief and to the point.

Once you have completed writing the details of your first employment period, the others will be easier to write. Help the reader by maintaining a consistent writing style and layout.

Avoid the danger of writing too much, but if possible describe the type of business briefly and your role within each organisation where you were employed. It helps, too, if you can give some indication of your future career plans.

At all costs, avoid the temptation to create fancy borders, shading and boxes; they can be confusing and seriously limit the full impact of your work.

Presentation is important

Most CVs are divided into five sections as shown on page 10. A handwritten CV is not advisable; it should be typed. Just staple the pages together. Plastic covers and professionally bound CVs are unnecessary. Although presentation is very much a personal choice, simplicity is of the essence. While creative layouts may look attractive remember recruiters require facts and since they review lots and lots of CVs, the all-important facts must stand out amongst the others, otherwise valuable opportunities can be lost.

Deciding on your CV presentation

Give a thought to how your CV is handled and processed and perhaps the motivation of the recruiter. It will be reviewed, categorised, duplicated, triplicated, cut and pasted and so on. It may be transmitted by facsimile or mailed. It will usually be dealt with urgently. Photocopy and fax machines are excellent pieces of technology, but they have their limitations. They produce the best copies from black print on plain white paper.

CONDUCTING THE JOB SEARCH

How to manage your job search

The international job market is defined by the needs of employers abroad in search of particular skills. Employers overseas are not exempt from the problems faced by their counterparts in the United Kingdom and Ireland. Businesses fail and are seriously affected by recession, inflation and market trends. Alternatively, they grow and expand proportionately to their market share, enter developing markets, find success and so on. Just like everything else in our world, the international jobs market is one of constant change and skills are subject to trends.

British and Irish workers are considered competent, well trained, hard working and exceptionally good value for money by most foreign employers. So if your skills and experience are required in the international work place, you might find a successful conclusion to your job search earlier than anticipated.

However, the speculative approach to finding work abroad requires organisation, careful planning and an awareness of a few simple guidelines. In the first instance you will find Part Two of this book an invaluable source of information. Use it to prepare your list of companies to target with your newly prepared or revised CV.

LIVING THE EXPATRIATE LIFE

Preparing to go

Depending on your personal circumstances, the preparation required before departure can range from allocating twenty minutes to pack a small suitcase and catch the airport bus, to something similar to organising a huge military operation, a logistics nightmare. Whatever your circumstances, be sure to allow adequate time to complete all your arrangements including extra time for unexpected problems. The following is a checklist of things to do, to help you plan for a trouble-free departure:

- Arrange a full health check and arrange a three month supply of current medicines.

- Discuss your contract and other important legal matters with a solicitor.

- Discuss your financial plans with an accountant, especially taxation legislation, offshore savings and investments.

- Make arrangements with your bank and building society for regular payments of standing orders, community tax, mortgage, and insurance premiums.

- Finalise travel arrangements.

- Shop for vital supplies.

- Liaise with your new employer to ensure all arrangements for your arrival are going to plan. Get full clarification of accommodation, furnishings, food, healthcare, transportation, education for dependants – the list is endless. What about books and equipment required for the job, protective clothing and equipment and tools?

- Plan carefully all the items you need to pack, including clothes and accessories, shortwave radio, photographic equipment and books.

Planning your personal finances

Probably the most important reason for working abroad is the money, but amassing vast sums does not come easily to most people. Self-discipline is the key. Without hesitation, you must establish a good practical saving routine and spending your hard earned money immediately will take a back seat. Expatriates tend to have an inordinate desire to spend. If you like the odd treat or perhaps buying unusual items, then saving might be difficult. The wisest expatriates save their money carefully. By all means spend it and enjoy it, but have a plan to return home showing a net profit. There are excellent advantages to earning large sums of money overseas and it is good sense to take professional advice from an accountant who is experienced and qualified to advise on offshore financial matters, savings and taxation.

You have arrived

Your first objective is to settle into your new home and place of work. It may take months to find a balance. It's difficult to cope with cultural differences, but persevere. Working and living abroad is not all fun and happiness; it's real life in a different location. But once you have integrated socially and become acclimatised to the changes in your new situation, it becomes your new home from home and hopefully for as long as necessary. Don't become a recluse. Go out and socialise and cultivate new and interesting friends.

Social survival is crucial to a long and happy expatriate life. To achieve successful integration, be aware of a new simple facts. Expatriates prefer to stay in any one place for long periods of time. That may sound surprising. After all it seems logical to associate mobility with travel overseas. However, there are disadvantages to moving around frequently. Moving on means starting all over again and having to go through the ordeal of resettling another time! This could be the reason why expatriates have an innate determination to survive and to stay put.

Do tread carefully in the early days of your new life abroad. Parents often advise their children 'to choose friends carefully'. When abroad and in the process of doing just that, these are indeed wise words and out there on the global streets of expatriate land, they have a real and true meaning. The better type of people to cultivate are individuals with a sensible non-excitable approach to life. Among your fellow expatriates, these type of people tend to be those who have been in the same place for a long time, years rather than months. To survive as an expatriate abroad means you have an exceptional understanding of the rules of self preservation. That's good and certainly the right company!

Eventually they will introduce you into other similar circles and then you can begin to get the best out of your new situation.

Find out about local clubs and business and activity groups. Visit your embassy or consulate and any other official representation. Get to know the people of your host country. This is a perfect opportunity to learn about another culture. Learn the language, the geography, sample the food, read about the way of life and benefit from the wealth of interesting things to learn and do.

Arrangements for your dependants

Your employer will usually provide for your contractually nominated dependants and may cover all educational, healthcare, accommodation and travel expenses. However, it might be wise to consider checking out the country first, perhaps staying alone for three months.

Dependants add complications. While husband and wife may be happy overseas, for example, the children may not like being away from home and miss their familiar surroundings and school friends. Also the facilities may not be adequate and therefore joining you is out of the question! Alternatively, having the family with you makes life much more enjoyable as an expatriate. All of the family will benefit especially if you are working and living in an interesting country, with good facilities, interesting countryside and lots of friends and things to do. Your greatest enemy is boredom. Avoid it and don't let it into your life. Keep busy and happy.

Travelling around

Possibly one of the best opportunities to travel is while working abroad. Usually employers offer their expatriate employees generous travel entitlement. Make the most of it; travel as often as you can afford and go as far as possible. See the world. The memories last a lifetime and when you eventually arrive home you will have a multitude of interesting stories to tell your family and friends.

Part Two Section 1
Consultancy Services

Accord Group Tyzack, 10 Hallam Street, London W1N 6DS, England. *Tel*: (0171) 580 2924. *Fax*: (0171) 631 5317.

Category: Search consultancy.

Recruitment specialty: Senior executive and management personnel for the financial services, manufacturing, consumer goods (FMCG), media, information technology (IT), telecommunications, sales and marketing specialty areas and sectors.

Locations: Asia, Australia, Canada, Europe, Far East, New Zealand, South America, United Kingdom and United States.

Acer Consultants Ltd, Chancellor Court, Occam Road, The Surrey Research Park, Guildford, Surrey GU2 5XS, England. *Tel*: (01483) 35000. *Fax*: (01483) 302961.

Category: Recruitment consultancy.

Recruitment specialty: Engineers – all professional disciplines including: environmental, civil and building structures, water, railways, highways and maritime. Project Managers – individuals with specialty experience of project management process. Technicians – individuals of HND, OND and NVQs educational levels with experience of CAD systems. Graduates – from various disciplines including those already mentioned.

Locations: Australia, Canada, Asia, Europe, Far East, Ireland, Middle East, New Zealand, South America, United Kingdom and United States.

ADA/Austin Knight BV, Donauweg 8d, 1043 AJ Amsterdam, Postbus 57176, 1040 BB Amsterdam, Netherlands. *Tel*: 00 312 0587 2666. *Fax*: 00 312 0611 1339.

Category: Recruitment advertising consultancy.

Recruitment specialty: Executive, management and technical in commercial, financial, industrial and public sectors.

Locations: Canada, Europe, United Kingdom and United States.

Additional information: Services offered to their clients are: recruitment advertising, search and selection, communications and business psychology.

Adamson & Partners Ltd, 10 Lisbon Square, Leeds LS1 4LY, England. *Tel*: (0113) 244 0939 or (0113) 244 1212. *Fax*: (0113) 242802.

Category: Recruitment consultancy.

Recruitment specialty: Senior executive personnel in the international financial and pharmaceutical sectors, as well as healthcare particularly technical appointments. Other specialty areas include senior executives for trade marks and patents.

Locations: Canada, Europe, Far East, Ireland, Middle East, Near East, South America, United Kingdom and United States.

Adderley Featherstone Plc, Bowcliss Court, Bowcliss Hall, Bramham, Leeds, West Yorkshire LS23 6LW, England. *Tel*: (01132) 444074. *Fax*: (01937) 841403.

Other offices: 5 in the United Kingdom.

Category: Human resources and executive search and selection consultancy.

Recruitment specialty: Executive, management and technical personnel in most sectors.

Locations: United Kingdom and worldwide.

Ahnkwon & Seihwa, 17th Floor, Korean Investment Trust Building, 27–1 Yoido-dong, Youngdeungpo-ku, Seoul, South Korea.

Category: Accountancy practice and management consultancy.

Recruitment specialty: Most accountancy specialist areas, including auditing, taxation, accountancy, business services, insolvency and corporate advisory services.

Location: Asia.

Aker Oil & Gas Technology (UK) Plc, Aker House, Blackness Road, Altens, Aberdeen AB1 4LH, Scotland. *Tel*: (01224) 403100. *Fax*: (01224) 890662.

Category: Recruitment consultancy.

Recruitment specialty: Professionals in design engineering, technical, procurement, safety, subsea petroleum drilling, petroleum processing and operational support personnel.

Locations: Asia, Australia, Canada, Europe, Far East, Ireland, Middle East, Near East, New Zealand, South America, United Kingdom and United States.

Alan Davis & Associates, 455 Main Road, Suite 201, Hudson, Québec JOP 1HO, Canada JOP 1HO. *Tel*: 00 514 458 3535. *Fax*: 00 514 458 3530.

Category: Recruitment consultancy.

Recruitment specialty: Professional management and technical levels in the aerospace, electronics, telecommunications, pharmaceutical, engineering and information technology (IT) industries.

Locations: Canada and United States.

Alasdair Graham Associates Ltd, 97 Ayr Road, Newton Mearns, Glasgow GL77 6RA, Scotland. *Tel*: (0141) 639 3345. *Fax*: (0141) 639 2918.

Category: Recruitment consultancy.

Recruitment specialty: Senior executive, management and technical personnel

for the oil and gas, petrochemical, rail, construction, power, marine and water industries. Permanent and contract assignments.
Locations: Africa, Asia, Canada, Europe, Far East, Middle East, Near East, South America, United Kingdom and United States.

Alba International (IOM) Ltd, Alba House, Princes Street, Douglas, Isle of Man, United Kingdom. *Tel*: (01624) 621293. *Fax*: (01624) 626177.
Category: Recruitment consultancy.
Recruitment specialty: Personnel for the petrochemical industry, oil and gas, associated project management. Consultants for computing (check out – mainframes, PCs, networks, hardware, software, IT etc.) and construction industries.
Locations: Asia, Far East, Middle East, Near East and South America.

Alexander Mann Associates Plc, Alexander House, 9/11 Fulwood Place, London WC1V 6HG, England. *Tel*: (0171) 242 9000. *Fax*: (0171) 242 9001.
Category: Recruitment consultancy.
Recruitment specialty: Senior management and technical personnel for the financial and investment banking sectors.
Locations: Asia, Canada, Europe, Middle East, United Kingdom and United States.

Amanda Barrington Appointments, 33 Southampton Street, Covent Garden, London WC2E 7HE, England. *Tel*: (0171) 379 7007. *Fax*: (0171) 379 3267.
Category: Recruitment consultancy.
Recruitment specialty: Secretaries within the advertising, TV, film and media, banking and commerce sectors.
Locations: Australia, Canada, New Zealand, United Kingdom and United States.

AMS Management Systems, 51/57 Gresham Street, London EC2V 7JH. England. Tel: (0171) 710 6600. Fax: (0171) 710 6700.
Other offices: 47 overseas.
Category: Business and IT consultancy.
Recruitment specialty: IT/computing such as software engineers, telecommunications, datacommunications etc, in most skills and sectors.
Locations: Canada, Europe and United States.

Andromedia, Via Longoni, 2, 20159 Milano, Italy. *Tel*: 00 39 2668 2644. *Fax*: 00 39 2668 2648.
Category: Human resource and management consultancy.
Recruitment specialty: Senior executive, management and technical personnel in most industries and sectors.
Locations: Europe.
Additional information: Andromedia is a member of European Human Resource Consultants (EHRC). The services provided by this company

include: human resources consultancy in all the known specialty areas, management development programmes, corporate strategy, executive recruitment, total staffing, performance programmes etc.

Anglo Arabian Services, London House, 53/54 Haymarket, London SW1Y 4RP, England. *Tel:* (0171) 925 0177. *Fax:* (0171) 930 4261.
Category: Recruitment consultancy.
Recruitment specialty: General management, financial, sales, marketing, engineering and technical personnel.
Locations: Africa, Asia, Europe, Far East, Middle East and United Kingdom.
Additional information: Recruiting personnel by means of search, selection and advertising.

Antal International, Unit 8, Alice Court, 116 Putney Bridge Road, London SW15 2NQ, England. *Tel:* (0181) 874 2744. *Fax:* (0181) 871 2211.
Category: Recruitment consultancy.
Recruitment specialty: Personnel for permanent and contract positions, senior to middle management levels in financial and general management. Also sales and marketing executives in various sectors.
Locations: Asia, Central and Eastern Europe and Far East.

Anthony Benjamin International, Sun House, 31/35 Sun Street, London EC2M 2PY, England. *Tel:* (0171) 377 7510. *Fax:* (0171) 377 7511.
Category: Human resources consultancy.
Recruitment specialty: Personnel of middle to senior management levels in the voice/data communication, IT and cable television industries for the United Kingdom and abroad.
Locations: Canada, Europe, Far East, Ireland, South America, United Kingdom and United States.
Additional information: A specialist human resources consultancy recruiting by means of search, selection and outsourcing.

Aquinas Ltd, 117 Two Mile Hill Road, Kingswood, Bristol, Avon BS15 1BH, England. *Tel:* (0117) 961 3535. *Fax:* (0117) 961 3303.
Category: Recruitment consultancy.
Recruitment specialty: Engineering, management and technical personnel for the oil and gas, petrochemical, power generation and engineering design specialty areas and industries.
Locations: Europe, Far East, Middle East and United Kingdom.

Arthur Andersen, 1 Surrey Street, London WC2R 2PS, England. *Tel:* (0171) 438 3000.
Other offices: 7 in the United Kingdom.
Category: Management consultancy.
Recruitment specialty: Professional services personnel with experience in internal audit, risk management etc.
Locations: United Kingdom and worldwide.

Arthur Morris & Company, Century House, Richmond Road, Hamilton, Bermuda.
Category: Accountancy practice and management consultancy.
Recruitment specialty: Most accountancy specialist areas including: auditing, taxation, accountancy, business services, insolvency and corporate advisory services.
Location: Bermuda.

ASA International, 498 Union Street, Aberdeen AB1 1TS, Scotland. *Tel*: (01224) 648062. *Fax*: (0131) 226 5110.
Category: Recruitment executive search consultancy.
Recruitment specialty: Senior executive, management and technical personnel for the legal and financial services specialty areas, including: legal practitioners, accountants, accountancy technicians, secretarial, administrative, clerical etc.
Locations: Africa, Australia, Canada, Europe, Far East, Middle East, Near East, New Zealand, South America, United Kingdom and United States.

ASA International, 63 George Street, Edinburgh EH2 2JG, Scotland. *Tel*: (0131) 226 6222. *Fax*: (0131) 226 5110.
Category: Recruitment executive search consultancy.
Recruitment specialty: Senior executive, management and technical personnel for the legal and financial services specialty areas, including: legal practitioners, accountants, accountancy technicians, secretarial, administrative, clerical etc.
Locations. Africa, Australia, Canada, Europe, Far East, Middle East, Near East, New Zealand, South America, United Kingdom and United States.

ASA International, 69 St Vincent Street, Glasgow G2 5TF, Scotland. *Tel*: (0141) 221 4166. *Fax*: (0131) 226 5110.
Category: Recruitment executive search consultancy.
Recruitment specialty: Senior executive, management and technical personnel for the legal and financial services specialty areas, including: legal practitioners, accountants, accountancy technicians, secretarial, administrative, clerical etc.
Locations: Africa, Australia, Canada, Europe, Far East, Middle East, Near East, New Zealand, South America, United Kingdom and United States.

ASA International, Glenrothes House, North Street, Glenrothes KY2 5PB, Scotland. *Tel*: (01592) 752312. *Fax*: (0131) 226 5110.
Category: Recruitment executive search consultancy.
Recruitment specialty: Senior executive, management and technical personnel for the legal and financial services specialty areas, including: legal practitioners, accountants, accountancy technicians, secretarial, administrative, clerical etc.
Locations: Africa, Australia, Canada, Europe, Far East, Middle East, Near East, New Zealand, South America, United Kingdom and United States.

Ashbrittle Ltd, Ashbrittle House, Lower Dagnall Street, St Albans, Hertfordshire AL3 4PA, England. *Tel*: (01727) 854854. *Fax*: (01727) 865557.
Category: Recruitment consultancy.
Recruitment specialty: Management and technical personnel for the construction, building, civil engineering and process/oil industries etc.
Locations: Europe, Far East, Middle East, Near East and United Kingdom.

Ashton Penny Partnership Ltd, Suite 201, Albany House, 324/326 Regent Street, London W1R 6AA, England. *Tel*: (0171) 580 8490.
Category: Management consultancy.
Recruitment specialty: Senior executive and management levels in most industries and sectors.
Locations: Eastern Europe.

Aston Zoraster Ltd, Westminster House, 58 London Street, Reading, Berkshire RG1 4SQ, England. *Tel*: (01734) 566123. *Fax*: (01734) 596222.
Category: Recruitment consultancy.
Recruitment specialty: Senior executive and technical personnel for the banking and finance, IT/computing, datacommunications, electronics, FMCG, food, high technology, logistics, manufacturing, retail, telecommunications, transportation and distribution industries, public sector and non-executive directors.
Locations: United Kingdom.
Additional information: Anston Zoraster Ltd has expertise in all the following functional disciplines – engineering, general management, finance, facilities management, human resources, information technology (IT), management consulting, market research, production, quality assurance, sales and marketing. Also, management development, training, team building, management audit, competency based assessment, and psychometric assessments.

Audiobyte Business Consultants, The Blackfriars Foundry, 156 Blackfriars Road, London SE1 8EN, England. *Tel*: (0181) 721 7117. *Fax*: (0181) 721 7107.
Category: Recruitment consultancy.
Recruitment specialty: IT contract and permanent personnel in connectivity, communications, database development, front end developers especially in banking and associated markets, AS/400 operations and RPG.
Locations: Asia, Australia, Canada, Europe, New Zealand, United Kingdom and United States.

Austin Knight Canada Inc, 1 Yonge Street, Suite 1403, Toronto, Ontario M5E 1J9, Canada. *Tel*: 00 1 416 366 5666. *Fax*: 00 1 416 366 7903/9610.
Category: Recruitment advertising consultancy.
Recruitment specialty: Executive, management and technical personnel in the commercial, financial, industrial and public sectors.

Locations: Canada, Europe, United Kingdom and United States.
Additional information: Services offered to their clients are: recruitment advertising, search and selection, communications and business psychology.

Austin Knight/Carre Turenne SA, 129 rue de Turenne, 75003 Paris, France. *Tel*: 00 33 1 4804 7878. *Fax*: 00 33 1 4804 5378.
Category: Recruitment advertising consultancy.
Recruitment specialty: Executive, management and technical personnel in the commercial, financial, industrial and public sectors.
Locations: Canada, Europe, United Kingdom and United States.
Additional information: Services offered to their clients are: recruitment advertising, search and selection, communications and business psychology.

Austin Knight Inc, 1524G Cloverfield Boulevard, Santa Monica, CA 90404, United States. *Tel*: 00 1 310 264 0117. *Fax*: 00 1 310 264 0677.
Category: Recruitment advertising consultancy.
Recruitment specialty: Executive, management and technical personnel in the commercial, financial, industrial and public sectors.
Locations: Canada, Europe, United Kingdom and United States.
Additional information: Services offered to their clients are: recruitment advertising, search and selection, communications and business psychology.

Austin Knight Inc, 1601 Fifth Avenue, Seattle, WA 98101, United States. *Tel*: 00 1 206 233 9840. *Fax*: 00 1 206 233 9785.
Category: Recruitment advertising consultancy.
Recruitment specialty: Executive, management and technical personnel in the commercial, financial, industrial and public sectors.
Locations: Canada, Europe, United Kingdom and United States.
Additional information: Services offered to their clients are: recruitment advertising, search and selection, communications and business psychology.

Austin Knight Inc, 2nd Floor, 10 Tremont Street, Boston, MA 02108, United States. *Tel*: 00 1 617 371 4100. *Fax*: 00 1 617 371 4114.
Category: Recruitment advertising consultancy.
Recruitment specialty: Executive, management and technical personnel in the commercial, financial, industrial and public sectors.
Locations: Canada, Europe, United Kingdom and United States.
Additional information: Services offered to their clients are: recruitment advertising, search and selection, communications and business psychology.

Austin Knight Inc, 303 West Erie, Chicago, Illinois 60610, United States. *Tel*: 00 1 312 337 5599. *Fax*: 00 1 312 337 6704.
Category: Recruitment advertising consultancy.
Recruitment specialty: Executive, management and technical personnel in the commercial, financial, industrial and public sectors.
Locations: Canada, Europe, United Kingdom and United States.

Additional information: Services offered to their clients are: recruitment advertising, search and selection, communications and business psychology.

Austin Knight Inc, Knightway House, 29 West 35th Street, New York, NY 10001, United States. *Tel*: 00 1 212 695 5055. *Fax*: 00 1 212 695 5164.
Category: Recruitment advertising consultancy.
Recruitment specialty: Executive, management and technical personnel in the commercial, financial, industrial and public sectors.
Locations: Canada, Europe, United Kingdom and United States.
Additional information: Services offered to their clients are: recruitment advertising, search and selection, communications and business psychology.

Austin Knight Inc, PO Box 2126, 100 Shoreline Highway, Sausalito, CA 94965, United States. *Tel*: 00 1 415 331 5600. *Fax*: 00 1 415 331 7860.
Category: Recruitment advertising consultancy.
Recruitment specialty: Executive, management and technical personnel in the commercial, financial, industrial and public sectors.
Locations: Canada, Europe, United Kingdom and United States.
Additional information: Services offered to their clients are: recruitment advertising, search and selection, communications and business psychology.

Austin Knight Pty Ltd, Level 2, 424 St Kilda Road, Melbourne, VIC 3004, Australia. *Tel*: 00 613 820 4222. *Fax*: 00 613 820 4660.
Category: Recruitment advertising consultancy.
Recruitment specialty: Executive, management and technical personnel in the commercial, financial, industrial and public sectors.
Locations: Canada, Europe, United Kingdom and United States.
Additional information: Services offered to their clients are: recruitment advertising, search and selection, communications and business psychology.

Austin Knight Pty Ltd, Sanyo House, Level 6, 122/130 Arthur Street, North Sydney, NSW 2060, Australia. *Tel*: 00 612 957 5533. *Fax*: 00 612 929 5228/ 4224.
Category: Recruitment advertising consultancy.
Recruitment specialty: Executive, management and technical personnel in the commercial, financial, industrial and public sectors.
Locations: Canada, Europe, United Kingdom and United States.
Additional information: Services offered to their clients are: recruitment advertising, search and selection, communications and business psychology.

Austin Knight Pty Ltd, Level 18, QVI Building, 250 St George's Terrace, Perth, WA 6000, Australia. *Tel*: 00 619 321 4600. *Fax*: 00 619 321 1292.
Category: Recruitment advertising consultancy.
Recruitment specialty: Executive, management and technical personnel in the commercial, financial, industrial and public sectors.
Locations: Canada, Europe, United Kingdom and United States.

Additional information: Services offered to their clients are: recruitment advertising, search and selection, communications and business psychology.

Austin Knight UK Ltd, 7th Floor, Tricorn House, 51/53 Hagley Road, Edgbaston, Birmingham B16 8TP, England. *Tel*: (0121) 456 1378. *Fax*: (0121) 456 1510.

Category: Recruitment advertising consultancy.

Recruitment specialty: Executive, management and technical personnel in the commercial, financial, industrial and public sectors.

Locations: Canada, Europe, United Kingdom and United States.

Additional information: Services offered to their clients are: recruitment advertising, search and selection, communications and business psychology.

Austin Knight UK Ltd, 11th Floor, Castlemead, Lower Castle Street, Bristol BS1 3AG, England. *Tel*: (0117) 922 1891. *Fax*: (0117) 922 1117.

Category: Recruitment advertising consultancy.

Recruitment specialty: Executive, management and technical personnel in the commercial, financial, industrial and public sectors.

Locations: Canada, Europe, United Kingdom and United States.

Additional information: Services offered to their clients are: recruitment advertising, search and selection, communications and business psychology.

Austin Knight UK Ltd, Riverside House, 31 Cathedral Road, Cardiff CF1 9HB, England. *Tel*: (01222) 373222. *Fax*: (01222) 394509.

Category: Recruitment advertising consultancy.

Recruitment specialty: Executive, management and technical personnel in the commercial, financial, industrial and public sectors.

Locations: Canada, Europe, United Kingdom and United States.

Additional information: Services offered to their clients are: recruitment advertising, search and selection, communications and business psychology.

Austin Knight UK Ltd, Nelson House, 23/27 Moulsham Street, Chelmsford. Essex CM2 0XG, England. *Tel*: (01245) 350250. *Fax*: (01245) 350498.

Category: Recruitment advertising consultancy.

Recruitment specialty: Executive, management and technical personnel in the commercial, financial, industrial and public sectors.

Locations: Canada, Europe, United Kingdom and United States.

Additional information: Services offered to their clients are: recruitment advertising, search and selection, communications and business psychology.

Austin Knight UK Ltd, Royal Exchange House, 100 Queen Street, Glasgow G1 3DL, Scotland. *Tel*: (0141) 248 6171. *Fax*: (0141) 248 6176.

Category: Recruitment advertising consultancy.

Recruitment specialty: Executive, management and technical personnel in the commercial, financial, industrial and public sectors.

Locations: Canada, Europe, United Kingdom and United States.

Additional information: Services offered to their clients are: recruitment advertising, search and selection, communications and business psychology.

Austin Knight UK Ltd, St George House, Great George Street, Leeds, West Yorkshire LS1 3DL, England. *Tel*: (0113) 234 0740. *Fax*: (0113) 234 0885.
Category: Recruitment advertising consultancy.
Recruitment specialty: Executive, management and technical personnel in commercial, financial, industrial and public sectors.
Locations: Canada, Europe, United Kingdom and United States.
Additional information: Services offered to their clients are: recruitment advertising, search and selection, communications and business psychology.

Austin Knight UK Ltd, Knightway House, 20 Soho Square, London W1A 1DS, England. *Tel*: (0171) 437 9261. *Fax*: (0171) 439 3410.
Category: Recruitment advertising consultancy.
Recruitment specialty: Executive, management and technical personnel in the commercial, financial, industrial and public sectors.
Locations: Canada, Europe, United Kingdom and United States.
Additional information: Services offered to their clients are: recruitment advertising, search and selection, communications and business psychology.

Austin Knight UK Ltd, Ship Canal House, 98 King Street, Manchester M2 4WD, England. *Tel*: (0161) 834 8723. *Fax*: (0161) 832 7783.
Category: Recruitment advertising consultancy.
Recruitment specialty: Executive, management and technical personnel in the commercial, financial, industrial and public sectors.
Locations: Canada, Europe, United Kingdom and United States.
Additional information: Services offered to their clients are: recruitment advertising, search and selection, communications and business psychology.

Axone Consultants, 7 bis avenue de la Créativité, BP 333, 59666 Villeneuve d'Ascq cedex, France. *Tel*: 00 33 2047 3221. *Fax*: 00 33 2047 3211.
Category: Human resource and management consultancy.
Recruitment specialty: Senior executive, management and technical personnel, in most industries and sectors.
Locations: Europe.
Additional information: Axone Consultants is a member of European Human Resource Consultants (EHRC). The services provided by this company include: human resources consultancy in all the known specialty areas, management development programmes, corporate strategy, executive recruitment, total staffing, performance programmes etc.

Barchester Royce Ltd, Chesham House, 150 Regent Street, London W1R 5FA, England. *Tel*: (0171) 439 6286. *Fax*: (0171) 734 4166.
Category: Recruitment consultancy.
Recruitment specialty: Senior executive, management, project management

within the IT, accountancy, property, construction, petrochemical and engineering curtain walling industries.

Locations: Asia, Europe, Far East, Middle East, Near East and United Kingdom.

Additional information: This company has over twenty years' experience in most recruitment disciplines for medium to large organisations worldwide.

Barnett Consulting Services Ltd, Providence House, River Street, Windsor, Berkshire SL4 1QT, England. *Tel*: (01753) 856723. *Fax*: (01753) 866297.

Category: Management consultancy.

Recruitment specialty: Senior executive, management and technical personnel within the engineering, finance, sales and marketing industries.

Locations: Asia, Canada, Europe, United Kingdom and United States.

Barry Latchford Associates, 10 Sedley Place, London W1R 1HG, England. *Tel*: (0171) 629 7594. *Fax*: (0171) 495 1153.

Category: Recruitment consultancy.

Recruitment specialty: Executive and management in most industries and sectors.

Locations: United Kingdom and overseas.

Berkeley Scott Group, The, Berkeley House, 11/13 Ockford Road, Godalming, Surrey GU7 1OU, England. *Tel*: (01483) 414141. *Fax*: (01483) 414457.

Category: Management consultancy.

Recruitment specialty: The hospitality industry, hotel and restaurant managers, general managers, deputy managers, sales, marketing and training staff, executive/head/sous/pastry chefs, restaurant and bar managers, housekeepers and engineers.

Locations: Africa, Asia, Far East, Ireland, Middle East and United Kingdom.

BFC Consultancy Services Ltd, Redhill House, Hope Street, Saltney, Chester CH4 8BU, England. *Tel*: (01244) 680600. *Fax*: (01244) 678001.

Category: Management consultancy.

Recruitment specialty: General and specific discipline management consultants.

Locations: Africa, Canada, United Kingdom and United States.

Bilinguagroup, Suite 1, 49 Maddox Street, London W1R 9LA, England. *Tel*: (0171) 493 6446. *Fax*: (0171) 493 0168.

Category: Recruitment consultancy.

Recruitment specialty: Most levels of bilingually skilled personnel, bilingual secretaries, personal assistants (PAs), translators, interpreters, receptionists, bilingual sales. Solicitors, legal executives and other legal personnel for private practice and industry. Senior executives for the banking, finance, publishing, advertising and export industries and specialty areas.

Locations: Europe, Far East and United Kingdom.

Additional information: Bilinguagroup is an international recruitment consultancy, specialising in the recruitment of bilingual personnel. Assignments can be on a permanent or temporary basis. All Western European languages are covered, plus Arabic, Chinese, Eastern European, Russian, Japanese etc.

Bouresli Auditing Office, PO Box 20966, Safat, 13070 Kuwait.
Category: Accountancy practice and management consultancy.
Recruitment specialty: Most accountancy specialist areas, including auditing, taxation, accountancy, business services, insolvency and corporate advisory services.
Location: Middle East.

Boyce Agency Ltd, Liberty House, 22 Regent Street, London W1R 5DE, England. *Tel*: (0171) 287 6060. *Fax*: (0171) 494 4652.
Category: Recruitment consultancy.
Recruitment specialty: Administrative and secretarial bilingual personnel including translators, interpreters etc. across most sectors including banking etc.
Locations: Europe and United Kingdom.

Boyden Executive Search & Selection, 24 Queen Anne's Gate, London SW1H 9AA, England. *Tel*: (0171) 222 9033. *Fax*: (0171) 222 8838.
Other offices: 64 overseas.
Category: Executive search and selection consultancy.
Recruitment specialty: Senior executive and management levels in most industries.
Locations: United Kingdom and worldwide.

Brown & Root Ltd, 150 The Broadway, Wimbledon, London SW19 1RX, England. *Tel*: (0181) 544 5000.
Category: Management and engineering consultancy.
Recruitment specialty: Engineering and project management, management, civil, mechanical and electrical engineers and other technical personnel for the construction industry.
Locations: Africa, Europe, Middle East and United Kingdom.

Brunel Recruitment, 80 Prospect Hill, Redditch B97 5BY, England. *Tel*: (01527) 584430. *Fax*: (01527) 584173.
Category: Recruitment consultancy.
Recruitment specialty: Senior and managerial engineers such as: civil, design and project, and senior executive engineers within most industries and sectors.
Locations: Asia, Canada, Europe, Ireland, United Kingdom and United States.

Bull Thompson International Ltd, 8 Upper St Martins Lane, London WC2H 9DH, England. *Tel*: (0171) 240 3561. *Fax*: (0171) 836 9812.
Category: Recruitment consultancy.

Recruitment specialty: Senior executive, management and technical in general commercial, engineering, distribution, cable TV, telecommunications, IT, retail, FMCG, pharmaceutical, health care, leisure, hotels, entertainment and finance.

Locations: Australia, Canada, Europe, Far East, Ireland, New Zealand, United Kingdom and United States.

Additional information: Salary ranges usually within £25,000–£120,000.

Cambridge Collocation, 6 Ross Street, Cambridge CB1 3BX, England. *Tel*: (01223) 249606. *Fax*: (01223) 414474.

Category: Recruitment consultancy.

Recruitment specialty: Registered nurses.

Locations: United Kingdom.

Campbell Birch Executive Recruitment, Parr House, 52 Broadway, Bracknell, Berkshire RG12 1AG, England. *Tel*: (01344) 424 117. *Fax*: (01344) 360 534.

Category: Search and selection consultancy.

Recruitment specialty: Commercial services – contracts/commercial professionals, all levels risk analysts, bid specialists, legal advisers and managers, barristers, project and programme managers. Finance and administration – qualified and part-qualified accountants, company secretaries, economists and financial analysts, human resources/personnel, training, administrators, sales administration, non-technical support and help desk. Sales and marketing – all levels, business and market analysts, public relations. Purchasing and logistics – purchasing/procurement, materials control, logistics, warehousing and distribution, stock control/inventory, transportation managers. Information technology (IT) – analysts, programmers, system developers and managers, project managers, consultants and interim managers. Technical and engineering – design and development personnel, systems and networks, quality, manufacturing, production, production and application engineers, technical authors, construction, civil engineering, mechanical and site engineers. Interim managers and temporary staff – bid specialists, interim managers etc.

Locations: Australia, Canada, Europe, Far East, Ireland, New Zealand, South America, United Kingdom and United States.

Additional information: Campbell Birch Executive Recruitment is organised into seven well supported departments: Commercial Services, Finance and Administration, Sales and Marketing, Purchasing and Logistics, Information Technology (IT), Technical and Engineering and Management Services/Contractors. The firm complies with the quality management system BS5750 and is dedicated to providing a professional service to clients.

Capita Recruitment Services, Great West House, Great West Road, Brentford, Middlesex TW8 9DF, England. *Tel*: (0181) 560 9997. *Fax*: (0181) 560 9788.

Category: Recruitment and management consultancy.

Recruitment specialty: Senior to middle management within the finance, IT and project management industries to both interim management assignments and in search and selection campaigns in public and utility sectors.
Locations: Africa, Europe, Ireland and United Kingdom.

Cappo International Ltd, Cappo House, 38/40 High Street, West Wickham, Kent BR4 0NJ, England. *Tel*: (0181) 776 1850. *Fax*: (0181) 777 9952.
Category: Recruitment consultancy.
Recruitment specialty: Senior and supervisory process, mechanical, instrumentation and electrical technical personnel within the chemical, oil and gas industries.
Locations: Asia, Europe, Far East, Middle East and United Kingdom.

Career Management International (CMI), 43 Fitzwilliam Square, Dublin D2, Republic of Ireland. *Tel*: 00 353 1 676 5722. *Fax*: 00 353 1 676 5774.
Category: Recruitment consultancy.
Recruitment specialty: Senior management, engineering and technical support personnel for the construction, design and project management industry specialty areas. Including: design and construction teams, land and hydrographic survey teams, project managers for oil/construction and manufacturing projects, telecommunications engineers, technical sales, buyers etc.
Locations: Africa, Asia, Canada, Europe, Far East, Ireland, Middle East, Near East, Philippines, South America, United States and United Kingdom.

Cargill Technical Services Ltd, Knowle Hill Park, Fairmile Lane, Cobham, Surrey KT11 2PD, England. *Tel*: (01932) 861000. *Fax*: (01932) 861900.
Category: Agricultural management consultancy.
Recruitment specialty: Specialists in agriculture, agro-industry, agribusiness, economics, marketing, privatisation sociology/anthropology, natural resources development, rural development, cotton, land and water resources, food sciences, post-harvest technology, organisations/institutions, SME development, livestock, and agronomy.
Locations: Africa, Asia, Caribbean, Central America, Eastern Europe, Far East, Middle East, Near East, South America, Western Europe.

Castlebay, The APL Centre, Stevenston, Ayrshire KA20 3LR, Scotland. *Tel*: (01294) 605 466. *Fax*: (01294) 605 486.
Category: Engineering consultancy.
Recruitment specialty: Management, engineering and other technical personnel for the oil, gas and petrochemical industries. Engineers, technical support and management etc.
Locations: Europe, Far East, Middle East and United Kingdom.

CB Linnell Ltd, 7 College Street, Nottingham NG1 5AQ, England. *Tel*: (0115) 941 1238 1238. *Fax*: (0115) 948 4742.

Category: Management consultancy.
Recruitment specialty: Senior executive and management particularly in the industrial sector.
Location: United Kingdom.
Additional information: Salary ranges usually within £30,000–£120,000.

CCL Recruitment International Ltd, 298 High Street, Dovercourt, Harwich, Essex CO12 3PJ, England. *Tel*: (01255) 506001. *Fax*: (01255) 506002.
Category: Recruitment consultancy.
Recruitment specialty: Senior executive, management and technical personnel for the automotive industry.
Locations: Africa, Far East, Middle East, Near East and United Kingdom.

CDI International Ltd, Capital House, Houndwell Place, Southampton, Hampshire SO14 1HU, England. *Tel*: (01703) 223511. *Fax*: (01703) 227911.
Other offices: 5 in the United Kingdom.
Category: Recruitment consultancy.
Recruitment specialty: Technical personnel in the aerospace, automotive, information technology (IT), petrochemical and manufacturing industries.
Locations: Africa, Asia, Canada, Europe, Far East, Ireland, Middle East, United Kingdom and United States.

Certes Computing Ltd, Arthur House, Roman Way, Coleshill, Warwickshire B46 1HQ, England. *Tel*: (01675) 467475. *Fax*: (01675) 467314.
Category: Recruitment consultancy.
Recruitment specialty: Management, engineering and technical support personnel for the IT/computing industry. Permanent and contract assignments, most specialists across most sectors.
Locations: Canada, Europe, Far East, Middle East, United Kingdom and United States.

Charity People, Leeming House, Vicar Lane North, Leeds, West Yorkshire LS2 7JF, England. *Tel*: (0113) 234 6969. *Fax*: (0113) 245 8222.
Category: Recruitment and management consultancy.
Recruitment specialty: Senior executive, secretarial, clerical, administrative personnel in financial, personnel, IT, marketing and fund raising areas/industries. Specialising in the 'not for profit' sector.
Locations: Asia, Australia, Canada, Europe, New Zealand, Middle East, United Kingdom and United States.

Charity People, Station House, 150 Waterloo Road, London SE1 8SB, England. *Tel*: (0171) 620 0062. *Fax*: (0171) 633 0331.
Category: Recruitment and management consultancy.
Recruitment specialty: Senior executive, secretarial, clerical, administrative personnel in financial, personnel, IT, marketing and fund raising areas/industries. Specialising in the 'not for profit' sector.

Locations: Asia, Australia, Canada, Europe, New Zealand, Middle East, United Kingdom and United States.

Christopher Murray Ltd, The Old Post Office, George Street, Bath BA1 2EB, England. *Tel*: (01225) 444117. *Fax*: (01225) 444042.
Category: Management consultancy.
Recruitment specialty: Executive, management and technical serving most sectors in financial, legal, insurance, actuarial, manufacturing, agriculture, sales and marketing, engineering and the motor trade.
Locations: Europe and United Kingdom.

Chuo Audit Corporation, Kasumigaseki Building, 32nd Floor, 3-2-5-Kasumigaseki, Chiyoda-ku, Tokyo 100, Japan.
Category: Accountancy practice and management consultancy.
Recruitment specialty: Most accountancy specialist areas including: auditing, taxation, accountancy, business services, insolvency and corporate advisory services.
Location: Asia.

Circuit Resources Ltd, 22/23 Old Burlington Street, London W1X 1RL, England. *Tel*: (0171) 439 1213. *Fax*: (0171) 439 1413.
Category: Recruitment consultancy.
Recruitment specialty: Senior executive, management and technical personnel for the sales, marketing and technical support sectors within the IT/computing and communications industries.
Locations: Africa, Canada, Europe, Far East, Ireland, Middle East, United Kingdom and United States.

CLEAS, 6 Place de la République Dominicaine, 75017 Paris, France. *Tel*: 00 33 1 4267 3511. *Fax*: 00 33 1 4267 6589.
Category: International human resources consultancy.
Recruitment specialty: Executive, management, technical in most sectors including oil and gas exploration and production.
Locations: Africa and Europe.

CMG Plc, Telford House, Tothill Street, London SW1H 9NB, England. *Tel*: (0171) 233 0288. *Fax*: (0171) 222 8792.
Other offices: 9 overseas.
Category: Management consultancy.
Recruitment specialty: IT/computing most skills.
Locations: United Kingdom and worldwide.

Cognos International GmbH, Kielortallee 1, 20144 Hamburg, Germany. *Tel*: 00 49 4 0419 0904. *Fax*: 00 49 4 0419 09444.
Category: Human resource and management consultancy.
Recruitment specialty: Senior executive, management and technical personnel,

in most industries and sectors.

Location: Europe.

Additional information: Cognos International GmbH is a member of European Human Resource Consultants (EHRC). The services provided by this company include: human resources consultancy in all the known specialty areas, management development programmes, corporate strategy, executive recruitment, total staffing, performance programmes etc.

Cole Henry Associates Ltd, Airport House, Purley Way, Croydon, Surrey CR0 0XZ, England. *Tel*: (0181) 781 6930. *Fax*: (0181) 781 6932.

Category: Recruitment consultancy.

Recruitment specialty: Senior to junior management levels in areas of support and human resources personnel. Retail sales and service industry including wholesale and distribution of a wide variety of product types.

Location: United Kingdom.

Colombo-Fiduciaria SA, Via San Salvatore 10, PO Box 44, 6902 Lugano-Paradiso, Switzerland.

Category: Accountancy practice and management consultancy.

Recruitment specialty: Most accountancy specialist areas, including auditing, taxation, accountancy, business services, insolvency and corporate advisory services.

Location: Europe.

Commissioning & Technical Services Ltd, Design House, Butts Road, Thornton Cleveleys, Lancashire FY5 4HX, England. *Tel*: (01253) 864 509. *Fax*: (01253) 866 665.

Category: Recruitment consultancy.

Recruitment specialty: Senior management, engineering and technical personnel for the nuclear, petrochemical, water, construction, aerospace, defence and general engineering industries.

Locations: Canada, Europe, Far East, Ireland, Middle East, United Kingdom and United States.

Computer People International, Victory House, 7 Selsdon Way, London E14 9GL, England. *Tel*: (0171) 510 2000. *Fax*: (0171) 510 2291.

Other offices: 9 in the UK and 5 overseas.

Category: Recruitment management consultancy.

Recruitment specialty: IT/computing all areas especially rare skills.

Locations: Canada, Europe, United Kingdom and United States.

Computer Team Group Ltd, 1 St Ann Street, Manchester M2 7LG, England. *Tel*: (0161) 834 7435. *Fax*: (0161) 834 7436.

Category: Recruitment consultancy.

Recruitment specialty: IT/computing personnel at most levels and with a wide band of skills. Specialists areas: systems and programming, network and communications, operations, consultancy, PC support, help desk, voice and data, LAN and WAN specialists, cabling systems engineers. Also personnel for the public finance and commercial sectors and industries such as manufacturing, oil and gas, chemicals etc.

Locations: Europe, Ireland and United Kingdom.

Conker Ltd, 15 Riverview Road, Chiswick Road, London W4 3QH, England. *Tel*: (0181) 994 1038. *Fax*: (0181) 742 0045.

Category: Recruitment consultancy.

Recruitment specialty: Management and technical in most sectors.

Location: Middle East.

Consult, 13 Broad Street, Alresford, Hampshire SO24 9AR, England. *Tel*: (01962) 735 577. *Fax*: (01962) 735 007.

Category: Human resources consultancy.

Recruitment specialty: Senior executive and management levels in human resources and financial services.

Locations: Europe and United Kingdom (including off shore).

CONTAX Gesellschaft für Betriebsberatung mbH, Feuerbachstrasse 8, 60325 Frankfurt, Germany.

Category: Accountancy practice and management consultancy.

Recruitment specialty: Most accountancy specialist areas including: auditing, taxation, accountancy, business services, insolvency and corporate advisory services.

Location: Europe.

CONTAX Gesellschaft für Betriebsberatung mbH, Zellescher Weg 24, 01217 Dresden, Germany.

Category: Accountancy practice and management consultancy.

Recruitment specialty: Most accountancy specialist areas including: auditing, taxation, accountancy, business services, insolvency and corporate advisory services.

Location: Europe.

Contracts Consultancy (CCL) Ltd, London House, 68 Upper Richmond Road, London SW15 2RP, England. *Tel*: (0181) 871 2994. *Fax*: (0181) 871 9461.

Category: Recruitment consultancy.

Recruitment specialty: Senior and other technical personnel for the oil and gas, power, engineering, construction and high technology industries. Project managers and engineers and cost and planning/pipeline and subsea/procurement and logistics etc.

Locations: Africa, Asia, Australia, Canada, Europe, Far East, Ireland, Middle East, Near East, New Zealand, South America, United Kingdom and United States.

CTA International Search & Selection, Staverton House, 3/5 East Hampstead Road, Wokingham, Berkshire RG40 2EH, England. *Tel*: (01734) 771100. *Fax*: (01734) 771223.
Other offices: 30 overseas.
Category: International search and selection consultancy.
Recruitment specialty: IT/computing most skills in networking and communications.
Locations: United Kingdom and worldwide.

CTC Consulting, Centre de Séminaires, CH-1565 Vallon FR, Switzerland. *Tel*: 00 41 3767 2500. *Fax*: 00 41 3767 2404.
Category: Human resource and management consultancy.
Recruitment specialty: Senior executive, management and technical personnel in most industries and sectors.
Location: Europe.
Additional information: CTC Consulting is a member of European Human Resource Consultants (EHRC). The services provided by this company include: human resources consultancy in all the known specialty areas,, management development programmes, corporate strategy, executive recruitment, total staffing, performance programmes etc.

Dalroth & Partners Ltd, Nightingale House, 46/48 East Street, Epsom, Surrey KT1 1HQ, England. *Tel*: (01872) 726299. *Fax*: (01872) 744020.
Category: Recruitment consultancy.
Recruitment specialty: Senior executive, management and technical personnel for the IT/computing industry, engineers, technical authors and other skills including programming, systems, software and hardware, sales, support and training.
Locations: Europe, Middle East and United Kingdom.

Dart Resourcing Group, MDA House, The Grove, Slough, Berkshire SL1 1RH, England. *Tel*: (01753) 534610/693633/693611.
Category: Recruitment consultancy.
Recruitment specialty: IT/computing specialists, IT multi-media industries, engineering programming, design analysis, telecommunications, CAD-CAM, PC and networking.
Locations: Europe, Ireland, Middle East and United Kingdom.

Dawood Consultants Plc, Dawood House, 28 Mayday Road, Thornton Heath, Surrey CR7 7HL, England. *Tel*: (0181) 683 2126 (10 lines). *Fax*: (0181) 683 4357.
Category: Recruitment consultancy.
Recruitment specialty: Executive, management, engineers and technical personnel for the IT/computing and general engineering industries.
Locations: Australia, Europe, Ireland, Middle East, New Zealand and United Kingdom.

Denge Denetim Yeminli Mali Musavirlik Anonim Sirketi, Piyale Pasa Bulvari, Kastel Is Merkezi Blok 2 Kat 6, Kasimpasa 80370 Istanbul, Turkey.
Category: Accountancy practice and management consultancy.
Recruitment specialty: Most accountancy specialist areas including: auditing, taxation, accountancy, business services, insolvency and corporate advisory services.
Location: Europe.

DH Associates, Wrights House, 102/104 High Street, Great Missenden, Buckinghamshire HP16 0BE, England. *Tel*: (01494) 862007. *Fax*: (01494) 862009.
Category: Recruitment consultancy.
Recruitment specialty: Senior to middle management in the catering industry overseas. In addition, similar personnel in maintenance, logistics and purchasing, retail (supermarkets) and catering (hotels) appointments in the United Kingdom.
Locations: Africa, Asia, Europe (CIS), Far East, Ireland, Middle East, Near East, South America, United Kingdom.
Additional information: Overseas appointments are often in hardship areas, in jungles, swamps, deserts, offshore rigs, war zones, mines etc.

DHA Resourcing Solutions, 32 Birmingham Road, Studley, Warwickshire B80 7BG, England. *Tel*: (01527) 857672. *Fax*: (01527) 854534.
Category: Management consultancy.
Recruitment specialty: Senior to middle management including board appointments in most sectors and specialist areas.
Locations: Europe, Ireland and United Kingdom.
Additional information: DHA is a strategic partner of the People Agenda Ltd, very difficult and esoteric assignment requirements are welcomed.

Dickens Hazell & Associates Ltd, RPL House, Ward Road, Mount Farm, Milton Keynes MK1 1JA, England. *Tel*: (01908) 374074. *Fax*: (01908) 374978.
Category: Recruitment consultancy.
Recruitment specialty: Executive, management and technical.
Location: United Kingdom.

Digby Morgan Consulting, London House, 53/54 Haymarket, London SW1Y 4RP, England. *Tel*: (0171) 321 0640. *Fax*: (0171) 930 4261.
Category: Management consultancy.
Recruitment specialty: Executive, management and technical in most sectors.
Locations: United Kingdom and worldwide.

DM Management Consultants Ltd, 19 Clarges Street, London W1Y 7PG, England. *Tel*: (0171) 499 8030. *Fax*: (0171) 948 6306.
Category: Management consultancy.

Recruitment specialty: Senior management in direct marketing, database marketing, home shopping, catalogue sectors including information technology (IT) operational functions and fulfilment specialists.
Locations: Canada, Europe, United Kingdom and United States.

Douglas Llambias, 410 Strand, London WC2R 0NS, England. *Tel*: (0171) 836 8501.
Category: Recruitment consultancy.
Recruitment specialty: Executive and management personnel for the finance, accountancy, banking and general management specialty areas.
Locations: Africa, Asia, Australia, Eastern Europe, Far East, Middle East, Near East, New Zealand and United Kingdom.

DP Group, The, 6th Floor, Berkley House, 73 Upper Richmond Road, London SW15 2SZ, England. *Tel*: (0181) 877 1121. *Fax*: (0181) 877 1104.
Category: Recruitment consultancy.
Recruitment specialty: Senior executive, management and engineering personnel for the IT/computing industry, project managers, senior consultants, senior computer audit, senior communications specialists.
Locations: Europe, Ireland and United Kingdom.
Additional information: The DP Group's clients include management consultancies, and international finance organisations. Salary range £20,000–£150,000.

Dr Helmut Fischer & Dr Bertram Fischer, Rankestrasse 56, 90461 Nürnberg, Germany.
Category: Accountancy practice and management consultancy.
Recruitment specialty: Most accountancy specialist areas including: auditing taxation, accountancy, business services, insolvency and corporate advisory services.
Location: Europe.

Dr W Meili & Partner AG, Lavaterstrasse 40, PO Box 375, CH-8027 Zürich, Switzerland.
Category: Accountancy practice and management consultancy.
Recruitment specialty: Most accountancy specialist areas including: auditing, taxation, accountancy, business services, insolvency and corporate advisory services.
Location: Europe.

Dr W Schlage & Company, Jungfernstieg 7, 20354 Hamburg, Germany.
Category: Accountancy practice and management consultancy.
Recruitment specialty: Most accountancy specialist areas including: auditing, taxation, accountancy, business services, insolvency and corporate advisory services.
Location: Europe.

Drake International, Charles House, 5 Regent Street, London SW1Y 4LR, England. *Tel*: (0171) 437 6900. *Fax*: (0171) 434 1255.
Other offices: 32 in the United Kingdom.
Category: Recruitment and human resources consultancy.
Recruitment specialty: Most levels and sectors, secretarial, administrative and support, bilingual, accountancy, sales and marketing, industrial, catering, occupational health etc.
Locations: Africa, Asia, Australia, Canada, Europe, New Zealand, United Kingdom and United States.

 DRAX Dearman Associates, Charlotte House, 14 Windmill Street, London W1P 2DY, England. *Tel*: (0171) 209 1000. *Fax*: (0171) 209 0001.
Category: Recruitment consultancy.
Recruitment specialty: Executive and management personnel in many industries.
Locations: Asia, Europe (Russian Federation and Eastern Europe), Far East, Ireland, United Kingdom and United States.

Dutton International Ltd, Victoria Court, Penny Street, Lancaster, Lancashire LA1 1XN, England. *Tel*: (01524) 39753/845888. *Fax*: (01524) 844488/ 381898.
Category: Recruitment search and selection consultancy.
Recruitment specialty: Senior executive and management within information technology (IT), accountancy, legal and contract catering specialty areas. In addition, senior management and technical personnel in the power generation, petrochemical, civil engineering, electromechanical, instrumentation and technical industries.
Locations: Europe and United Kingdom.

Eagling Computer Services Ltd, 4 Cromwell Road, Stevenage, Hertfordshire SG2 9HT, England. *Tel*: (01438) 353262. *Fax*: (01438) 314619.
Category: Management and recruitment consultancy.
Recruitment specialty: IT/computing including most hardware and software platforms, placement levels from IT directors to trainees for permanent and contract assignments and for fixed term employees, interim managers and management consultants.
Locations: Africa, Australia, Canada, Europe, New Zealand, United Kingdom and United States.
Additional information: Provides additional services, search and selection, outsourcing, outplacement, competency psychometric testing.

Earl Associates, Lakeside, Common Road, Weston Colville, Cambridge CB1 5NS, England. *Tel*: (01223) 290343. *Fax*: (01223) 290090.
Category: Recruitment consultancy.
Recruitment specialty: Executive, management and technical personnel such as: general managers, sales and marketing management, hardware and software engineers and engineering managers.

Location: United Kingdom.

Ellis Employment, 15 College Green, Dublin 2, Republic of Ireland. *Tel*: 00 353
    1 679 3561. *Fax*: 00 353 1 679 3717.
Category: Recruitment consultancy.
Recruitment specialty: Senior executive, management and technical personnel,
    in IT/computing, financial services, hospitality, legal, healthcare, sales and
    marketing, accountancy and specialist areas. Permanent or temporary
    assignments.
Locations: Far East, Ireland and Near East.

Emigration Consultancy Services, De Salis Court, Hampton Lovett, Droitwich,
    Worcestershire WR9 0NX, England. *Tel*: (01905) 795949. *Fax*: (01905)
    795557.
Category: Emigration consultancy.
Recruitment specialty: Most skills and sectors.
Locations: Australia, Canada, New Zealand and United States.
Additional information: Assist people to obtain permanent residency in Australia,
    New Zealand and Canada. A comprehensive service is provided, including
    assistance in finding employment.

Engineering Resource Management, Salisbury House, 15/17 The Broadway, Old
    Hatfield, Hertfordshire, AL9 5H7, England. *Tel*: (01707) 272828/264311.
    Fax: (01707) 272828.
Category: Engineering consultancy.
Recruitment specialty: Engineering within construction, civil engineering,
    M&E, utilities, power generation and petrochemical industries.
Locations: Asia, Australia, Canada, Europe, Far East, Ireland, Middle East,
    New Zealand, United Kingdom and United States.

Ennismore Partnership Ltd, 48/50 Mortimer Street, London W1N 7DG,
    England. *Fax*: (0171) 436 7677.
Category: International search and selection consultancy.
Recruitment specialty: Executive and management in sales, marketing and
    other sectors.
Locations: Middle East and United Kingdom.

ERAS, 105 Denmark Street, Diss, Norfolk IP22 3LF, England. Tel: (01379)
    652171. *Fax*: (01379) 644225.
Category: Management consultancy.
Recruitment specialty: Senior to middle management in most sectors excluding
    financial services, banking and specialist IT areas.
Locations: Canada, Europe, United Kingdom and United States.
Additional information: Other services offered to clients include modular
    services, full consultancy services and search and selection.

ESDU International Plc, 27 Corsham Street, London N1 6UQ, England. *Tel*: (0171) 490 5151. *Fax*: (0171) 490 2701.

Category: Employer.

Recruitment specialty: Technical personnel in computing and mathematical sciences, aerospace engineering in mechanical, chemical and structural disciplines.

Location: United Kingdom.

Additional information: Additional services provided to clients are: engineering design data and methodology in looseleaf binders and software for use in aerospace, process and mechanical engineering industries.

Euro Secretaries, 2 Beechworth Close, London NW3 7UT, England. *Tel*: (0171) 435 0718/(0374) 920790. *Fax*: (0171) 794 0249.

Category: Recruitment consultancy.

Recruitment specialty: Monolingual and multilingual secretarial personnel with recognised qualifications and appropriate experience.

Locations: Europe and United Kingdom.

Euro Elite Consultants, Western Australia House, 113/116 The Strand, London WC2R 0AA, England. *Tel*: (0171) 240 4440. *Fax*: (0171) 379 7208.

Category: Recruitment agency.

Recruitment specialty: Engineering and technical support personnel for the public and private sectors on a permanent and temporary basis. Specialist skills and occupational areas include: roads, drainage, bridge and structural design, traffic and transportation, water treatment/supply and design, marine and coastal design, rail, clerks of works, surveyors, resident engineers, draughting technicians, CAD operators, inspectors, geotechnical, architects, laboratory technicians etc.

Locations: Australia, Europe, Far East, Ireland, Middle East, New Zealand and United Kingdom.

Eurolink Group, 56 Old Steine, Brighton BN1 1NH, England. *Tel*: (01273) 202316. *Fax*: (01273) 723078.

Other offices: 7 in the United Kingdom and 9 overseas.

Category: Recruitment agency and management consultancy.

Recruitment specialty: IT/computing both permanent and contract personnel.

Locations: Europe and United Kingdom.

Euromedica Plc, Enterprise House, Vision Park, Histon, Cambridge CB4 4ZR, England. *Tel*: (01223) 235333. *Fax*: (01223) 235305.

Other offices: 4 in Europe.

Category: Executive search consultancy.

Recruitment specialty: Senior executive and management personnel for the pharmaceutical, healthcare and bioscience industries.

Locations: Asia, Europe, Middle East and United Kingdom.

Additional information: Euromedica Plc has offices in France, Benelux,

Germany and Spain and 20 consultants throughout Europe.

European Human Resource Consultants, 63 rue de Rivoli, 75001 Paris, France. *Tel*: 00 33 1 4221 4905. *Fax*: 00 33 1 4221 4956.
Category: Human resource and management consultancy.
Recruitment specialty: Senior executive, management and technical personnel in most industries and sectors.
Location: Europe.
Additional information: European Human Resource Consultants is a network of independent consultancies. It is registered in Paris under EU law as a European economic interest group and has members in 7 EU countries and an associate member in Switzerland. EHRC members employ nearly 800 staff in about 100 locations in 15 countries.

European Project Consultants, Tower House, Fishergate, York YO1 4UA, England. *Tel*: (01904) 624442. *Fax*: (01904) 624187.
Category: Management consultancy.
Recruitment specialty: Project, commercial and construction management in oil and gas, chemicals/pharmaceuticals, cryogenics, telecommunications, transportation and infrastructure projects.
Locations: Africa, Asia, Europe (Scandinavia), Far East, Middle East and United Kingdom.

Eurosearch Associates, 20 North Street, Leatherhead, Surrey KT22 7AS, England. (01372) 361144. *Fax*: (01372) 377250.
Category: Recruitment consultancy.
Recruitment specialty: Executive, management and technical.
Locations: Africa, Europe and United Kingdom.

Executive Choice, Mead Cottage, Memorial Avenue, Shiplake, Oxfordshire RG9 4DF, England. *Tel*: (01734) 403095. Fax: (01734) 403095.
Category: Recruitment consultancy.
Recruitment specialty: Banking systems both retail and wholesale, including dealing room systems and investment job categories in roles such as: senior management, sales and marketing executives, client consultants, project managers and client service personnel.
Locations: Africa, Asia, Europe, Far East, Middle East and United Kingdom.

Executive Recruitment Services, Boundary Way, Hemel Hempstead, Hertfordshire HP2 7RX, England. *Tel*: (01442) 231691. *Fax*: (01442) 230063.
Category: Recruitment consultancy.
Recruitment specialty: Computing, electronics and high technology industries. Also legal professions predominantly from graduate level upwards.
Locations: Canada, Europe, Middle East, United Kingdom and United States.

Fairstaff Agency Ltd, 29/31 Oxford Street, London W1R 1RE, England. *Tel*: (0171) 439 2051. *Fax*: (0171) 287 0850.
Category: Recruitment consultancy.
Recruitment specialty: Specialists in the healthcare and commercial sectors at most levels. Also specialist area placements such as: medical secretaries and receptionists, ward and clinic clerks for private and national health service (NHS) and most administrative placements in both permanent and temporary assignments.
Location: United Kingdom.

Fastec, Butstone House, West Street, Banwell, Avon BS24 6DA, England. *Tel*: (01934) 822492. *Fax*: (01934) 823504/823946.
Category: Design and engineering consultancy.
Recruitment speciality: Engineering and technical support personnel.
Locations: United Kingdom and overseas.

FHELP Marketing, Henriette Villa, Common Mead Avenue, Gillingham, Dorset SP8 4NB, England. *Tel*: (01747) 822651. *Fax*: (01747) 825845.
Category: Recruitment consultancy.
Recruitment specialty: Petrochemical engineers and technicians in processing, refining, chemicals etc. Healthcare personnel including doctors, dentists, paramedics, nursing staff and recreational support especially diving.
Locations: Africa, Canada, Europe, Middle East, Near East, United Kingdom and United States.

FM Recruitment, Greencoat House, Francis Street, London SW1P 1DH, England. *Tel*: (0171) 828 3344. *Fax*: (0171) 828 3355.
Category: Recruitment consultancy.
Recruitment specialty: Management and technical personnel for the hotel, catering and leisure industries. Specialist areas: accounting, finance and systems for long and short term assignments.
Locations: Africa, Asia, Caribbean, Europe, Far East, Ireland, Middle East, Near East and United Kingdom.
Additional information: Applicants must possess appropriate industry experience. Salary ranges £15,000–£100,000.

Focus Executive Ltd, Focus House, Tubbs Lane, Highclere, Newbury, Berkshire RG20 9RD, England. *Tel*: (01635) 254979. *Fax*: (01635) 254002.
Category: Management consultancy.
Recruitment specialty: Senior executive and management levels for the networking and communications specialist areas. Mostly sales, marketing and support placements.
Locations: Europe and United Kingdom.
Additional information: Focus Executive Ltd is a specialist consultancy in business start-up scenarios.

FSS Group, Charlotte House, 14 Windmill Street, London W1P 2DY, England. *Tel*: (0171) 209 1000. *Fax*: (0171) 209 0001.
Category: Recruitment consultancy.
Recruitment specialty: Senior management and technical personnel for the finance and accountancy specialties, qualified and part-qualified accountants etc.
Locations: Asia, Central and Eastern Europe, Far East, Ireland, Middle East, United Kingdom and United States.

FSS Europe, Charlotte House, 14 Windmill Street, London W1P 2DY, England. *Tel*: (0171) 209 1000. *Fax*: (0171) 209 0001.
Category: Search and selection consultancy.
Recruitment specialty: Senior management and technical personnel for the finance, sales and marketing and general management specialty areas.
Locations: Central and Eastern Europe, Ireland and United Kingdom.

Gatton Consulting Group Ltd, Gatton Place, St Matthew's Road, Redhill, Surrey RH1 1TA, England. *Tel*: (01737) 774100. *Fax*: (01737) 772949.
Category: Recruitment consultancy.
Recruitment specialty: IT/computing contract personnel most skills and levels, such as: senior project managers, consultants, programmers etc.
Locations: Europe, Ireland and United Kingdom.

Global Reflex Corporation (GRC) Ltd, 28 Parnell Street, Clonmel, County Tipperary, Republic of Ireland. *Tel*: 00 353 52 27177/25646. *Fax*: 00 353 52 24787.
Category: Recruitment consultancy.
Recruitment specialty: Management and technical personnel within the oil and gas, power generation, water and civil construction specialist areas. Project managers, QS, quality assurance and control (QA/QC), planning/design/instrumentation/electrical and mechanical engineers and technicians.
Locations: Africa, Asia, Europe, Far East, Ireland, Middle East and United Kingdom.

Goh Tan & Company, Suite A & B, 4th Floor, Wisma Hajjah Fatimah, 22/23 Jalan Sultam, Bandar Seri Begawan 2085, Brunei Darussalam.
Category: Accountancy practice and management consultancy.
Recruitment specialty: Most accountancy specialist areas including: auditing, taxation, accountancy, business services, insolvency and corporate advisory services.
Location: Brunei.

Goldsmith Fox PKF, 234-238 Armagh Street, Christchurch, New Zealand.
Category: Accountancy practice and management consultancy.
Recruitment specialty: Most accountancy specialist areas including: auditing, taxation, accountancy, business services, insolvency and corporate advisory

services.

Location: New Zealand.

Goodman Graham & Associates 74 Wimpole Street, London W1M 7DD, England. *Tel*: (0171) 317 1100. *Fax*: (0171) 317 1111.

Category: Executive search consultancy.

Recruitment specialty: Senior executive, management and technical personnel within the information technology (IT), communications, IS, financial services and media sectors.

Locations: Asia, Australia, Canada, Europe, Far East, Ireland, Near East, New Zealand, South America, United Kingdom and United States.

Additional information: Goodman Graham is an executive search and management selection and search firm serving the information industries. The firm works in partnership with blue chip corporations and smaller high growth, fast technology companies across most functions in the United Kingdom and Europe. Clients include leading companies in the IT, communications, IS, financial services and media sectors.

Goodman Graham & Associates, 8 Beaumont Gate, Shenley Hill, Radlett, Hertfordshire WD7 7AR, England. *Tel*: (01923) 855515, Fax: (01923) 854791.

Category: Management selection and search consultancy.

Recruitment specialty: Senior executive, management and technical personnel within the information technology (IT), communications, IS, financial services and media sectors.

Locations: Asia, Australia, Canada, Europe, Far East, Ireland, Near East, New Zealand, South America, United Kingdom and United States.

Additional information: Goodman Graham is an executive search and management selection and search firm serving the information industries. The firm works in partnership with blue chip corporations and smaller high growth, fast technology companies across most functions in the United Kingdom and Europe. Clients include leading companies in the IT, communications, IS, financial services and media sectors.

GPW Search & Selection, Worsley House, North Road, St Helens, Isle of Wight WA10 2BL, England. *Tel*: (01744) 23454. *Fax*: (01744) 451766.

Category: Recruitment consultancy.

Recruitment specialty: Senior executive, management, technical and trades personnel predominantly for the engineering and automotive industries.

Locations: Canada, Europe, United Kingdom and United States.

Grafton Recruitment, 35/37 Queens Square, Belfast BT1 3FG, Northern Ireland. *Tel*: (01232) 242824. *Fax*: (01232) 242897.

Category: Employment consultancy.

Recruitment specialty: Senior executive, management and technical personnel for most sectors.

Locations: Canada, Central and Eastern Europe, Ireland, Middle East, United Kingdom and United States.

Griffon Management Ltd, Tower House, Fishergate, York YO1 4UA, England. *Tel*: (01904) 620772. *Fax*: (01904) 620773.
Category: Executive search consultancy.
Recruitment specialty: Senior executive and management levels in the chemical, food and associated industries.
Locations: Canada, Europe, Ireland and United States.

Hamilton Parker Associates, Lyons House, 2 Station Road, Frimley, Surrey GU16 5HF, England. *Tel*: (01276) 418208. *Fax*: (01276) 418209.
Category: Recruitment agency and human resources consultancy.
Recruitment specialty: Information technology (IT), electronics, datacommunications and telecommunications specialist areas. Also general and line management, sales and marketing, projection management, technical support, design engineering, research and development etc.
Locations: Canada, Europe, United Kingdom and United States.
Additional information: Hamilton Parker Associates provides human resource consultancy services in all of the above areas.

Hanover Fox International, 8 Hanover Street, London W1R 9HF, England. *Tel*: (0171) 290 2622. *Fax*: (0171) 290 2636.
Category: Executive search and selection consultancy.
Recruitment specialty: Executive, senior management and technical personnel for a wide range of industries.
Location: United Kingdom.

Hanover Matrix Ltd, 11/12 Hanover Square, London W1R 9HD, England. *Tel*: (0171) 495 7711. *Fax*: (0171) 495 0826.
Category: Recruitment consultancy.
Recruitment specialty: Sales and sales related personnel most levels and market sectors, including: IT/computing, telecommunications and information.
Location: United Kingdom.

Harel Drouin & Associés, 507 Place d'Armés, Bureau 800, Montréal, Québec, H2Y 2W8, Canada.
Category: Accountancy practice and management consultancy.
Recruitment specialty: Most accountancy specialist areas, including auditing, taxation, accountancy, business services, insolvency and corporate advisory services.
Location: Canada.

Hawtal Whiting Holdings Plc, Phoenix House, Christopher Martin Road, Basildon, Essex SS14 3EZ, England. *Tel*: (01268) 531155. *Fax*: (01268) 531140.

Category: Recruitment consultancy.

Recruitment specialty: Engineering and support personnel for the transportation, automotive and associated industries including styling, computing, structural analysis, quality control and manufacturing.

Locations: Asia, Australia, Canada, Europe, Far East, Ireland, New Zealand, South America, United Kingdom and United States.

Haztek Executive Search, Premier House, 10 Greycoat Place, London SW1P 1SB, England. *Tel*: (0171) 222 8866. Fax: (0171) 223 2847.

Category: Transport and engineering consultancy.

Recruitment specialty: Specialist and chartered engineers such as: chemical engineers, process and safety on/off shore, aeronautical engineers, railway design engineers, safety/reliability/risk and assessment engineers, pharmaceutical process engineers. All placements up to director level.

Locations: Australia, Europe, Far East, Middle East, New Zealand and United Kingdom.

Head Hunt International Ltd, 68 Harcourt Street, Dublin 2, Republic of Ireland. *Tel*: 00 353 1 478 0222. *Fax*: 00 353 1 478 1663.

Category: Recruitment consultancy.

Recruitment specialty: Executive, management, technical etc. personnel within the sales and marketing, information technology services (IT), technical/engineering, linguistics and financial services specialist areas and in most sectors.

Locations: Australia, Canada, Europe, Far East, Ireland, Middle East, New Zealand, United Kingdom and United States.

Hellinger, Hahnemann, Schulte-Gross & Partner, Birkenwaldstrasse 157, 71091 Stuttgart, Germany.

Category: Accountancy practice and management consultancy.

Recruitment specialty: Most accountancy specialist areas including: auditing, taxation, accountancy, business services, insolvency and corporate advisory services.

Location: Europe.

Herst Austin Rowley, 30 St George Street, London W1R 9FA, England. *Tel*: (0171) 629 1223. *Fax*: (0171) 409 7872.

Other offices: 7 overseas.

Category: Search and selection consultancy.

Recruitment specialty: Senior executive and management personnel for most industries and sectors.

Locations: Eastern Europe, United States and Western Europe.

Heston (Middle East) Ltd, The Parade, Market Square, Castletown, Isle of Man IM9 1LQ, United Kingdom. *Tel*: (01624) 82 4595. *Fax*: (01624) 82 5657.

Category: Recruitment consultancy.
Recruitment specialty: Senior engineering and technical personnel for the oil and gas industry, project managers, engineers, technicians, supervisors etc. Also technical and support to the construction industry.
Location: Middle East.

Hewitt Associates, Romeland House, Romeland Hill, St Albans, Hertfordshire AL3 4EZ, England. *Tel*: (01727) 866233. *Fax*: (01727) 831022.
Other offices: 64 overseas.
Category: Human resources consultancy.
Recruitment specialty: Human resources professionals especially compensation reward specialists.
Locations: Africa, Asia, Australia, Canada, Europe, Far East, Ireland, Middle East, Near East, New Zealand, South America, United Kingdom and United States.

Hill & Company, 41 Valleybrook Drive, Suite 200, Toronto, Ontario M3B 2S6, Canada.
Category: Accountancy practice and management consultancy.
Recruitment specialty: Most accountancy specialist areas, including auditing, taxation, accountancy, business services, insolvency and corporate advisory services.
Location: Canada.

Hill McGlynn, Prospect House, Meridians Cross, Ocean Village, Southampton SO14 3TJ, England. *Tel*: (01703) 221 122.
Category: Recruitment consultancy.
Recruitment specialty: Engineers for building and civil engineering, geotechnical and materials, quantity surveying, project management, both mainstream contracting and consulting engineers etc.
Locations: Africa, Asia, Europe, Far East, Middle East, Near East, Indian subcontinent and United Kingdom.

Hillman Saunders Ltd, 78/79 Leadenhall Street, London EC3A 3DH, England. *Tel*: (0171) 929 0707. *Fax*: (0171) 929 1666.
Category: Recruitment consultancy.
Recruitment specialty: Management personnel for the insurance, financial services and legal specialty areas.
Locations: Africa, Europe, Ireland and United Kingdom.

Hoggett Bowers, 7/9 Breams Building, off Chancery Lane, London EC4A 1DY, England. *Tel*: (0171) 430 9000. *Fax*: (0171) 405 5995.
Category: Search and selection consultancy.
Recruitment specialty: Senior executive and management personnel for the financial, accountancy, information technology (IT), defence, aerospace, oil, gas and petrochemical industries.

Locations: Africa, Asia, Australia, Canada, Europe, Far East, Ireland, Middle East, Near East, New Zealand, United Kingdom and United States.

Horton International, 10 Tower Lane, Avon, CT 06001, United States. *Tel*: 00 1 860 674 8701. *Fax*: 00 1 860 676 9735.
Other offices: 2 in the United Kingdom and 28 overseas.
Category: Recruitment consultancy.
Recruitment specialty: General management in the financial services, construction, information technology (IT), aerospace and automotive industries; energy – electricity, oil, gas; utilities – electricity, gas, water, telecommunications including high tech electronics software engineering etc.
Locations: Asia, Australia, Canada, Europe, Far East, Ireland, Middle East, Near East, New Zealand, South America, United Kingdom and United States.

Horton International, 11th Floor, City Centre House, Union Street, Birmingham B2 4SR, England. *Tel*: (0121) 631 4555. *Fax*: (0121) 631 2306.
Other offices: 1 in the United Kingdom and 29 overseas.
Category: Recruitment consultancy.
Recruitment specialty: General management in the financial services, construction, information technology (IT), aerospace and automotive industries; energy – electricity, oil, gas; utilities – electricity, gas, water, telecommunications including high tech electronics software engineering etc.
Locations: Asia, Australia, Canada, Europe, Far East, Ireland, Middle East, Near East, New Zealand, South America, United Kingdom and United States.

Horton International, 15 Scotts Road, #05-05 Thong Teck Building, Singapore 228218. *Tel*: 00 65 738 6511. *Fax*: 00 65 738 6860.
Other offices: 2 in the United Kingdom and 28 overseas.
Category: Recruitment consultancy.
Recruitment specialty: General management in the financial services, construction, information technology (IT), aerospace and automotive industries; energy – electricity, oil, gas; utilities – electricity, gas, water, telecommunications including high tech electronics software engineering etc.
Locations: Asia, Australia, Canada, Europe, Far East, Ireland, Middle East, Near East, New Zealand, South America, United Kingdom and United States.

Horton International, 21/F Silom Complex Building, 191 Silom Road, Bangkok 10500, Thailand. *Tel*: 00 66 2 231 3940. *Fax*: 00 66 2 231 3662.
Other offices: 2 in the United Kingdom and 28 overseas.
Category: Recruitment consultancy.
Recruitment specialty: General management in the financial services, construction, information technology (IT), aerospace and automotive industries; energy – electricity, oil, gas; utilities – electricity, gas, water, telecommunica-

tions including high tech electronics software engineering etc.
Locations: Asia, Australia, Canada, Europe, Far East, Ireland, Middle East, Near East, New Zealand, South America, United Kingdom and United States.

Horton International, 3 rue Troyon, 75017 Paris, France. *Tel*: 00 33 1 4766 4318. *Fax*: 00 33 1 4380 2993.
Other offices: 2 in the United Kingdom and 28 overseas.
Category: Recruitment consultancy.
Recruitment specialty: General management in the financial services, construction, information technology (IT), aerospace and automotive industries; energy – electricity, oil, gas; utilities – electricity, gas, water, telecommunications including high tech electronics software engineering etc.
Locations: Asia, Australia, Canada, Europe, Far East, Ireland, Middle East, Near East, New Zealand, South America, United Kingdom and United States.

Horton International, 3/22 Prabhaderi Industrial Estate, Veer Savarkar Marg, Bombay 400 025, India. *Tel*: 00 91 22 4362341. *Fax*: 00 91 22 4300127.
Other offices: 2 in the United Kingdom and 28 overseas.
Category: Recruitment consultancy.
Recruitment specialty: General management in the financial services, construction, information technology (IT), aerospace and automotive industries; energy – electricity, oil, gas; utilities – electricity, gas, water, telecommunications including high tech electronics software engineering etc.
Locations: Asia, Australia, Canada, Europe, Far East, Ireland, Middle East, Near East, New Zealand, South America, United Kingdom and United States.

Horton International, 33 Sloan Street, Roswell, GA 30075, United States. *Tel*: 00 1 770 640 1533. *Fax*: 00 1 770 640 6242.
Other offices: 2 in the United Kingdom and 28 overseas.
Category: Recruitment consultancy.
Recruitment specialty: General management in the financial services, construction, information technology (IT), aerospace and automotive industries; energy – electricity, oil, gas; utilities – electricity, gas, water, telecommunications including high tech electronics software engineering etc.
Locations: Asia, Australia, Canada, Europe, Far East, Ireland, Middle East, Near East, New Zealand, South America, United Kingdom and United States.

Horton International, 333 So Grand Avenue, Suite #2980, Los Angeles, CA 90071, United States. *Tel*: 00 1 213 628 2580. *Fax*: 00 1 213 628 2581.
Other offices: 2 in the United Kingdom and 28 overseas.
Category: Recruitment consultancy.
Recruitment specialty: General management in the financial services, construc-

tion, information technology (IT), aerospace and automotive industries; energy – electricity, oil, gas; utilities – electricity, gas, water, telecommunications including high tech electronics software engineering etc.

Locations: Asia, Australia, Canada, Europe, Far East, Ireland, Middle East, Near East, New Zealand, South America, United Kingdom and United States.

Horton International, 38 Grosvenor Gardens, London SW1W 0EB, England. *Tel*: (0171) 730 2122. *Fax*: (0171) 730 0261.

Other offices: 1 in the United Kingdom and 29 overseas.

Category: Recruitment consultancy.

Recruitment specialty: General management in the financial services, construction, information technology (IT), aerospace and automotive industries; energy – electricity, oil, gas; utilities – electricity, gas, water, telecommunications including high tech electronics software engineering etc.

Locations: Asia, Australia, Canada, Europe, Far East, Ireland, Middle East, Near East, New Zealand, South America, United Kingdom and United States.

Horton International, 666 Fifth Avenue, 37th Floor, New York NY 10103, United States. *Tel*: 00 1 212 541 3900. *Fax*: 00 1 212 541 3902.

Other offices: 2 in the United Kingdom and 28 overseas.

Category: Recruitment consultancy.

Recruitment specialty: General management in the financial services, construction, information technology (IT), aerospace and automotive industries; energy – electricity, oil, gas; utilities – electricity, gas, water, telecommunications including high tech electronics software engineering etc.

Locations: Asia, Australia, Canada, Europe, Far East, Ireland, Middle East, Near East, New Zealand, South America, United Kingdom and United States.

Horton International, 6th Floor, The Valero Tower, 122 Valero Street, Salcedo Village, Makati, Metro Manila, Philippines. *Tel*: 00 63 2 893 7891/7985. *Fax*: 00 63 2 893 8031.

Other offices: 2 in the United Kingdom and 28 overseas.

Category: Recruitment consultancy.

Recruitment specialty: General management in the financial services, construction, information technology (IT), aerospace and automotive industries; energy – electricity, oil, gas; utilities – electricity, gas, water, telecommunications including high tech electronics software engineering etc.

Locations: Asia, Australia, Canada, Europe, Far East, Ireland, Middle East, Near East, New Zealand, South America, United Kingdom and United States.

Horton International, 814 Gordon Woods Road, Wilmington, NC 28405, United States. *Tel*: 00 1 910 792 1103. *Fax*: 00 1 910 792 1105.

Other offices: 2 in the United Kingdom and 28 overseas.

Category: Recruitment consultancy.

Recruitment specialty: General management in the financial services, construction, information technology (IT), aerospace and automotive industries; energy – electricity, oil, gas; utilities – electricity, gas, water, telecommunications including high tech electronics software engineering etc.

Locations: Asia, Australia, Canada, Europe, Far East, Ireland, Middle East, Near East, New Zealand, South America, United Kingdom and United States.

Horton International, Av. Ibirapuera 2064-10°, 04028-001 São Paulo, Brazil. *Tel/Fax*: 00 55 11 575 5551.

Other offices: 2 in the United Kingdom and 28 overseas.

Category: Recruitment consultancy.

Recruitment specialty: General management in the financial services, construction, information technology (IT), aerospace and automotive industries; energy – electricity, oil, gas; utilities – electricity, gas, water, telecommunications including high tech electronics software engineering etc.

Locations: Asia, Australia, Canada, Europe, Far East, Ireland, Middle East, Near East, New Zealand, South America, United Kingdom and United States.

Horton International, Barranca del Muerto, No 472 Col Alpes, Mexico DF 01010. *Tel*: 00 525 593 8766. *Fax*: 00 525 593 8969.

Other offices: 2 in the United Kingdom and 28 overseas.

Category: Recruitment consultancy.

Recruitment specialty: General management in the financial services, construction, information technology (IT), aerospace and automotive industries; energy – electricity, oil, gas; utilities – electricity, gas, water, telecommunications including high tech electronics software engineering etc.

Locations: Asia, Australia, Canada, Europe, Far East, Ireland, Middle East, Near East, New Zealand, South America, United Kingdom and United States.

Horton International, Box 7026, S-103 86 Stockholm, Sweden. *Tel*: 00 46 8 613 1660. *Fax*: 00 46 8 791 8121.

Other offices: 2 in the United Kingdom and 28 overseas.

Category: Recruitment consultancy.

Recruitment specialty: General management in the financial services, construction, information technology (IT), aerospace and automotive industries; energy – electricity, oil, gas; utilities – electricity, gas, water, telecommunications including high tech electronics software engineering etc.

Locations: Asia, Australia, Canada, Europe, Far East, Ireland, Middle East, Near East, New Zealand, South America, United Kingdom and United States.

Horton International, Katona Jozsef u. 3.11/18, 1137 Budapest, Hungary. *Tel/ Fax:* 00 361 269 3737.
Other offices: 2 in the United Kingdom and 28 overseas.
Category: Recruitment consultancy.
Recruitment specialty: General management in the financial services, construction, information technology (IT), aerospace and automotive industries; energy – electricity, oil, gas; utilities – electricity, gas, water, telecommunications including high tech electronics software engineering etc.
Locations: Asia, Australia, Canada, Europe, Far East, Ireland, Middle East, Near East, New Zealand, South America, United Kingdom and United States.

Horton International, Lagerstrasse 14, CH-8600 Dubendorf, Switzerland. *Tel:* 00 411 821 0515. *Fax:* 00 411 821 0517.
Other offices: 2 in the United Kingdom and 28 overseas.
Category: Recruitment consultancy.
Recruitment specialty: General management in the financial services, construction, information technology (IT), aerospace and automotive industries; energy – electricity, oil, gas; utilities – electricity, gas, water, telecommunications including high tech electronics software engineering etc.
Locations: Asia, Australia, Canada, Europe, Far East, Ireland, Middle East, Near East, New Zealand, South America, United Kingdom and United States.

Horton International, Level 2, 36 Albert Road, South Melbourne, Vic 3205, Australia. *Tel:* 00 61 3 9696 0800. *Fax:* 00 61 3 9682 1000.
Other offices: 2 in the United Kingdom and 28 overseas.
Category: Recruitment consultancy.
Recruitment specialty: General management in the financial services, construction, information technology (IT), aerospace and automotive industries; energy – electricity, oil, gas; utilities – electricity, gas, water, telecommunications including high tech electronics software engineering etc.
Locations: Asia, Australia, Canada, Europe, Far East, Ireland, Middle East, Near East, New Zealand, South America, United Kingdom and United States.

Horton International, Malesingel 27 A 3581 BH, Utrecht, Netherlands. *Tel:* 00 31 3 0236 9136. *Fax:* 00 31 3 0236 9199.
Other offices: 2 in the United Kingdom and 28 overseas.
Category: Recruitment consultancy.
Recruitment specialty: General management in the financial services, construction, information technology (IT), aerospace and automotive industries; energy – electricity, oil, gas; utilities – electricity, gas, water, telecommunications including high tech electronics software engineering etc.
Locations: Asia, Australia, Canada, Europe, Far East, Ireland, Middle East, Near East, New Zealand, South America, United Kingdom and United States.

Horton International, Monte Esquinza, 44 3° B 28010, Madrid, Spain. *Tel*: 00 34 1 319 2122/9091. *Fax*: 00 34 1 319 8942.
Other offices: 2 in the United Kingdom and 28 overseas.
Category: Recruitment consultancy.
Recruitment specialty: General management in the financial services, construction, information technology (IT), aerospace and automotive industries; energy – electricity, oil, gas; utilities – electricity, gas, water, telecommunications including high tech electronics software engineering etc.
Locations: Asia, Australia, Canada, Europe, Far East, Ireland, Middle East, Near East, New Zealand, South America, United Kingdom and United States.

Horton International, Plaza PP, Lantai 11, Jalan Raga Gedong 57, Jakarta, Timur, Indonesia. *Tel*: 00 62 21 840 3990. *Fax*: 00 62 21 840 3991.
Other offices: 2 in the United Kingdom and 28 overseas.
Category: Recruitment consultancy.
Recruitment specialty: General management in the financial services, construction, information technology (IT), aerospace and automotive industries; energy – electricity, oil, gas; utilities – electricity, gas, water, telecommunications including high tech electronics software engineering etc.
Locations: Asia, Australia, Canada, Europe, Far East, Ireland, Middle East, Near East, New Zealand, South America, United Kingdom and United States.

Horton International, Presnienski val 24-16, 123557 Moscow, Russia. *Tel*: 00 07 7 095 253 4586. *Fax*: 00 07 7 095 253 4442.
Other offices: 2 in the United Kingdom and 28 overseas.
Category: Recruitment consultancy.
Recruitment specialty: General management in the financial services, construction, information technology (IT), aerospace and automotive industries; energy – electricity, oil, gas; utilities – electricity, gas, water, telecommunications including high tech electronics software engineering etc.
Locations: Asia, Australia, Canada, Europe, Far East, Ireland, Middle East, Near East, New Zealand, South America, United Kingdom and United States.

Horton International, Rambla de Cataluna, 121. 1° 08008, Barcelona, Spain.
Other offices: 2 in the United Kingdom and 28 overseas.
Category: Recruitment consultancy.
Recruitment specialty: General management in the financial services, construction, information technology (IT), aerospace and automotive industries; energy – electricity, oil, gas; utilities – electricity, gas, water, telecommunications including high tech electronics software engineering etc.
Locations: Asia, Australia, Canada, Europe, Far East, Ireland, Middle East, Near East, New Zealand, South America, United Kingdom and United States.

Horton International, Room 1901, 19/F Queen's Place, 74 Queen's Road, Central Hong Kong. *Tel*: 00 852 2525 9127. *Fax*: 00 852 2521 6056. *Other offices*: 2 in the United Kingdom and 28 overseas. *Category*: Recruitment consultancy. *Recruitment specialty*: General management in the financial services, construction, information technology (IT), aerospace and automotive industries; energy – electricity, oil, gas; utilities – electricity, gas, water, telecommunications including high tech electronics software engineering etc. *Locations*: Asia, Australia, Canada, Europe, Far East, Ireland, Middle East, Near East, New Zealand, South America, United Kingdom and United States.

Horton International, Room 1218, Block B, Lucky Tower, 3 Dong Shan Huan, Bei Lu Chao,Yang District, Beijing, People's Republic of China. *Tel*: 00 86 10 461 6391. *Fax*: 00 86 10 461 6392. *Other offices*: 2 in the United Kingdom and 28 overseas. *Category*: Recruitment consultancy. *Recruitment specialty*: General management in the financial services, construction, information technology (IT), aerospace and automotive industries; energy – electricity, oil, gas; utilities – electricity, gas, water, telecommunications including high tech electronics software engineering etc. *Locations*: Asia, Australia, Canada, Europe, Far East, Ireland, Middle East, Near East, New Zealand, South America, United Kingdom and United States.

Horton International, Rue Copermic 6A, 1180 Brussels, Belgium. *Tel/Fax*: 00 32 2 374 0860. *Other offices*: 2 in the United Kingdom and 28 overseas. *Category*: Recruitment consultancy. *Recruitment specialty*: General management in the financial services, construction, information technology (IT), aerospace and automotive industries; energy – electricity, oil, gas; utilities – electricity, gas, water, telecommunications including high tech electronics software engineering etc. *Locations*: Asia, Australia, Canada, Europe, Far East, Ireland, Middle East, Near East, New Zealand, South America, United Kingdom and United States.

Horton International, Rusterstrasse, 1 PO Box 170250, 60325 Frankfurt, Germany. *Tel*: 00 49 6 9714 0060. *Fax*: 00 49 6 9714 00625. *Other offices*: 2 in the United Kingdom and 28 overseas. *Category*: Recruitment consultancy. *Recruitment specialty*: General management in the financial services, construction, information technology (IT), aerospace and automotive industries; energy – electricity, oil, gas; utilities – electricity, gas, water, telecommunications including high tech electronics software engineering etc. *Locations*: Asia, Australia, Canada, Europe, Far East, Ireland, Middle East,

Near East, New Zealand, South America, United Kingdom and United States.

Horton International, Shugetsu, Building 6F, 3-12-7 Kita Aoyama, Minato-ku, Tokyo 107, Japan. *Tel*: 00 813 3486 2711. *Fax*: 00 813 3486 2722.
Other offices: 2 in the United Kingdom and 28 overseas.
Category: Recruitment consultancy.
Recruitment specialty: General management in the financial services, construction, information technology (IT), aerospace and automotive industries; energy – electricity, oil, gas; utilities – electricity, gas, water, telecommunications including high tech electronics software engineering etc.
Locations: Asia, Australia, Canada, Europe, Far East, Ireland, Middle East, Near East, New Zealand, South America, United Kingdom and United States.

Horton International, Suite B & C, 10th Floor, 629 Ling Ling road, Shanghai 200030, People's Republic of China. *Tel*: 00 86 21 486 4796. *Fax*: 00 86 21 486 4797.
Other offices: 2 in the United Kingdom and 28 overseas.
Category: Recruitment consultancy.
Recruitment specialty: General management in the financial services, construction, information technology (IT), aerospace and automotive industries; energy – electricity, oil, gas; utilities – electricity, gas, water, telecommunications including high tech electronics software engineering etc.
Locations: Asia, Australia, Canada, Europe, Far East, Ireland, Middle East, Near East, New Zealand, South America, United Kingdom and United States.

Horton International, ul. Koszykowa 60/62, 00-673 Warsaw, Poland. *Tel*: 00 482 628 4836. *Fax*: 00 482 622 0124.
Other offices: 2 in the United Kingdom and 28 overseas.
Category: Recruitment consultancy.
Recruitment specialty: General management in the financial services, construction, information technology (IT), aerospace and automotive industries; energy – electricity, oil, gas; utilities – electricity, gas, water, telecommunications including high tech electronics software engineering etc.
Locations: Asia, Australia, Canada, Europe, Far East, Ireland, Middle East, Near East, New Zealand, South America, United Kingdom and United States.

Horton International, Via Paolo da Cannobio, 8 20122 Milano, Italy. *Tel*: 00 39 2 8645 5500. *Fax*: 00 39 2 8645 6000.
Other offices: 2 in the United Kingdom and 28 overseas.
Category: Recruitment consultancy.
Recruitment specialty: General management in the financial services, construction, information technology (IT), aerospace and automotive industries;

energy – electricity, oil, gas; utilities – electricity, gas, water, telecommunications including high tech electronics software engineering etc.
Locations: Asia, Australia, Canada, Europe, Far East, Ireland, Middle East, Near East, New Zealand, South America, United Kingdom and United States.

Hoskyns Consulting, 130 Shaftesbury Avenue, London W1V 8HH, England.
Category: Management consultancy.
Recruitment specialty: Executive and management in most sectors.
Locations: Middle East and United Kingdom.

Howgate Sable & Partners, Arkwright House, Parsonage Gardens, Manchester M3 2LF, England. *Tel*: (0161) 839 2000. *Fax*: (0161) 839 0064.
Other offices: 3 in the United Kingdom.
Category: Executive search and selection consultancy.
Recruitment specialty: Executive and senior management in most sectors.
Location: United Kingdom.

Hughes Castell, 602 East Town Building, 41 Lockhart Road, Wanchai, Hong Kong. *Tel*: 00 852 2520 1168.
Category: Recruitment consultancy.
Recruitment specialty: Senior legal personnel for the banks and public limited companies (plcs).
Locations: Asia, Australia, Europe, Far East, Ireland, Middle East, New Zealand, United Kingdom and United States.

Humana International Group Plc, The, 231 Tottenham Court Road, London W1P 9AE, England. *Tel*: (0171) 636 7636. *Fax*: (0171) 636 7666.
Other offices: 70 in the United Kingdom and 30 overseas.
Category: Recruitment consultancy.
Recruitment specialty: Executive, management and technical personnel, in a wide band of levels, in most business, banking and commercial sectors.
Locations: Asia, Canada, Europe, Far East, Ireland, Middle East, Near East, United Kingdom and United States.

Hunter Personnel Contracts Ltd, 24 St Peters Road, Bournemouth, Dorset BH1 2LN, England. *Tel*: (01202) 298322. *Fax*: (01202) 298383.
Category: Recruitment consultancy.
Recruitment specialty: Senior executive, management and technical placements, specialising in tunnelling, mining and heavy civil engineering. Personnel placed in permanent or contract assignments. Specialist skills areas are: engineers, administration, consultants, ground personnel, production mining/tunnelling/structural engineers, quantity surveyors, quality control, electrical and mechanical engineers.
Locations: Africa, Asia, Australia, Canada, Europe, Far East, Ireland, Middle East, New Zealand, United Kingdom and United States.

Hunter Search & Selection, 18 The Green, Richmond, Surrey TW9 1PX, England. *Tel*: (0181) 332 7242. *Fax*: (0181) 848 3151.
Category: Search and selection consultancy.
Recruitment specialty: Senior executive and management levels in IT, merchant banking, management consultancy, commerce and defence specialist areas.
Locations: Canada, Europe, United Kingdom and United States.

Hunter Staff Consultants, Buxton House, Buxton Square, Leigh-on-Sea, Essex SS9 3UD, England. *Tel*: (01702) 557561.
Category: Management consultancy.
Recruitment specialty: Senior executive, management and technical personnel in most industries and sectors.
Locations: Middle East and United Kingdom.

Hunters Search & Selection, 33 Southampton Street, Covent Garden, London WC2E 7HE, England. *Tel*: (0171) 240 2400. *Fax*: (0171) 379 3267.
Category: Search and selection consultancy.
Recruitment specialty: Recruitment consultants up to MD level within IT, banking, insurance and accountancy.
Locations: Australia, Canada, New Zealand, United Kingdom and United States.

Hunterskil Howard, Aalsterweg 5, PO Box 155, 5600 AD Eindhoven, Netherlands. *Tel*: 00 31 40 294 8686. *Fax*: 00 31 40 212 0260.
Category: Recruitment consultancy.
Recruitment specialty: Engineers and technical personnel for the aerospace, telecommunications, high technology and industrial electronics, consumer electronics and IT/computing industries and specialty areas.
Location: Europe.

Hutchinson's Recruitment Consultants, 33 Princes Gate Mews, London SW7 2PR, England. *Tel*: (0171) 581 0010. *Fax*: (0171) 581 1011.
Category: Recruitment consultancy.
Recruitment specialty: Executive management and technical in most sectors.
Locations: Middle East and United Kingdom.

HZ Praha sro Ltd, Ceskomoravska 23, 180 56 Prague 9, Czech Republic.
Category: Accountancy practice and management consultancy.
Recruitment specialty: Most accountancy specialist areas including: auditing, taxation, accountancy, business services, insolvency and corporate advisory services.
Location: Czech Republic.

IBNIX Ltd, 12/18 Paul Street, London EC2A 4NX, England. *Tel*: (0171) 377 9995. *Fax*: (0171) 247 5471.
Category: Recruitment consultancy.

Recruitment specialty: IT/computing contract personnel in communications, PC networks, skills in OOD, relational databases, client server development etc.

Locations: Europe, Ireland, Middle East and United Kingdom.

Industrie-und Verkehrstreuhand GmbH, Maximilianstrasse 27, 80539 München, Germany.

Category: Accountancy practice and management consultancy.

Recruitment specialty: Most accountancy specialist areas, including: auditing, taxation, accountancy, business services, insolvency and corporate advisory services.

Location: Europe.

Information Management Resources (IMR) UK, Link House, St Mary's, Chesham, Buckinghamshire HP5 1HR, England. *Tel*: (01494) 791791.

Other offices: 5 overseas.

Category: Management consultancy.

Recruitment specialty: Management and technical personnel for the IT/computing industry. Skills such as: programming, analysis, databases, project management, hardware and software engineers etc.

Location: United States.

InfoSoft Inc, 10670 North Tantall Avenue, Cupertino, CA 95014, United States. *Tel*: 00 408 366 0900. *Fax*: 00 408 366 1329.

Category: Information technology consultancy.

Recruitment specialty: IT consultants, project managers, analysts, programmers etc in the provision of custom software development and IT consulting.

Location: United States.

INTEC UK Ltd, Rhodes House, 114 St Leonard Gate, Lancaster, Lancashire LA1 1NN, England. *Tel*: (01524) 62324. *Fax*: (01524) 33085.

Category: Recruitment consultancy.

Recruitment specialty: Senior management and technical personnel, project management, quality consultants, inspectors, engineers, safety and environmental specialists.

Locations: Africa, Asia, Europe, Far East, Ireland, Middle East, Near East, South America and United Kingdom.

Intercai Mondiale Ltd, Walton House, The Courtyard, West Street, Marlow, Buckinghamshire SL7 2LS, England. *Tel*: (01628) 478470. *Fax*: (01628) 478472.

Category: Management and telecommunications consultancy.

Recruitment specialty: Executive consultants in business/financial planning, marketing, economics, telecommunications, customer service etc.

Locations: Europe, United Kingdom and United States.

InterExec Career Management, 1 Warwick Row, London SW1E 5ER, England. *Tel*: (0171) 630 0155. *Fax*: (0171) 630 0114/0117.
Other offices: 14 in the United Kingdom.
Category: Human resources consultancy.
Recruitment specialty: Senior executive, management, technical and support personnel in most levels and sectors.
Locations: Australia, Europe, Far East, Near East, New Zealand, South America and United Kingdom.
Additional information: InterExec Career Management assists all levels of personnel to focus on relevant career objectives, whether in employment or moving to new positions. Senior executives can receive impartial advice through the firm's workshop programme. More junior levels of staff can participate in career care courses in the Career Partnership Division. The Executive Outplacement Division handles individuals whereas technical management and middle management are advised by professional advisers in the Job Counsellors Division. Overall InterExec Career Management are able to assist personnel departments to manage change more effectively and enhance the morale and careers of the remaining members of the workforce.

Intermanagement Group, Head Office, 159 High Street, Huntingdon, Cambridgeshire PE18 6TF, England. *Tel*: (01480) 455455. *Fax*: (01480) 52201.
Category: Recruitment consultancy.
Recruitment specialty: IT/computing, software engineering, electronics and telecommunications engineering, operations, business development, sales and marketing, electrical and mechanical engineering, banking, insurance and finance. Permanent, contract and consultancy assignments.
Locations: Africa, Europe, Far East, Middle East and United Kingdom.

International Auditing S.A., 120 Vassilissis Sophias Avenue, 115 26 Athens, Greece.
Category: Accountancy practice and management consultancy.
Recruitment specialty: Most accountancy specialist areas including: auditing, taxation, accountancy, business services, insolvency and corporate advisory services.
Location: Europe.

International Management & Marketing Consulting (IMMC) Ltd, H-1054 Budapest, Alkotrnany u 10, Hungary. *Tel*: 00 36 1 131 0378. *Fax*: 00 36 1 153 2726.
Category: Executive search and selection consultancy.
Recruitment specialty: Senior executive, management and technical personnel in most industries and sectors.
Location: Europe.
Additional information: IMMC Ltd is a member of European Human Resource Consultants (EHRC).

Intertech Computer Consultants Ltd, Chester House, Harlands Road, Haywards Heath, West Sussex RH16 1TD, England. *Tel*: (01444) 450405. *Fax*: (01444) 457 1123.
Category: Recruitment consultancy.
Recruitment specialty: IT/computing permanent and contract personnel in most skills such as: IBM mainframe, UNIX, ICL/DEC/AS400, ORACLE/INGRES/SYBASE/INFORMIX, networking, communications, PC support and development, client server, OO, GVI, GSM, analysis, management and consultancy roles.
Locations: Canada, Europe, United Kingdom and United States.

IPS Group Ltd, Lloyd's Avenue House, 6 Lloyd's Avenue, London EC3N 3ES, England. *Tel*: (0171) 481 8111. *Fax*: (0171) 481 0994.
Category: Recruitment consultancy.
Recruitment specialty: Management and technical personnel in most specialty areas within the insurance industry.
Locations: Africa, Asia, Australia, Canada, Europe, Far East, Ireland, Middle East, Near East, New Zealand, South America, United Kingdom and United States.

IQS International, The Honours, 70/80 Akeman Street, Tring, Hertfordshire HP23 6AJ, England. *Tel*: (01442) 891170. *Fax*: (01442) 891017.
Category: Quality management consultancy.
Recruitment specialty: Senior executive, management and technical in most sectors with emphasis on quality management systems, ISO9000, training and development, CE marking etc.
Location: United Kingdom.

ISIS Consultants, Old Bank House, 79 Broad Street, Chipping Sodbury, Bristol BS17 6AD, England. *Tel*: (01454) 329 944. *Fax*: (01454) 329 955.
Category: Recruitment consultancy.
Recruitment specialty: Senior executive, management, engineering and technical personnel for the information technology (IT), communications, aerospace, defence, electronics, chemicals, construction, environmental, process control, manufacturing, transportation, utilities, energy etc. industries.
Locations: Europe and United Kingdom.

Jacob Partnership, The, AW House, Chaul End Lane, Luton, Bedfordshire LU4 8EG, England. *Tel*: (01582) 566789. *Fax*: (01582) 560033.
Category: Recruitment consultancy.
Recruitment specialty: Engineering and technical support personnel for the construction, automotive, HVAC, validation, IT/computing, technical sales industries and specialist areas. Contract and permanent assignments, mechanical, electrical, electronic, design, project engineers and technicians.
Locations: Europe, Ireland, Middle East and United Kingdom.

Jacob Partnership, The, Spring Bridge Mews, Ealing, London W5 2AB, England. *Tel*: (0181) 566 5998. *Fax*: (0181) 566 5933.
Category: Recruitment consultancy.
Recruitment specialty: Engineering and technical support personnel for the construction, automotive, HVAC, validation, IT/computing, technical sales industries and specialist areas. Contract and permanent assignments, mechanical, electrical, electronic, design, project engineers and technicians.
Locations: Europe, Ireland, Middle East and United Kingdom.

James Baker Associates, 46 Queens Road, Reading, Berkshire RG1 4BD, England. *Tel*: (0118) 950 5022. *Fax*: (0118) 950 5056.
Category: Recruitment and human resources consultancy.
Recruitment specialty: Senior executive to lower management levels specialising in the information technology (IT) industry. Specialists range from software development to sales etc.
Locations: Australia, Canada, Europe (Scandinavia), Middle East, New Zealand, United Kingdom and United States.

James Lambert Consulting Inc, 84 Marylebone High Street, London W1M 3DE, England. *Tel*: (0181) 449 1125. *Fax*: (0181) 245 5810.
Category: Management consultancy.
Recruitment specialty: Senior technical personnel with excellent communication and presentation skills for the data warehousing (DW), BPR, change management, system migration, DB and client server specialist areas.
Locations: Canada, United Kingdom and United States.
Additional information: Candidates must hold a recognised degree qualification preferably with previous board level experience.

Jawaby Oil Service, 15/17 Lodge Road, London NW8 7JA, England. *Tel*: (0171) 314 6000. Fax: (0171) 266 2298.
Category: Management consultancy.
Recruitment specialty: Oil exploration, production and support.
Location: Middle East.
Additional information: This company offers work opportunities in Libya. Forward CVs to the recruitment department.

JED Consultants, 166 Upper New Walk, Leicester, Leicestershire LE1 7QA, England. *Tel*: (0116) 233 8866. *Fax*: (0116) 233 8867.
Category: Recruitment consultancy.
Recruitment specialty: Senior executive, management, technical personnel for the automotive, aerospace, energy, power, oil and gas and high technology industries. Technical consultants and electrical/mechanical engineers, project and production managers in most levels from new graduates to directors.
Locations: Europe and United Kingdom.

Job Maeglerne, 7G1 Lundtoftevej, DK-2800 Kgs Lyngby, Denmark. *Tel*: 00 45 4593 0012. Fax: 00 45 4593 0880.

Category: Human resource and management consultancy.

Recruitment specialty: Senior executive, management and technical personnel in most industries and sectors.

Location: Europe

Additional information: Job Maeglerne is a member of European Human Resource Consultants (EHRC). The services provided by this company include: human resources consultancy in all the known specialty areas, management development programmes, corporate strategy, executive recruitment, total staffing, performance programmes etc.

John Richards Associates, 130 High Street, Newport, Shropshire, TF10 7BH, England. *Tel*: (01952) 825247 (6 lines). *Fax*: (01952) 825249.

Category: Recruitment consultancy.

Recruitment specialty: Senior executive and management personnel for the sales and marketing and export specialty areas of building products and materials. Sales directors, executives, managers, export and product managers etc.

Locations: Europe, Middle East and United Kingdom.

Jonathan Lee Technical Recruitment, The Maltings, Mount Road, Stourbridge, West Midlands DY8 1HZ, England. *Tel*: (01384) 397555. *Fax*: (01384) 379396.

Category: Recruitment consultancy.

Recruitment speciality: Senior executive, management, technical and graduate trainee personnel for the aerospace, rail, domestic appliance, light engineering, capital goods and equipment, electronics and process industries.

Locations: Australia, Canada, Europe, New Zealand, United Kingdom and United States.

Additional information: Jonathan Lee Technical Recruitment also handle advertised and headhunt assignments.

Kanoo Group Ltd, The Glassmill, 1 Battersea Road, London SW11 3BG, England.

Category: Management consultancy.

Recruitment specialty: Executive and management.

Location: Middle East.

Keith Townrow & Partners, Aztec Centre, Aztec West, Bristol BS12 4TD, England. *Tel*: (01454) 614373. *Fax*: (01454) 615015.

Category: Human resources consultancy.

Recruitment specialty: Senior executives for specialising in the food and drink industries.

Locations: Europe and United Kingdom.

Additional information: Other client services include: executive search and selection, management assessment, psychometric analysis, non-executive directors and interim managers.

Keystone Recruitment Consultants, Head Office, Keystone House, 272/276 Pentonville Road, London N1 9JY, England. *Tel*: (0171) 278 3400/837 6444. *Fax*: (0171) 278 2558/7299.
Category: Recruitment consultancy.
Recruitment specialty: Senior executive, management and technical personnel for the hotel and catering industry. Permanent and temporary basis for non-senior secretarial, printing, hotel and catering staff.
Locations: Africa, Asia, Europe, Far East, Ireland, Middle East and United Kingdom.

Keystone Recruitment Consultants, 107 Muswell Hill, London N10 3HS, England. *Tel*: (0181) 883 8322. *Fax*: (0181) 883 4268.
Category: Recruitment consultancy.
Recruitment specialty: Senior executive, management and technical personnel for the hotel and catering industry. Permanent and temporary basis for non-senior secretarial, printing, hotel and catering staff.
Locations: Africa, Asia, Europe, Far East, Ireland, Middle East and United Kingdom.

Keystone Recruitment Consultants, 176 Liverpool Street, Bishopsgate, London EC2 M4NQ, England. *Tel*: (0171) 283 5914. *Fax*: (0171) 283 7780.
Category: Recruitment consultancy.
Recruitment specialty: Senior executive, management and technical personnel for the hotel and catering industry. Permanent and temporary basis for non-senior secretarial, printing, hotel and catering staff.
Locations: Africa, Asia, Europe, Far East, Ireland, Middle East and United Kingdom.

Keystone Recruitment Consultants, 219 Oxford Street, London W1R 1AH, England. *Tel*: (0171) 434 1301. *Fax*: (0171) 494 3762.
Category: Recruitment consultancy.
Recruitment specialty: Senior executive, management and technical personnel for the hotel and catering industry. Permanent and temporary basis for non-senior secretarial, printing, hotel and catering staff.
Locations: Africa, Asia, Europe, Far East, Ireland, Middle East and United Kingdom.

Kilvington Saville & Partners Ltd, Minerva House, 34 North Street, Rugby, Warwickshire CV21 2AL, England. *Tel*: (01788) 541 306. *Fax*: (01788) 552 142.
Category: Recruitment consultancy.
Recruitment specialty: Most management levels within the high technology, consumer electronics, IT, telecommunications industries etc.

Locations: Asia, Canada, Eastern Europe, Ireland, Middle East, United Kingdom, United States and Western Europe.

Knight Chapman Ltd, 11 Garrick Street, London WC2E 9AR, England. *Tel*: (0171) 379 7879. *Fax*: (0171) 497 2133.
Category: Executive search and selection consultancy.
Recruitment specialty: Executive, management and technical in most sectors.
Locations: Far East and United Kingdom.

KPMG Management Consultants, Stokes Place, St Stephen's Green, Dublin 2, Republic of Ireland. *Tel*: 00 353 1 708 1800/1000. *Fax*: 00 353 1 708 1880/ 1122.
Category: Executive search and selection consultancy.
Recruitment specialty: Senior executive, management and technical personnel, most levels and sectors.
Locations: Europe and Ireland.

Kramer Westfield, The Old Pound House, London Road, Sunningdale, Berkshire SL5 0DS, England. *Tel*: (01344) 875087. *Fax*: (01344) 874877.
Category: Search and selection consultancy.
Recruitment specialty: Senior management and technical personnel for the telecommunications and software engineering industry and general management, marketing etc.
Locations: Asia, Australia, Canada, Europe, New Zealand, United Kingdom and United States.

Leading Edge Consulting, Chesham House, 150 Regent Street, London W1R 5FA, England. *Tel*: (01273) 326337. *Fax*: (01273) 821271.
Category: Recruitment consultancy.
Recruitment specialty: Senior information technology (IT) permanent appointments in most sectors.
Locations: Asia, Australia, Canada, Europe, Far East, New Zealand, United Kingdom and United States.

Liebrecht Persona Iwerbung GmbH, Mendelssohnstrasse 75/77, 6000 Frankfurt 1, Germany. *Tel*: 00 49 6974 0255. *Fax*: 00 49 6975 2401.
Category: Recruitment advertising consultancy.
Recruitment specialty: Executive, management and technical in commercial, financial, industrial and public sectors.
Locations: Canada, Europe, United Kingdom and United States.
Additional information: Services offered to their clients are: recruitment advertising, search and selection, communications and business psychology.

Ling Recruitment International, Kulite House, Stroudley Road, Basingstoke, Hampshire RG24 8WG, England. *Tel*: (01256) 56565. *Fax*: (01256) 812864.
Category: Recruitment consultancy.

Recruitment specialty: Management and engineering personnel for the petro-chemical, civil, electrical, water treatment, design and construction industries.
Locations: Europe, Far East, Middle East, Near East and United Kingdom.

LJB & Company, The Maples, 144 Liverpool Road, London N1 1LA, England. *Tel*: (0171) 609 7769. *Fax*: (0171) 607 7378.
Category: Recruitment and search and selection consultancy.
Recruitment specialty: Senior management and technical personnel for the construction, building services and IT/computing industries. Site engineers and agents, project managers, quantity surveyors, CAD operators, HVAC design engineers, electrical design engineers, project engineers, M&E supervisors etc. Also, cable and telecommunications specialists, software engineers etc.
Locations: Europe, Far East and United Kingdom.

LKRC, Evelyn House, 62 Oxford Street, London W1N 9LB, England. *Tel*: (0171) 323 2323. *Fax*: (0171) 323 4563.
Category: Recruitment consultancy.
Recruitment specialty: Senior management, technical and administrative support for the information technology (IT), banking and management consultancy industries and specialty areas. Skilled personnel in IT/computing, investment banking, management consultants, graduates, secretarial, administrative etc.
Location: United Kingdom.

Logica United Kingdom Ltd, 75 Hampstead Road, London NW1 2PL, England.
Other offices: 17 overseas.
Category: IT/computing consultancy.
Recruitment specialty: IT/computing skills in systems integration and software engineering.
Locations: United Kingdom and worldwide.

Macmillan Davies Consultants, Salisbury House, Bluecoats, Hertfordshire SG14 1PU, England. *Tel*: (01992) 552552. *Fax*: (01992) 505301.
Category: Recruitment consultancy.
Recruitment specialty: Senior executive and specialists in telecommunications, information technology (IT), manufacturing, engineering, energy, utilities, financial services, pharmaceuticals and FMCG industry sectors.
Locations: Asia, Canada, Europe, Far East, United Kingdom and United States.

Maine Tucker Recruitment Consultants, 18/21 Jermyn Street, London SW1Y 6HP, England. *Tel*: (0171) 734 7341. *Fax*: (0171) 734 3260.
Category: Recruitment consultancy.
Recruitment specialty: Secretarial and support personnel senior to junior levels,

PA secretaries, WP operators, receptionists. Also editorial assistants, trainee graduates, office managers etc.
Locations: Europe and United Kingdom.

Management Match International, 90/92 Great Portland Street, London W1N SP3, England. Tel: (0171) 323 3635. Fax: (0171) 323 5380.
Category: Recruitment consultancy.
Recruitment specialty: Marketing executives, all levels.
Locations: Europe, Middle East and United Kingdom.

Management Search International, Suite 904, Commercial Tower, Holiday Inn Centre, PO Box 51686, Dubai, United Arab Emirates. *Tel*: 00 9 714 314777. *Fax*: 00 9 714 315464.
Other offices: 1 in the United Kingdom and 2 overseas.
Category: Executive search and selection consultancy.
Recruitment specialty: Senior executive and management personnel for the oil and gas, construction, retail management, telecommunications, FMCG, law, specialty chemicals, finance and banking, electro-mechanical engineering industries and specialty areas.
Locations: Africa, Asia, Middle East and Near East.
Additional information: Salary levels from US$60,000.

Marchfield Engineering (Resources) Ltd, Globe House, Welsh Row, Nantwich, Cheshire CW5 5EW, England. *Tel*: (01270) 611323. *Fax*: (01270) 611324.
Category: Recruitment consultancy.
Recruitment specialty: Senior to junior design, engineering, commissioning and construction personnel. Skills in 3D CAD, PDS, ACAO, PDMS etc.
Locations: Africa, Asia, Australia, Canada, Europe (Scandinavia), Far East, Ireland, Middle East, Near East, New Zealand, South America, United Kingdom and United States.

Marque Executive Resourcing, 4 Hepton Court, York Road, Leeds, West Yorkshire LS9 6PN, England. *Tel*: (0113) 248 0110. *Fax*: (0113) 248 7642.
Category: Executive search and selection consultancy.
Recruitment specialty: Executive and management personnel in most sectors.
Locations: Asia, Canada, Far East, United Kingdom and United States.

Marren & Partners, Royal Buildings, 1A Cecil Road, Hale, Altrincham, Cheshire WA15 9NY, England. *Tel*: (0161) 927 9149. *Fax*: (0161) 929 5449.
Category: Recruitment consultancy.
Recruitment specialty: General management; human resources; financial services – broker consultants, investment specialists, actuaries; marketing specialists; fashion retail – shop management, buyers, merchandisers, allocators.
Locations: Europe and United Kingdom.

Martin Jarvie Underwood & Hall, 3rd Floor, 85 The Terrace, Wellington, New Zealand.
Category: Accountancy practice and management consultancy.
Recruitment specialty: Most accountancy specialist areas including: auditing, taxation, accountancy, business services, insolvency and corporate advisory services.
Location: New Zealand.

Mascotech Engineering Europe Ltd, Canewdon House, Locks Hill, Rochford, Essex SS9 1NE, England. *Tel*: (01702) 541881. *Fax*: (01702) 540993.
Category: Engineering consultancy and employer.
Recruitment specialty: Engineers and technical support personnel for the automotive industry. CAD designers, EUCLID, ISEMSURF, PDGS CATIA, CADDS4X, CADDS5. Most engineering disciplines, electrical, test and development engineers, finite element analysts, NVH testing, programme coordinators, cost analysis, timing and release analysts, programme managers.
Locations: Europe, Far East, Middle East, Near East, South America and United Kingdom.
Additional information: Suitably qualified and experienced candidates are welcome to forward their detailed CVs to the Recruitment Supervisor in the recruitment department.

McCourt Newton Consulting Group Ltd, Lidgett House, 56 Lidgett Lane, Garforth, Leeds, West Yorkshire LS25 1LL, England. *Tel*: (0113) 287 2855. *Fax*: (0113) 232 0683.
Category: Management recruitment consultancy.
Recruitment specialty: Senior management and technical support personnel for the manufacturing sector, particularly for the plastics, packaging and food specialist areas.
Locations: Europe, Ireland and United Kingdom.

MCD, 2 Truda pl. 3rd Floor, St Petersburg 190000, Russia.
Category: Accountancy practice and management consultancy.
Recruitment specialty: Most accountancy specialist areas including: auditing, taxation, accountancy, business services, insolvency and corporate advisory services.
Location: Eastern Europe.

McGregor Boyall Associates, 114 Middlesex Street, London E1 7JH, England. *Tel*: (0171) 247 7444. *Fax*: (0171) 297 7975.
Category: Recruitment consultancy.
Recruitment specialty: IT/computing permanent and contract placements in financial markets. Contract only placements in sales, trading and researched financial markets. Also, IT vendor placements in management, sales, marketing and technical areas, non-financial and user markets.

Locations: Canada, Europe, United Kingdom, United States and worldwide.

McMillan Montague Ltd, 2nd Floor, 4 City Road, Finsbury Square, London EC1Y 2AA, England. *Tel*: (0171) 588 8118. *Fax*: (0171) 638 7646.
Category: Recruitment and search consultancy.
Recruitment specialty: Senior executives and management levels up to managing director and sales and technical directors, senior sales and support executives within IT and computing vendors and integrators. Vertical markets include: finance, banking, EIS ROBMS, FM and systems integration, DIP workflow, BPR etc.
Locations: Africa, Australia, Canada, Europe, Far East, New Zealand, United Kingdom and United States.

Merc Partners, Number Twelve, Richview Office Park, Clonskeagh, Dublin 14, Republic of Ireland. *Tel*: 00 353 1 283 0114. *Fax*: 00 353 1 283 0550.
Category: Management consultancy.
Recruitment specialty: Senior management to middle management levels through advertised selection, within most sectors and including financial services, healthcare, electronics, telecommunications and software.
Locations: Ireland, Middle East and United Kingdom.

Merz & McLellan Ltd, Amber Court, William Armstrong Drive, Newcastle-upon-Tyne NE4 7YQ, England. *Tel*: (0191) 226 1899. *Fax*: (0191) 226 1104.
Category: Recruitment engineering consultancy.
Recruitment specialty: Senior engineering and technical support personnel for the power generation, distribution, transmission engineering industries. Also design and site construction, commissioning sectors.
Locations: Africa, Asia, Far East, Middle East and United Kingdom.

Metzger Recruitment Consultants Ltd, The Wharf Business Centre, Bourne End, Buckinghamshire SL8 5RY, England. *Tel*: (01628) 528828.
Category: Management consultancy.
Recruitment specialty: Sales, marketing and facilities management.
Locations: Europe, Ireland and United Kingdom.

Michael J Stevens Human Resource Consultancy, The Manse, Honey Hill, Gamlingay, Sandy, Bedfordshire SG19 3JU, England. *Tel*: (01767) 651555.
Fax: (01767) 650909.
Category: Human resources consultancy.
Recruitment specialty: Sales, marketing and other general areas at executive level.
Locations: Europe and United Kingdom.
Additional information: Speculative candidate enquiries are not required.

Millar Associates, 6 Sloane Street, London SW1X 9LE, England. *Tel*: (0171) 823 2222. *Fax*: (0171) 823 2208.

Category: International search and selection consultancy.

Recruitment specialty: Executive, management and technical in most sectors.

Locations: Asia and United Kingdom.

Miller Brand & Co Ltd, 36 Spital Square, London E1 6DY, England. *Tel*: (0171) 377 5661. *Fax*: (0171) 377 5437.

Category: Human resources consultancy.

Recruitment specialty: Senior executive and management levels in organisation structure and development, rewards and benefits, manpower planning development, personnel locums, executive leasing.

Locations: Asia, Europe, Far East, Ireland and United Kingdom.

MKA Management Consulting Ltd, Tectonic Place, Holyport Road, Holyport, Maidenhead, Berkshire SL6 2YE, England. *Tel*: (01628) 798015. *Fax*: (01628) 798138.

Other offices: 6 overseas.

Category: Management consultancy.

Recruitment specialty: Chief executives, directors, senior and middle management and technical personnel for aviation, brewing, building products, engineering, construction, food/drinks, FMCG, IT, telecommunications, metals, trading, pharmaceuticals, oil and gas, plastics, hotel/leisure and retail industries.

Locations: Australia, Canada, Europe, Far East, Middle East, New Zealand, United Kingdom and United States.

Montaner & Asociados, Balmes, 209, 2°.1°., 08006 Barcelona, Spain. *Tel*: 00 34 3415 7600. *Fax*: 00 34 3415 6610.

Category: Human resource and management consultancy.

Recruitment specialty: Senior executive, management and technical personnel in most industries and sectors.

Location: Europe.

Additional information: Montaner & Asociados is a member of European Human Resource Consultants (EHRC). The services provided by this company include: human resources consultancy in all the known specialty areas, management development programmes, corporate strategy, executive recruitment, total staffing, performance programmes etc.

Montreal Associates (Systems) Ltd, City Gate House, 399/425 Eastern Avenue, Gants Hill, Ilford, Essex I92 6LR, England. *Tel*: (0181) 518 2211. *Fax*: (0181) 518 3898.

Category: Recruitment consultancy.

Recruitment specialty: IT/computing skills and specialists areas include: management and technical personnel working on open systems, mainframe and SAP consultants, incorporating most other programming languages, operating systems, databases, hardware manufacturers and applications. Serving client industries such as: banking, insurance, petrochemical, retail,

government utilities, project management and software engineering.
Locations: Asia, Australia, Canada, Europe, Far East, Ireland, Middle East, Near East, New Zealand, South America, United Kingdom and United States.

Moore Control & Engineering Plc, Crofton House, Crofton Road, Portrack, Stockton-on-Tees, Cleveland TS18 2QZ, England. *Tel*: (01642) 678678. *Fax*: (01642) 603333.
Category: Recruitment consultancy.
Recruitment specialty: Senior engineers and other technical personnel within the petrochemical, oil and gas, chemical, power generation, retail and steel production industries. Mechanical, civil, structural, design, installation, inspection, commissioning engineers and technicians.
Locations: Canada, Europe, Far East, Near East, South America, United Kingdom and United States.

Morgan Bainbridge Ltd, 345 Station Road, Harrow, Middlesex, HA1 2AA, England. *Tel*: (0181) 863 7260. *Fax*: (0181) 445 6161.
Category: Executive search and selection and human resources consultancy.
Recruitment specialty: Senior executive, management and technical personnel for the healthcare, FMCG, information technology (IT), retail, chemicals, print, packing, financial services industries and specialty areas.
Locations: Africa, Asia, Australia, Canada, Europe, Far East, Ireland, New Zealand, United Kingdom and United States.

Morgan & Banks Plc, Brettenham House, Lancaster Place, London WC2E 7EN, England. *Tel*: (0171) 240 1040. *Fax*: (0171) 240 1052.
Category: Management and human resource consultancy.
Recruitment specialty: Senior executive and management levels in most sectors.
Locations: Asia, Australia, Europe, Far East, New Zealand and United Kingdom.
Additional information: Morgan & Banks Plc's other services include: search and selection across most sectors, career transition management, psychological testing, management and human resources consulting.

Morgan & Day (Europe) Ltd, The Old Coach House, 5a Holywell Hill, St Albans, Hertfordshire AL1 1EU, England. *Tel*: (01727) 836266. *Fax*: (01727) 837989.
Category: Recruitment consultancy.
Recruitment specialty: Engineers, trainers and other senior technical and support personnel for the oil and gas, petrochemical, heavy industrial, food processing and pharmaceutical industries and specialty areas.
Locations: Africa, Europe, Far East, Middle East and United Kingdom.

Morris Brankin & Company, West Wind Building, George Town, Grand Cayman, Cayman Islands, British West Indies.

Category: Accountancy practice and management consultancy.
Recruitment specialty: Most accountancy specialist areas including: auditing, taxation, accountancy, business services, insolvency and corporate advisory services.
Location: West Indies.

Motor Trade Selection, Sheen Lane House, 254 Upper Richmond Road West, London SW14 8AG, England. *Tel*: (0181) 392 1818. *Fax*: (0181) 876 4631.
Category: Recruitment consultancy.
Recruitment specialty: Senior executive to middle management levels, especially sales roles in the retail motor industry.
Locations: Africa, Asia, Europe, Far East, Middle East and United Kingdom.
Additional information: Motor Trade Selection publish annual salary surveys for the industry.

Mott MacDonald Ltd, St Anne House, 20/26 Wellesley Road, Croydon, Surrey CR9 2UL, England. *Tel*: (0181) 686 5041/(0127) 336 5000/(0122) 346 0600. *Fax*: (0181) 681 5706/(0127) 336 5100/(0122) 346 1007.
Other offices: 5 in the United Kingdom.
Category: Engineering consultancy and employer.
Recruitment specialty: Most levels of civil, mechanical, electrical, structural and environmental engineers, from experienced chartered engineers to recent graduates.
Locations: Africa, Asia, Australia, Europe, Far East, Middle East, Near East, New Zealand and United Kingdom.
Additional information: Average annual salary level £40,000.

MRK Consulting, 1 School Lane, Bagshot, Surrey GU19 5BP, England. *Tel*: (01276) 476866. *Fax*: (01276) 479666.
Category: Recruitment consultancy.
Recruitment specialty: Senior executive, management, engineers and other technical personnel for the IT/computing industry. Focusing mainly on IBM hardware, open systems, client server, computer networks LAN & WAN, multi-vendor environment, digital, HP, SUN microsystems etc in the computer industry and customer service sectors. Skills include: operational analysts, business analysts, programmers, application planners, rapid application development, DPMs, IS managers, operations/project/service management, quality, PC and open system engineers, communications broker sales, hardware and software sales, training, digital, installations, de-installations, PCMs, UNIX network, CNEs, ATM, IBM systems, databases, visual basic, SDK, C, C++, ORACLE, INGRES, SYBASE, IEF, SAP, RPG 400s, AS400s, designers, testers and development engineers etc. Assignments available on a permanent and contract basis.
Locations: Africa, Asia, Australia, Canada, Europe, Far East, Ireland, Middle East, Near East, New Zealand, South America, United Kingdom and United States.

Additional information: MRK Consulting provide consultancy services for the information technology (IT) industry, including IT service market research, multi-vendor service support, market analysis, strategic research and specialist projects.

MSL International Ltd, Quadrant Court, 50 Calthorpe Road, Edgbaston, Birmingham B15 1TH, England. *Tel*: (0121) 454 8864.
Other offices: 8 in the United Kingdom.
Category: Management consultancy.
Recruitment specialty: Senior executive and management levels in most industries and sectors.
Locations: United Kingdom and worldwide.

Multicom UK Ltd, The Coach House, rear of 32 Evesham Road, Cheltenham, Gloucestershire GL52 2AB, England. *Tel*: (01242) 261275. *Fax*: (01242) 261971.
Category: Recruitment consultancy.
Recruitment specialty: Technical computing personnel, programmers, authors for high technology projects, in-house etc.
Locations: United Kingdom and Northern Europe including Scandinavia.
Additional information: Multicom UK Ltd offer a full technical publications service, including technical translations and media transfer facilities.

Network Recruitment, Kennett House, 108/110 London Road, Headington, Oxfordshire OX3 9AW, England. *Tel*: (01865) 742822. *Fax*: (01865) 741777.
Category: Recruitment consultancy.
Recruitment specialty: Most levels and sectors including: commercial, technical, industrial, sales and marketing and print.
Locations: United Kingdom.

Nicholas Associates Ltd, Reginald Arthur House, Percy Street, Rotherham, South Yorkshire S65 1ED, England. *Tel*: (01709) 360900. *Fax*: (01709) 370037.
Category: Recruitment consultancy.
Recruitment specialty: Managerial and technical personnel predominantly for the construction industry on a permanent and contract basis.
Locations: Europe, Far East, Ireland, Middle East, Near East and United Kingdom.

Nichols Consultancy Ltd, The, 11 Eghams Court, Boston Drive, Bourne, Buckinghamshire SL8 5YS, England. *Tel*: (01628) 810717. *Fax*: (01628) 810829.
Category: Executive search consultancy.
Recruitment specialty: Senior executive and management levels, sales and marketing, training, human resources etc. in most sectors.
Locations: Africa, Europe, Far East, Middle East, Near East and United

Kingdom.

Additional information: Executive search, advertising, group selection, training and development for management development – teams, leadership, change, customer service, sales and marketing. Strategic consultancy – planning, design, TNA, performance, succession, career development, outplacement etc.

Nicholson International, 34/36 High Holborn, London WC1V 6AS, England. *Tel*: (0171) 404 5501. *Fax*: (0171) 404 8128.

Other offices: 20 overseas.

Category: Search and selection consultancy.

Recruitment specialty: Executive and senior management levels in most industries and sectors.

Locations: United Kingdom and worldwide.

Norma Consulting, Av. 5 de Outubro, 122-7°, 1000 Lisboa, Portugal. *Tel*: 00 351 1 796 7604/7608. *Fax*: 00 351 1 797 3948.

Category: Human resource and management consultancy.

Recruitment specialty: Senior executive, management and technical personnel in most industries and sectors.

Location: Europe.

Additional information: Norma Consulting is a member of European Human Resource Consultants (EHRC). The services provided by this company include: human resources consultancy in all the known specialty areas, management development programmes, corporate strategy, executive recruitment, total staffing, performance programmes etc.

NPA Management Services Ltd, 12 Well Court, London WC4M 9DN, England. *Tel*: (0171) 248 3812. *Fax*: (0171) 221 4538.

Category: Management consultancy.

Recruitment specialty: Senior executive and management levels in international banking. Also, treasury, asset and liability management, risk assessment and management, securities, trading, sales, foreign exchange and derivatives sales.

Locations: Europe, Far East, Middle East and United Kingdom.

NRC Recruitment Specialist, 23 Ely Place, Dublin 2, Republic of Ireland. *Tel*: 00 353 1 676 8644. *Fax*: 00 353 1 676 8662.

Category: Recruitment management consultancy.

Recruitment specialty: Senior executive, management and technical levels in accountancy, food, materials/logistics/procurement, printing and packaging, engineering, technical engineering, agriculture, electronics, manufacturing, quality assurance, warehousing, human resources, administration/clerical, and secretarial (PAs, WP operators etc.).

Locations: Canada, Europe, Ireland and United States.

Additional information: NRC provides additional services in management consulting and career guidance.

Nucleus Associates, Hebron House, 51 Boundary Road, West Bridgford, Nottingham NG2 7BZ, England. *Tel/Fax*: (0115) 9452717.
Category: Executive search and selection consultancy.
Recruitment specialty: Senior executive and management personnel in specialist areas such as: telecommunications, datacommunications, networking SDH, ATM, wireless, voice response, CIT, ACD, public and private switching, mobile, mainboard, sector sales, marketing, technical, human resources etc.
Locations: Asia, Canada, Europe, United Kingdom and United States.

O'Loughlin Partnership, 2 Sandyford Downs, Sandyford, County Dublin, Republic of Ireland. *Tel*: 00 353 1 670 9277. *Fax*: 00 353 1 670 9280.
Category: Executive search consultancy.
Recruitment specialty: Senior technical executive personnel for the pharmaceutical, chemical, plastic processing, material science, beverage, medical devices and cosmetics industries.
Locations: Canada, Europe, Ireland, United Kingdom and United States.

Onstream Ltd, 583 Bath Road, Longford, near Heathrow, Middlesex UB7 0EH, England. *Tel*: (01753) 680077. *Fax*: (01753) 689194.
Category: Recruitment engineering consultancy.
Recruitment specialty: Engineering and technical personnel for the oil and gas, petrochemical and civil industries.
Locations: Africa, Asia, Europe, Far East, Middle East and United Kingdom.

PA Consulting Group, 4th Floor, 2 Caxton Street, London SW1H 0QE, England. *Tel*: (0171) 730 9000. *Fax*: (0171) 730 6198.
Other offices: 4 in the United Kingdom and 45 and 2 technology centres overseas.
Category: Management consultancy.
Recruitment specialty: Senior executives, non-executive directors, interim managers in most sectors.
Locations: Asia, Australia, Eastern Europe, Far East, Ireland, Middle East, New Zealand, United Kingdom and Western Europe.
Additional information: PA Consulting Group employs 2,000 employees in 45 offices and 2 technology centres around the world and 200 recruiters worldwide. Working in all sectors of the economy providing recruitment personnel with perspectives and insights into a wide range of business and public sector enterprises. Speculative enquiries are not required.

Pannell Kerr Forster, #808, 8th Floor, Wisma HLA, Jalan Raja Chulan, 50200 Kuala Lumpur, West Malaysia.
Category: Accountancy practice and management consultancy.
Recruitment specialty: Most accountancy specialist areas including; auditing, taxation, accountancy, business services, insolvency and corporate advisory

services.
Locations: Malaysia.

Pannell Kerr Forster, 106/107 Lamaha Street, North Cummingsburg, George-town, Guyana.
Category: Accountancy practice and management consultancy.
Recruitment specialty: Most accountancy specialist areas including: auditing, taxation, accountancy, business services, insolvency and corporate advisory services.
Locations: Guyana.

Pannell Kerr Forster, 109 Boulevard Antoine Gauthier, 33000 Bordeaux, France.
Category: Accountancy practice and management consultancy.
Recruitment specialty: Most accountancy specialist areas including: auditing, taxation, accountancy, business services, insolvency and corporate advisory services.
Locations: Western Europe.

Pannell Kerr Forster, 15 St Matthews Road, East London 5201, South Africa.
Category: Accountancy practice and management consultancy.
Recruitment specialty: Most accountancy specialist areas including: auditing, taxation, accountancy, business services, insolvency and corporate advisory services.
Locations: South Africa.

Pannell Kerr Forster, 181 Queens Road, Gaborone, Botswana.
Category: Accountancy practice and management consultancy.
Recruitment specialty: Most accountancy specialist areas including: auditing, taxation, accountancy, business services, insolvency and corporate advisory services.
Locations: Botswana.

Pannell Kerr Forster, 19 Abdallah Draz Street, Golfland, Heliopolis, Egypt.
Category: Accountancy practice and management consultancy.
Recruitment specialty: Most accountancy specialist areas including: auditing, taxation, accountancy, business services, insolvency and corporate advisory services.
Locations: Egypt.

Pannell Kerr Forster, 191 Flinders Street, Adelaide, South Australia, Australia 5000.
Category: Accountancy practice and management consultancy.
Recruitment specialty: Most accountancy specialist areas including: auditing, taxation, accountancy, business services, insolvency and corporate advisory services.

Locations: Australia.

Pannell Kerr Forster, 2 Boulevard de la Tremouille, 21000 Dijon, France.
Category: Accountancy practice and management consultancy.
Recruitment specialty: Most accountancy specialist areas including: auditing, taxation, accountancy, business services, insolvency and corporate advisory services.
Locations: Western Europe.

Pannell Kerr Forster, 20th Level, 1 York Street, Sydney, New South Wales, Australia 2000.
Category: Accountancy practice and management consultancy.
Recruitment specialty: Most accountancy specialist areas including: auditing, taxation, accountancy, business services, insolvency and corporate advisory services.
Locations: Australia.

Pannell Kerr Forster, 24 Rue de Cronstadt, 75015 Paris, France,
Category: Accountancy practice and management consultancy.
Recruitment specialty: Most accountancy specialist areas including: auditing, taxation, accountancy, business services, insolvency and corporate advisory services.
Locations: Western Europe.

Pannell Kerr Forster, 30 Achad Ha'am Street, Tel Aviv, Israel 65541.
Category: Accountancy practice and management consultancy.
Recruitment specialty: Most accountancy specialist areas including: auditing, taxation, accountancy, business services, insolvency and corporate advisory services.
Locations: Middle East.

Pannell Kerr Forster, 33 rue du Général Offenstein, 67100 Strasbourg, France.
Category: Accountancy practice and management consultancy.
Recruitment specialty: Most accountancy specialist areas including: auditing, taxation, accountancy, business services, insolvency and corporate advisory services.
Locations: Western Europe.

Pannell Kerr Forster, 397 rue Paradis, 13008 Marseille, France.
Category: Accountancy practice and management consultancy.
Recruitment specialty: Most accountancy specialist areas including: auditing, taxation, accountancy, business services, insolvency and corporate advisory services.
Locations: Western Europe.

Pannell Kerr Forster, 3rd Floor, 64 Kennedy Avenue, 1076 Nicosia, Cyprus.
Category: Accountancy practice and management consultancy.
Recruitment specialty: Most accountancy specialist areas including: auditing,
   taxation, accountancy, business services, insolvency and corporate advisory
   services.
Locations: Cyprus.

Pannell Kerr Forster, 5 Bd. Abdellatif Benkaddour, Casablanca, Morocco.
Category: Accountancy practice and management consultancy.
Recruitment specialty: Most accountancy specialist areas including: auditing,
   taxation, accountancy, business services, insolvency and corporate advisory
   services.
Locations: Morocco.

Pannell Kerr Forster, 55 University Avenue, 17th Floor, PO Box 27, Toronto,
Ontario M5J 2H7, Canada.
Category: Accountancy practice and management consultancy.
Recruitment specialty: Most accountancy specialist areas including: auditing,
   taxation, accountancy, business services, insolvency and corporate advisory
   services.
Locations: Canada.

Pannell Kerr Forster, 6 Lockett Avenue, Kingston 4, Jamaica.
Category: Accountancy practice and management consultancy.
Recruitment specialty: Most accountancy specialist areas including: auditing,
   taxation, accountancy, business services, insolvency and corporate advisory
   services.
Locations: Jamaica.

Pannell Kerr Forster, 6th Floor, Ufanisi House, Haile Selassie Avenue, Nairobi,
Kenya.
Category: Accountancy practice and management consultancy.
Recruitment specialty: Most accountancy specialist areas including: auditing,
   taxation, accountancy, business services, insolvency and corporate advisory
   services.
Locations: Africa.

Pannell Kerr Forster, 7th Floor, Manulife Tower, 169 Electric Road, North
Point, Hong Kong.
Category: Accountancy practice and management consultancy.
Recruitment specialty: Most accountancy specialist areas including: auditing,
   taxation, accountancy, business services, insolvency and corporate advisory
   services.
Locations: Hong Kong.

Pannell Kerr Forster, 800 West Pender Street, Suite 1120, Vancouver, British Colombia V6C 2V6, Canada.
Category: Accountancy practice and management consultancy.
Recruitment specialty: Most accountancy specialist areas including: auditing, taxation, accountancy, business services, insolvency and corporate advisory services.
Locations: Canada.

Pannell Kerr Forster, Adjodha Building, Laborie Street, Castries, St Lucia, West Indies.
Category: Accountancy practice and management consultancy.
Recruitment specialty: Most accountancy specialist areas including: auditing, taxation, accountancy, business services, insolvency and corporate advisory services.
Locations: West Indies.

Pannell Kerr Forster, Ahumada 341, Piso 4, Santiago, Chile.
Category: Accountancy practice and management consultancy.
Recruitment specialty: Most accountancy specialist areas including: auditing, taxation, accountancy, business services, insolvency and corporate advisory services.
Locations: Chile.

Pannell Kerr Forster, Al Ain Ahlia Insurance Company Building, 13th Floor, Opp. Hamdan Centre, Sheikh Hamdan Street, Abu Dhabi, United Arab Emirates.
Category: Accountancy practice and management consultancy.
Recruitment specialty: Most accountancy specialist areas including: auditing, taxation, accountancy, business services, insolvency and corporate advisory services.
Locations: Middle East.

Pannell Kerr Forster, Audiec-Checkaudit, S.A., Av. Diagonal 612 7-13, 08021 Barcelona, Spain.
Category: Accountancy practice and management consultancy.
Recruitment specialty: Most accountancy specialist areas including: auditing, taxation, accountancy, business services, insolvency and corporate advisory services.
Locations: Western Europe.

Pannell Kerr Forster, August-Bebel-Strasse 38, 04275 Leipzig, Germany.
Category: Accountancy practice and management consultancy.
Recruitment specialty: Most accountancy specialist areas, including auditing, taxation, accountancy, business services, insolvency and corporate advisory services.
Locations: Western Europe.

Pannell Kerr Forster, Av. Almirante Barroso, No. 2-13 Piso, Rio de Janeiro, Brazil.
Category: Accountancy practice and management consultancy.
Recruitment specialty: Most accountancy specialist areas including: auditing, taxation, accountancy, business services, insolvency and corporate advisory services.
Locations: Brazil.

Pannell Kerr Forster, Av. Magalhaes Lima n 5-r/c Dt, 1000 Lisbon, Portugal.
Category: Accountancy practice and management consultancy.
Recruitment specialty: Most accountancy specialist areas including: auditing, taxation, accountancy, business services, insolvency and corporate advisory services.
Locations: Western Europe.

Pannell Kerr Forster, Avenida 32 No. 18-32, Piso 2, Bogota, Colombia.
Category: Accountancy practice and management consultancy.
Recruitment specialty: Most accountancy specialist areas including: auditing, taxation, accountancy, business services, insolvency and corporate advisory services.
Locations: Colombia.

Pannell Kerr Forster, BP House, 30 Mechlin Street, Monrovia, Liberia.
Category: Accountancy practice and management consultancy.
Recruitment specialty: Most accountancy specialist areas including: auditing, taxation, accountancy, business services, insolvency and corporate advisory services.
Locations: Liberia.

Pannell Kerr Forster Nederland B.V., Boeingavenue 204, 1119 PN Schipol-Rijk, Amsterdam, Netherlands.
Category: Accountancy practice and management consultancy.
Recruitment specialty: Most accountancy specialist areas including: auditing, taxation, accountancy, business services, insolvency and corporate advisory services.
Locations: Western Europe.

Pannell Kerr Forster, Bogstadveien 50, 0366 Oslo, Norway.
Category: Accountancy practice and management consultancy.
Recruitment specialty: Most accountancy specialist areas including: auditing, taxation, accountancy, business services, insolvency and corporate advisory services.
Locations: Western Europe.

Pannell Kerr Forster, Calle El Progreso, Pasaje El Rosal No. 23, Apdo. Postal 2790 (CG), San Salvador, El Salvador.

Category: Accountancy practice and management consultancy.
Recruitment specialty: Most accountancy specialist areas including: auditing, taxation, accountancy, business services, insolvency and corporate advisory services.
Locations: El Salvador.

Pannell Kerr Forster, Corso Bueonos Aires n. 23, 201 24 Milan, Italy.
Category: Accountancy practice and management consultancy.
Recruitment specialty: Most accountancy specialist areas including: auditing, taxation, accountancy, business services, insolvency and corporate advisory services.
Locations: Western Europe.

Pannell Kerr Forster, European Union Office, Belliardstraat 205/4B, 1040 Brussels, Belgium.
Category: Accountancy practice and management consultancy.
Recruitment specialty: Most accountancy specialist areas including: auditing, taxation, accountancy, business services, insolvency and corporate advisory services.
Locations: Western Europe.

Pannell Kerr Forster, Farrar Avenue, Accra, Ghana.
Category: Accountancy practice and management consultancy.
Recruitment specialty: Most accountancy specialist areas including: auditing, taxation, accountancy, business services, insolvency and corporate advisory services.
Locations: Ghana.

Pannell Kerr Forster, FHS House, 15 Girton Road, Parktown, Johannesburg 2193, South Africa.
Category: Accountancy practice and management consultancy.
Recruitment specialty: Most accountancy specialist areas including: auditing, taxation, accountancy, business services, insolvency and corporate advisory services.
Locations: Africa.

Pannell Kerr Forster, FHS House, 27 Newton Street, Newton Park 6045, Port Elizabeth, South Africa.
Category: Accountancy practice and management consultancy.
Recruitment specialty: Most accountancy specialist areas including: auditing, taxation, accountancy, business services, insolvency and corporate advisory services.
Locations: Africa.

Pannell Kerr Forster, First Floor, Building 2, Chelston Park, Collymore Rock, St Michael, Barbados, West Indies.

Category: Accountancy practice and management consultancy.
Recruitment specialty: Most accountancy specialist areas including: auditing, taxation, accountancy, business services, insolvency and corporate advisory services.
Locations: West Indies.

Pannell Kerr Forster, Fouad Chehab Blvd, Atlas Centre, Sinelfil, Beirut, Lebanon.
Category: Accountancy practice and management consultancy.
Recruitment specialty: Most accountancy specialist areas including: auditing, taxation, accountancy, business services, insolvency and corporate advisory services.
Locations: Middle East.

Pannell Kerr Forster, Frederiksgade 1, DK-1265 København K, Denmark.
Category: Accountancy practice and management consultancy.
Recruitment specialty: Most accountancy specialist areas including: auditing, taxation, accountancy, business services, insolvency and corporate advisory services.
Locations: Western Europe.

Pannell Kerr Forster, Ghanem & Majid Building, MBD Area, Ruwi, Muscat, Sultanate of Oman.
Category: Accountancy practice and management consultancy.
Recruitment specialty: Most accountancy specialist areas including: auditing, taxation, accountancy, business services, insolvency and corporate advisory services.
Locations: Middle East.

Pannell Kerr Forster, Herfort Van Kerkom Hower Streit, Gereonstrasse 34–36, 50670, Köln, Germany.
Category: Accountancy practice and management consultancy.
Recruitment specialty: Most accountancy specialist areas including: auditing, taxation, accountancy, business services, insolvency and corporate advisory services.
Locations: Western Europe.

Pannell Kerr Forster, Jl.Barito 2 No. 31, Jakarta 12130, Indonesia.
Category: Accountancy practice and management consultancy.
Recruitment specialty: Most accountancy specialist areas including: auditing, taxation, accountancy, business services, insolvency and corporate advisory services.
Locations: Indonesia.

Pannell Kerr Forster, Kungsgatan 6, 211 49 Malmö, Sweden.
Category: Accountancy practice and management consultancy.

Recruitment specialty: Most accountancy specialist areas including: auditing, taxation, accountancy, business services, insolvency and corporate advisory services.
Locations: Western Europe.

Pannell Kerr Forster, Kungsgaten 36, S-111 35 Stockholm, Sweden.
Category: Accountancy practice and management consultancy.
Recruitment specialty: Most accountancy specialist areas including: auditing, taxation, accountancy, business services, insolvency and corporate advisory services.
Locations: Western Europe.

Pannell Kerr Forster, Lanchid u.5, H-1013 Budapest, Hungary.
Category: Accountancy practice and management consultancy.
Recruitment specialty: Most accountancy specialist areas including: auditing, taxation, accountancy, business services, insolvency and corporate advisory services.
Locations: Eastern Europe.

Pannell Kerr Forster, Le Thelemos, 12 quai de Commerce, CP 202-69336 Lyon Cedex 09, France.
Category: Accountancy practice and management consultancy.
Recruitment specialty: Most accountancy specialist areas including: auditing, taxation, accountancy, business services, insolvency and corporate advisory services.
Locations: Western Europe.

Pannell Kerr Forster, Level 21, 307 Queen Street, Brisbane, Queensland, Australia 4000.
Category: Accountancy practice and management consultancy.
Recruitment specialty: Most accountancy specialist areas including: auditing, taxation, accountancy, business services, insolvency and corporate advisory services.
Locations: Australia.

Pannell Kerr Forster, Level 11, CU Tower, 485 LaTrobe Street, Melbourne, Victoria, Australia 3000.
Category: Accountancy practice and management consultancy.
Recruitment specialty: Most accountancy specialist areas including: auditing, taxation, accountancy, business services, insolvency and corporate advisory services.
Locations: Australia.

Pannell Kerr Forster, Level 7, Griffin Centre, 28 The Esplanade, Perth, Western Australia, Australia 6000.
Category: Accountancy practice and management consultancy.

Recruitment specialty: Most accountancy specialist areas including: auditing, taxation, accountancy, business services, insolvency and corporate advisory services.
Locations: Australia.

Pannell Kerr Forster, Lob. No. 3, AG-18, Jebel Ali, Dubai, United Arab Emirates.
Category: Accountancy practice and management consultancy.
Recruitment specialty: Most accountancy specialist areas including: auditing, taxation, accountancy, business services, insolvency and corporate advisory services.
Locations: Middle East.

Pannell Kerr Forster, 1st Floor, Fisher Hoffman House, 17 New Church Street, Cape Town 8001, South Africa.
Category: Accountancy practice and management consultancy.
Recruitment specialty: Most accountancy specialist areas including: auditing, taxation, accountancy, business services, insolvency and corporate advisory services.
Locations: Africa.

Pannell Kerr Forster, Meliza Court, 4th & 7th Floors, 229 Arch. Makarios III Avenue, 3105 Limassol, Cyprus.
Category: Accountancy practice and management consultancy.
Recruitment specialty: Most accountancy specialist areas including: auditing, taxation, accountancy, business services, insolvency and corporate advisory services.
Locations: Cyprus.

Pannell Kerr Forster, Nebraska 62, Desp. 103, 202 Col. Napoles, 03810 Mexico, D.F., Mexico.
Category: Accountancy practice and management consultancy.
Recruitment specialty: Most accountancy specialist areas including: auditing, taxation, accountancy, business services, insolvency and corporate advisory services.
Locations: Mexico.

Pannell Kerr Forster (PKF), New Garden House, 78 Hatton Garden, London EC1N 8JA, England. *Tel*: (0171) 831 7393. *Fax*: (0171) 405 6736.
Other offices: 34 in the United Kingdom and 305 overseas.
Category: Management consultancy.
Recruitment specialty: Most accountancy specialist areas including: auditing, taxation, accountancy, business services, insolvency and corporate advisory services.
Additional services: In addition to the hotel and leisure related consultancy services, the company provides a wide range of other services, such as:

information technology (IT), human resources in executive recruitment and accountancy recruitment, financial and strategic planning etc. Speculative candidates can forward CVs directly to the London office or directly to any of their associated offices overseas. PKF is represented in virtually every offshore tax jurisdiction, their tax partners are carefully selected and trained and all services provided are solidly supported by a broad range of accounting, auditing, consulting and managerial executives.
Locations: Worldwide.

Pannell Kerr Forster Associates, New Garden House, 78 Hatton Garden, London EC1N 8JA, England. *Tel*: (0171) 831 7393.
Other offices: 34 in the United Kingdom and 305 overseas.
Category: Management consultancy.
Recruitment specialty: Senior management consultancy personnel in most industries and sectors.
Locations: Worldwide.

Pannell Kerr Forster, Ostra Martensgatan 15, S-223 61 Lund, Sweden.
Category: Accountancy practice and management consultancy.
Recruitment specialty: Most accountancy specialist areas including: auditing, taxation, accountancy, business services, insolvency and corporate advisory services.
Locations: Western Europe.

Pannell Kerr Forster, PO Box 1013, Bahrain.
Category: Accountancy practice and management consultancy.
Recruitment specialty: Most accountancy specialist areas including: auditing, taxation, accountancy, business services, insolvency and corporate advisory services.
Locations: Middle East.

Pannell Kerr Forster, Pannell House, Elizabeth Avenue, Nassau, Bahamas, West Indies.
Category: Accountancy practice and management consultancy.
Recruitment specialty: Most accountancy specialist areas including: auditing, taxation, accountancy, business services, insolvency and corporate advisory services.
Locations: West Indies.

Pannell Kerr Forster, PO Box 28150, Danhof, Bloemfontein 9310, South Africa.
Category: Accountancy practice and management consultancy.
Recruitment specialty: Most accountancy specialist areas including: auditing, taxation, accountancy, business services, insolvency and corporate advisory services.
Locations: Africa.

Pannell Kerr Forster, Regent House, 12 Wilberforce Street, Freetown, Sierra Leone.
Category: Accountancy practice and management consultancy.
Recruitment specialty: Most accountancy specialist areas including: auditing, taxation, accountancy, business services, insolvency and corporate advisory services.
Locations: Sierra Leone.

Pannell Kerr Forster, Rietbaan 2, 2908 LP Capelle aan den IJssel, Netherlands.
Category: Accountancy practice and management consultancy.
Recruitment specialty: Most accountancy specialist areas including: auditing, taxation, accountancy, business services, insolvency and corporate advisory services.
Locations: Western Europe.

Pannell Kerr Forster, Room 341, ul. Marszalkowska 1115, 00-102 Warsaw, Poland.
Category: Accountancy practice and management consultancy.
Recruitment specialty: Most accountancy specialist areas including: auditing, taxation, accountancy, business services, insolvency and corporate advisory services.
Locations: Eastern Europe.

Pannell Kerr Forster GmbH, Sozietat, Piorek Riese Thum, Platanenallee 11, 14050 Berlin, Germany.
Category: Accountancy practice and management consultancy.
Recruitment specialty: Most accountancy specialist areas including: auditing, taxation, accountancy, business services, insolvency and corporate advisory services.
Locations: Western Europe.

Pannell Kerr Forster, Stampgatan 14, S-411 01 Göteborg, Sweden.
Category: Accountancy practice and management consultancy.
Recruitment specialty: Most accountancy specialist areas including: auditing, taxation, accountancy, business services, insolvency and corporate advisory services.
Locations: Western Europe.

Pannell Kerr Forster, Suite 1201, 255 Ponce De Leon Avenue, Hato Rey, Puerto Rico 00917.
Category: Accountancy practice and management consultancy.
Recruitment specialty: Most accountancy specialist areas including: auditing, taxation, accountancy, business services, insolvency and corporate advisory services.
Locations: Puerto Rico.

Pannell Kerr Forster, Suite 1922, 320 West Street, Durban 4001, South Africa.
Category: Accountancy practice and management consultancy.
Recruitment specialty: Most accountancy specialist areas including: auditing, taxation, accountancy, business services, insolvency and corporate advisory services.
Locations: Africa.

Pannell Kerr Forster, Suite 206, Al Maidan Tower, Al Maktoum Street, Opposite Etisalat Building, PO Box 13094, Deira, Dubai, United Arab Emirates.
Category: Accountancy practice and management consultancy.
Recruitment specialty: Most accountancy specialist areas including: auditing, taxation, accountancy, business services, insolvency and corporate advisory services.
Locations: Middle East.

Pannell Kerr Forster, Sultan Rashed Al Dhariri Building, Flat No. 110, 1st Floor, Opp. Rustamani Building, King Faisal Street, Sharjah, United Arab Emirates.
Category: Accountancy practice and management consultancy.
Recruitment specialty: Most accountancy specialist areas including: auditing, taxation, accountancy, business services, insolvency and corporate advisory services.
Locations: Middle East.

Pannell Kerr Forster, Unit 11810 Cityland Condominium 10 Tower 1, 6815 Ayala Avenue cor. H.V. Dela Costa Ext., Makati, Metro Manila 1200, Philippines.
Category: Accountancy practice and management consultancy.
Recruitment specialty: Most accountancy specialist areas including: auditing, taxation, accountancy, business services, insolvency and corporate advisory services.
Locations: Philippines.

Paradigm Associates, Bishops Court, 17a The Broadway, Old Hatfield, Hertfordshire AL9 5MA, England. *Tel*: (01707) 266363. *Fax*: (01707) 266464.
Category: Recruitment consultancy.
Recruitment specialty: Senior executive, management, technical and support levels, in datacommuniations, telecommunications, sales and marketing, pre-sales and post-sales support and network design. Also: field engineers, trainers, human resource specialists etc.
Locations: Africa, Asia, Canada, Europe, Ireland, Middle East, United Kingdom and United States.

Parallel International, 1 Groveland Court, Bow Lane, London EC4M 9EH, England. *Tel*: (0171) 236 4288. *Fax*: (0171) 236 4277.
Other offices: 10 overseas.
Category: Recruitment consultancy.
Recruitment specialty: IT/computing personnel.
Locations: Europe and United Kingdom.

Parc Aviation Ltd, St Johns Court, Swords Road, Santry, Dublin 9, Republic of Ireland. *Tel*: 00 353 1 842 9933. *Fax*: 00 353 1 3284/6442/9389.
Category: Aviation manpower and services consultancy.
Recruitment specialty: Executive, technical and support personnel on a permanent and contract basis, most skills such as: pilots, technicians, support, flight crews etc. within the aviation industry.
Locations: Asia, Australia, Canada, Europe, Far East, Ireland, Middle East, Near East, New Zealand, South America, United Kingdom and United States.
Additional information: Parc Aviation operates in over 30 countries worldwide and provides human resource services to the aviation industry from its three main operating divisions, Flight Crew Leasing, Technical and Maintenance Manpower Leasing and Aviation Consultancy. It is part of the PARC group, providing other services to their clients in PARC Healthcare International and PARC Technical Services, active in over 30 countries. Consultancy services include: infrastructure development, legal advisory, psychometric testing, operational training, quality assurance/safety compliance with JAA regulations.

Parc Workforce, St Johns Court, Swords Road, Santry, Dublin 9, Republic of Ireland. *Tel*: 00 353 1 842 9933. *Fax*: 00 353 1 842 3284/6642/9389.
Category: Recruitment consultancy.
Recruitment specialty: Senior management, technical and support personnel in specialist industries such as: manufacturing, telecommunications, aviation, healthcare, IT/computing, construction design management. Also in the petrochemical industry, most engineering and technical disciplines including designers, technicians, CAD operators, surveyors etc.
Locations: Asia, Australia, Canada, Europe, Far East, Ireland, Middle East, Near East, New Zealand, South America, United Kingdom and United States.

Partners In Recruitment, St John's Innovation Park, Cowley Road, Cambridge CB4 4WS, England. *Tel*: (01223) 328935.
Category: Human resources consultancy.
Recruitment specialty: Management, technical and administrative support personnel for the packaging industry, materials, machinery, manufacturing and technology. Most levels of personnel, middle management, accountancy, administrative support etc.
Locations: Asia, Europe, Middle East and United Kingdom.

Partners In Recruitment, Suites 1 & 2, Meadow Lane Business Park, St Ives, Cambridgeshire PE17 4LG, England. *Tel*: (01480) 493344. *Fax*: (01480) 493343.
Category: Human resources consultancy.
Recruitment specialty: Management, technical and administrative support personnel for the packaging industry, materials, machinery, manufacturing and technology. Most levels of personnel, middle management, accountancy, administrative support etc.
Locations: Asia, Europe, Middle East and United Kingdom.

Pendleton Recruitment Consultants Ltd, Intercity House, 93/109 Victoria Street, Bristol BS1 6AX, England. *Tel*: (0117) 929 7851. *Fax*: (0117) 922 5529.
Category: Recruitment and human resources consultancy.
Recruitment specialty: Senior executive to junior management levels, specialising in the paper and packaging industries.
Locations: Africa, Asia, Europe, Far East and United Kingdom.
Additional information: The firm specialises in providing search and selection services on a retained assignment basis.

Penspen Ltd, Darpen House, 1 Citadel Place, London SE11 5EF, England. *Tel*: (0171) 582 5577. *Fax*: (0171) 587 0288.
Category: Management and engineering consultancy.
Recruitment specialty: Senior management, engineering and technical personnel for the oil and gas, chemical and water industries.
Locations: Africa, Asia, Europe, Far East, Middle East and United Kingdom.

Peter Glaser & Associates, Bramble Hill, Bramble Lane, Christchurch, Dorset BH23 5NB, England. *Tel*: (01425) 276622. *Fax*: (01425) 278278.
Category: Recruitment agency and human resources consultancy.
Recruitment specialty: Senior executive, management and technical personnel for the construction, water, waste, environmental, highways, pharmaceutical and petrochemical industries.
Locations: Africa, Asia, Europe, Far East, Ireland, Middle East, Near East, South America and United Kingdom.
Additional information: Peter Glaser & Associates offer clients advice planning and execution of resourcing assignments, including confidential search, advertising, register search and the supply of temporary specialist personnel.

Peter Stoner & Associates, 73 Pavilion Gardens, Staines, Middlesex TW18 1LT, England. *Tel/Fax*: (01784) 457787.
Category: Recruitment consultancy.
Recruitment specialty: Director to site engineer levels in the construction industry as quantity surveyors, engineers, site managers, project managers, contract managers etc.
Locations: Africa, Asia, Europe, Far East, Middle East and United Kingdom.

PHDS Engineering Group, Brookfoot House, Low Lane, Horsforth, West Yorkshire LS18 5PU, England. *Tel*: (0113) 258 2929/(01708) 250301/(0116) 242 4040. *Fax*: (0113) 258 2928/(01708) 641846/(0116) 242 4031.
Other offices: 4 in the United Kingdom.
Category: Search consultancy.
Recruitment specialty: Senior engineering and support technical personnel for the design, petrochemical, pharmaceutical and manufacturing industries.
Locations: Australia, Canada, Ireland, New Zealand, United Kingdom and United States.
Additional information: PHDS Engineering Group is not a contingency recruitment agency, the firm provides retainer search facilities within engineering disciplines.

Phil Vignoles Associates, 211 Piccadilly, London W1V 9LD, England.
Category: Recruitment consultancy.
Recruitment specialty: Executive and management consultants in most sectors.
Locations: Asia, Europe and United Kingdom.

PKF Consulting Limited, 7th Floor, Manulife Tower, 169 Electric Road, North Point, Hong Kong.
Category: Accountancy practice and management consultancy.
Recruitment specialty: Most accountancy specialist areas including: auditing, taxation, accountancy, business services, insolvency and corporate advisory services.
Location: Hong Kong.

PKF Euroconsult GmbH, Management Consultants, Jungfernstieg 7, 20354 Hamburg, Germany.
Category: Accountancy practice and management consultancy.
Recruitment specialty: Most accountancy specialist areas including: auditing, taxation, accountancy, business services, insolvency and corporate advisory services.
Location: Europe.

PKF Hellas Limited, Management Consultants, 64 Vassilissis Sophias Avenue, 115 28 Athens, Greece.
Category: Accountancy practice and management consultancy.
Recruitment specialty: Most accountancy specialist areas, including auditing, taxation, accountancy, business services, insolvency and corporate advisory services.
Locations: Europe.

Portman Price, 39 Hillcrest Avenue, Edgware, Middlesex HA8 8NZ, England. *Tel*: (0181) 905 4900. *Fax*: (0181) 905 4901.
Category: Management consultancy.
Recruitment specialty: Senior executive, management and technical personnel

for the information technology (IT), FMCG, property, healthcare, marketing services, management consultancy, retail and leisure industries and specialty areas.
Locations: Europe and United Kingdom.

Premier International Consultants, Suite 5, Greenwell Road, Tullos, Aberdeen AB1 4AX, Scotland. *Tel*: (01224) 877705. *Fax*: (01224) 879757.
Category: Recruitment consultancy.
Recruitment specialty: Most skilled personnel in most industries and sectors.
Location: Middle East.
Additional information: Premier International Consultants specialises in organising recruitment campaigns for clients through to candidate interviews.

Premmit Associates Ltd, 33 Eccleston Square, London SW1V 1PH, England. *Tel*: (0171) 834 7253. *Fax*: (0171) 834 3544.
Category: Recruitment agency and search and selection consultancy.
Recruitment specialty: Executive, management and technical personnel for the IT/computing, hardware and software engineering, electronics, defence, aerospace, pharmaceutical and biotech industries. Also: general sales and marketing, human resources, finance etc.
Locations: Canada, Europe, Middle East, Near East, United Kingdom and United States.

Price Waterhouse, No 1 London Bridge, London SE1 9QL, England. *Tel*: (0171) 939 3000. *Fax*: (0171) 403 5265.
Category: Executive search and selection consultancy.
Recruitment specialty: Executive, management and technical in most sectors, qualified accountants etc.
Locations: United Kingdom and worldwide.

Pro Fit Computer Recruitment, The Arena Forum, Stockley Park, Uxbridge, Middlesex UB11 1AA, England. *Tel*: (0181) 899 1757. *Fax*: (0181) 899 1751.
Category: Recruitment consultancy.
Recruitment specialty: IT/computing most skills such as: customer facing staff from technical help desk through to sales support, senior executive to management levels incorporating the following sectors of the industry: RDBMS, object database, data warehousing, OLAP, data access, 4GL, GUI, development and second generation application development tools for client server and enterprise wide development environments, help desk customer support systems, Internet access, systems management tools/ security/back-up, applications logistics process control, R3, documentation management, workflow, telecommunications, datacommunications.
Locations: Europe and United Kingdom.
Additional information: Services available range from general search, head hunting and advertised campaigns.

Professional & Engineering Consultants Ltd, Riverside House, 1/5 High Street, London Corner, Hertfordshire AL2 1LE, England. *Tel*: (01727) 824444/ (01634) 261773. *Fax*: (01727) 824390.
Category: Recruitment consultancy.
Recruitment specialty: Management and engineering personnel for the oil and gas, petrochemical, information technology (IT), pharmaceuticals, manufacturing, civil and architectural engineering industries. Engineer designers, project managers etc.
Locations: Africa, Asia, Europe, Far East, Ireland, Middle East and United Kingdom.

Project Management Professional Services Ltd, PMP House, Gardner Road, Maidenhead, Berkshire SL6 7RJ, England. *Tel*: (01628) 75444. *Fax*: (01628) 26203.
Category: Management consultancy.
Recruitment specialty: Project management most levels of personnel and skilled areas such as: planning, system and project engineers, project managers, cost controllers and estimators and document controllers etc.
Location: United Kingdom.

Quarry Dougall Group, 37/41 Bedford Row, London WC1R 4JH, England. *Tel*: (0171) 405 6062. *Fax*: (0171) 831 6394.
Other offices: 6 overseas.
Category: Recruitment consultancy.
Recruitment specialty: Specialist legal personnel in both private practice and commerce and industry, from newly qualified solicitors to partners and teams.
Locations: Asia, Australia, Canada, Europe, Far East, Ireland, New Zealand, United Kingdom and United States.
Additional information: Quarry Dougall is staffed fully by qualified lawyers who are able to combine their previous practical legal skills with extensive experience in recruitment and further professional training, including the MBA and IPD qualifications. Special Project Lawyer, a sister company, uses consultants with extensive experience of short term contract market to provide a professional service to clients seeking fixed-term cover. Other specialist divisions within the group advise a high profile client base on advertising, outplacement counselling and career management.

Quarry Dougall Retail Sales & Marketing, 37/41 Bedford Row, London WC1R 4JH, England. *Tel*: (0171) 405 6062. *Fax*: (0171) 831 6394.
Other offices: 6 overseas.
Category: Recruitment consultancy.
Recruitment specialty: Senior board level executives to middle management levels of personnel, buyers, merchandisers, general marketing managers, account directors etc, specifically for the retail, sales and marketing specialist areas.

Locations: Asia, Australia, Canada, Europe, Far East, Ireland, New Zealand, United Kingdom and United States.
Additional information: Salaries range from £15,000–£150,000.

Randall Massey Consultants, 7 Dorcan Business Village, Murdock Road, Dorcan, Swindon, Wiltshire SN3 5HY, England.
Category: Management consultancy.
Recruitment specialty: Senior executive and management levels in the top technology and electronic specialty areas.
Locations: Asia (including China, Hong Kong and Singapore), Australia, Canada, Europe, Far East, Ireland, New Zealand, United Kingdom and United States.

Reclamebureau Timmermans NV, Collegelaan 69, B-2140 Antwerpen, Belgium.
Tel: 00 32 3235 6064. *Fax*: 00 32 3235 4919.
Category: Recruitment advertising consultancy.
Recruitment specialty: Executive, management and technical in the commercial, financial, industrial and public sectors.
Locations: Canada, Europe, United Kingdom and United States.
Additional information: Services offered to their clients are: recruitment advertising, search and selection, communications and business psychology.

REL Consultancy Group Ltd, Park Gate, 21 Tothill Street, London SW1H 9LL, England.
Other offices: 12 overseas.
Category: Management consultancy.
Recruitment specialty: Executive and management personnel in most industries and sectors.
Location: Worldwide.

Renaissance Solutions Ltd, 22 Grafton Street, London W1X 3LD, England.
Tel: (0171) 629 2456. *Fax*: (0171) 290 3737.
Other offices: 5 overseas.
Category: Management consultancy.
Recruitment specialty: Computing consultants.
Locations: Europe, United Kingdom and United States.

Resources International Plc, 31 Bedford Square, London WC1 3EG, England.
Tel: (0171) 314 4200. *Fax*: (0171) 323 3094.
Category: Recruitment consultancy.
Recruitment specialty: Contract IT/computing personnel most levels and skills.
Locations: Asia, Australia, Canada, Europe, Far East, Ireland, Middle East, Near East, New Zealand, United Kingdom and United States.
Additional information: Resources International Plc provides a fully comprehensive recruitment service: planning, designing and conducting advertising campaigns; outplacement staff; career counselling; search and selection of IT;

corporate and general management personnel.

Reynell Legal Recruitment, 4th Floor, 55 Fetter Lane, London EC4A 1AA, England. *Tel*: (0171) 353 7007. *Fax*: (0171) 353 7008.
Category: Recruitment advertising consultancy.
Recruitment specialty: Legal personnel.
Locations: Canada, Europe, United Kingdom and United States.
Additional information: This company is associated with Austin Knight United Kingdom Ltd. Services offered to their clients are: recruitment advertising, search and selection, communications and business psychology.

Reynell Ltd, Park House, 5 Jubilee Avenue, London E4 9JD, England. *Tel*: (0181) 527 6100. *Fax*: (0181) 527 9940.
Category: Recruitment advertising consultancy.
Recruitment specialty: Executive, management and technical in the commercial, financial, industrial and public sectors.
Locations: Canada, Europe, United Kingdom and United States.
Additional information: This company is associated with Austin Knight United Kingdom Ltd. Services offered to their clients are: recruitment advertising, search and selection, communications and business psychology.

Right International Ltd, Coveham House, Downside Bridge Road, Cobham, Surrey KT11 3EP, England. *Tel*: (01932) 863939. *Fax*: (01932) 866433.
Category: Executive search consultancy.
Recruitment specialty: Executive and senior management in the following specialist areas: financial services, banking, insurance, information technology (IT) and telecommunications.
Locations: Canada, Europe, United Kingdom and United States.

Robert Walters Associates, 150 Broadway – Suite 2013, New York, NY 10036, United States. *Tel*: 00 1 212 704 9900. *Fax*: 00 1 212 704 4312.
Other offices: 2 in the United Kingdom and 4 overseas.
Category: Recruitment consultancy.
Recruitment specialty: Senior executive, management and technical personnel in most sectors.
Locations: Australia, Europe, New Zealand, United Kingdom and United States.

Robert Walters Associates, 25 Bedford Street, London WC2E 9HP, England. *Tel*: (0171) 379 3333. *Fax*: (0171) 915 8714.
Other offices: 1 in the United Kingdom and 5 overseas.
Category: Recruitment consultancy.
Recruitment specialty: Senior executive, management and technical personnel in most sectors.
Locations: Australia, Europe, New Zealand, United Kingdom and United States.

Robert Walters Associates, 42 Thames Street, Windsor, Berkshire SL4 1PR, England. *Tel*: (01753) 831515. Fax: (01753) 678908.
Other offices: 1 in the United Kingdom and 5 overseas.
Category: Recruitment consultancy.
Recruitment specialty: Senior executive, management and technical personnel in most sectors.
Locations: Australia, Europe, New Zealand, United Kingdom and United States.

Robert Walters Associates, Avenue Louise 66, Box 5, B-1000 Brussels, Belgium. *Tel*: 00 322 511 6688. *Fax*: 00 322 511 9969.
Other offices: 2 in the United Kingdom and 4 overseas.
Category: Recruitment consultancy.
Recruitment specialty: Senior executive, management and technical personnel in most sectors.
Locations: Australia, Europe, New Zealand, United Kingdom and United States.

Robert Walters Associates, Level 7 – Wang House, 195/201 Willis Street, Wellington, New Zealand. *Tel*: 00 644 384 1100. *Fax*: 00 644 384 1112.
Other offices: 2 in the United Kingdom and 4 overseas.
Category: Recruitment consultancy.
Recruitment specialty: Senior executive, management and technical personnel in most sectors.
Locations: Australia, Europe, New Zealand, United Kingdom and United States.

Robert Walters Associates, Level 15, 9 Castleragh Street, Sydney, NSW 2000, Australia. *Tel*: 00 612 231 3302. *Fax*: 00 612 231 3306.
Other offices: 2 in the United Kingdom and 4 overseas.
Category: Recruitment consultancy.
Recruitment specialty: Senior executive, management and technical personnel in most sectors.
Locations: Australia, Europe, New Zealand, United Kingdom and United States.

Robert Walters Associates, Riverstaete Amsteldijk 166, 1079 LH Amsterdam, Netherlands. *Tel*: 00 31 20 644 4655. *Fax*: 00 31 20 642 9005.
Other offices: 2 in the United Kingdom and 4 overseas.
Category: Recruitment consultancy.
Recruitment specialty: Senior executive, management and technical personnel in most sectors.
Locations: Australia, Europe, New Zealand, United Kingdom and United States.

Ross Melville PKF, Level 5, 50 Anzac House, Auckland, New Zealand.
Category: Accountancy practice and management consultancy.
Recruitment specialty: Most accountancy specialist areas including: auditing, taxation, accountancy, business services, insolvency and corporate advisory services.
Location: New Zealand.

Rowan Resources, Rowan House, Crown Business Park, Tredegar, Gwent NP2 4EF, Wales. *Tel*: (01495) 308621. *Fax*: (01495) 308609.
Cateogry: Human resources consultancy.
Recruitment specialty: Specialists in areas of engineering and senior management.
Locations: Africa, Asia, Far East, Middle East, Near East and United Kingdom.

Sales Placement Ltd, 5 Herbert Place, Dublin 2, Republic of Ireland. *Tel*: 00 353 1 668 5144. *Fax*: 00 353 1 676 3710.
Category: Recruitment consultancy.
Recruitment specialty: Senior executive, management, technical and trainee personnel within the sales and marketing, contract, FMCG, healthcare and pharmaceutical specialist areas and industries.
Locations: Africa, Canada, Europe, Ireland, Middle East, United Kingdom and United States.

Sales Placement Ltd, 9 Lower Crescent, Belfast BT7 1NR, Northern Ireland.
Category: Recruitment consultancy.
Recruitment specialty: Senior executive, management, technical and trainee personnel within the sales and marketing, contract, FMCG, healthcare, pharmaceutical specialist areas and industries.
Locations: Africa, Canada, Europe, Ireland, Middle East, United Kingdom and United States.

Sales Recruitment Specialist Ltd, Leigh House, 28/32 St Paul's Street, Leeds, West Yorkshire LS1 2PX, England. *Tel*: (0113) 242 7444. *Fax*: (0113) 244 3992.
Category: Recruitment consultancy.
Recruitment specialty: Sales personnel, field sales representatives, regional and key account management and telesales.
Location: United Kingdom.

SAS Executive Recruitment, The Old George Brewery, Rollestone Street, Salisbury SP1 1DX, England. *Tel*: (01722) 330099. *Fax*: (01722) 331313.
Category: Management consultancy.
Recruitment specialty: Senior executive, management and technical personnel within the telecommunications industry, such as: engineers, marketing executives, sales and management and in general management, accounts

and human resource personnel.
Locations: Middle East and United Kingdom.

SBS Ltd, Centre Point, 103 New Oxford Street, London WC1A 1DY, England. *Tel*: (0171) 240 7575. *Fax*: (0171) 240 7580.
Category: Recruitment consultancy.
Recruitment specialty: Senior management, engineers and technical personnel within the IT/computing industry. Specialist skills include: SYBASE, ORACLE, IBM hardware, INGRES, PC development and support, networking and SAP.
Locations: Eastern Europe, United Kingdom, Western Europe.

Shanahan Engineering Ltd, Beauparc, Monkstown Road, Blackrock, County Dublin, Republic of Ireland. *Tel*: 00 353 1 280 9888. *Fax*: 00 353 1 280 0952.
Category: Engineering consultancy.
Recruitment specialty: Consultants, contractors and project managers in the power generation, oil and gas industries. Specialist areas such as: installation, commissioning, operations and maintenance of power generation plant and oil and gas field plant. In addition: mechanical, electrical contols and instrumentation engineers, civil engineers with powergen experience.
Locations: Africa, Asia, Europe, Far East, Middle East, South America and United Kingdom.

Shaw & Hatton International Ltd, Ashridge Manor, Forest Road, Wokingham, Berkshire RG40 5SL, England. *Tel*: (01734) 774 177/(01734) 789 695. *Fax*: (01734) 770 422/(01734) 771 210.
Category: Recruitment consultancy.
Recruitment specialty: Engineering and support personnel for the oil and gas industry, onshore and offshore facilities.
Locations: Asia, Australia, Canada, Europe, Far East, Middle East, New Zealand, South America, United Kingdom and United States.

Sheila Burgess International, 4 Cromwell Place, London SW7 2JS, England. *Tel*: (0171) 584 6446. *Fax*: (0171) 584 1824.
Category: Recruitment consultancy.
Recruitment specialty: Bilingual secretaries and personal assistants.
Locations: Europe (Belgium, France and Germany).
Additional information: French language qualifications at degree level and with secretarial training, touch typing 45 words per minute minimum and word processing skills. All clients of Sheila Burgess International are international companies working in English and French languages and generally with a· US management style.

Sherwood Engineering Recruitment, Sherwood House, Aldwarne Road, Parkgate, Rotherham, South Yorkshire S62 6BU, England. *Tel*: (01709)

710800. *Fax*: (01709) 710880.
Category: Recruitment consultancy.
Recruitment specialty: Senior management, engineering and technical personnel for the engineering and construction industries. Project directors and managers, foremen/supervisors and other technical staff.
Locations: Africa, Asia, Canada, Europe, Far East, Ireland, Middle East, Near East, South America, United Kingdom and United States.

Silicon Valley Group, Consultants House, 60 High Street, Sandhurst, Surrey GU17 8DY, England. *Tel*: (01252) 877778. *Fax*: (01252) 875737.
Category: Recruitment consultancy.
Recruitment specialty: Management and technical personnel within the IT/ computing industry, specialising in ATC, ILS/reliability, information technology (IT), communications, quality assurance and networking. Skills include: project managers, analyst programmers, draughting technicians, technical authors and software, systems, electronics, test and mechanical engineers etc.
Locations: Canada, Europe, Far East, Ireland, Middle East, United Kingdom and United States.
Additional information: Silicon Valley Group is a recruitment consultancy and software house.

Simpson Crowden Consultants Ltd, 97/99 Park Street, London W1Y 3HA, England. *Tel*: (0171) 629 5909.
Category: Management consultancy.
Recruitment specialty: Executive, management and technical personnel in most industries and sectors.
Locations: Africa and United Kingdom.

Smythe Ratcliffe, 7th Floor, Marine Building, 355 Burrard Street, Vancouver, British Colombia V6C 2G8, Canada.
Category: Accountancy practice and management consultancy.
Recruitment specialty: Most accountancy specialist areas including: auditing, taxation, accountancy, business services, insolvency and corporate advisory services.
Location: Canada.

Spiers Ayres Townshend, Oxford House, 39 Broad Street, Wokingham, Berkshire RG40 1AU, England. *Tel*: (01734) 795550. *Fax*: (01734) 795188.
Category: Management consultancy.
Recruitment specialty: Senior management and executive in most industries and sectors.
Locations: Canada, Europe, Ireland, Middle East, United Kingdom and United States.

SSR Group Services, Select House, 400 Leabridge Road, London E10 7DY, England. *Tel*: (0181) 556 0996. *Fax*: (0181) 556 4493.
Other office: Moscow, Russia.
Category: Executive search consultancy.
Recruitment specialty: Management, engineers and technical personnel within general and contract engineering, facilities maintenance, security, health and safety, sales and marketing specialty areas and industries.
Locations: Africa, Asia, Eastern Europe, South America and United Kingdom.
Additional information: SSR Group Services offer executive search consultancy services to clients.

Staniforth Endsor & Partners Ltd, 3 The Courtyard, Ashley Road, Hale, Altrincham, Cheshire WN4 3NG, England. *Tel*: (0161) 929 1481. *Fax*: (0161) 929 8098.
Category: Recruitment agency and executive search and selection consultancy.
Recruitment specialty: Senior executive to middle management levels of personnel for most sectors.
Locations: Canada, Europe, Ireland, United Kingdom and United States.

Stats Support Services Ltd, Recruitment Division, South House 2, Bond Avenue, Bletchley, Milton Keynes, Buckinghamshire MK1 1SW, England. *Tel*: (01908) 271660. *Fax*: (01908) 271332.
Category: Recruitment consultancy.
Recruitment specialty: Technical documentation personnel such as: technical authors, editors, technical clerks, copy writers, graphic designers, technical illustrators, tracers, CAD operators, desktop publishing (DTP) and word processing (WP) operators and proofreaders. Permanent and contract assignments.
Locations: Europe and United Kingdom.
Additional information: Stats Support Services Ltd draw their own staff from a wide band of industries and skills. Their personnel possess a thorough understanding of client and candidate needs. A total turnkey service is provided, this includes: facilities management, project management, proposal bid support and preparation, technical and training documentation, training material, recruitment, translations and printing.

Stats Support Services Ltd, Technical Publications Division, South House 2, Bond Avenue, Bletchley, Milton Keynes, Buckinghamshire MK1 1SW, England. *Tel*: (01908) 271660. *Fax*: (01908) 271332.
Category: Technical publications consultancy.
Recruitment specialty: Technical documentation personnel such as: technical authors, editors, technical clerks, copy writers, graphic designers, technical illustrators, tracers, CAD operators, desktop publishing (DTP) and word processing (WP) operators and proofreaders. Permanent and contract assignments.
Locations: Europe and United Kingdom.

Additional information: This division specialises in the production of high quality technical and training documentation to various commercial and military specifications. Working with clients from the defence, engineering, aviation, power, utilities, information technology (IT), finance and telecommunications industries in the United Kingdom and in Europe. Technical authors, editors and copy writers come from various engineering and commercial backgrounds having gained valuable hands-on experience in using a wide range of equipment and software, allowing them to understand the end user's requirements more accurately. The authors are supported by in-house teams, consisting of technical illustrators, tracers, delineators, graphic designers, WP and DTP operators. Full reprographics and micrographic services are provided for the completed documentation, including translations into the majority of European languages.

Stats Support Services Ltd, Training Division, South House 2, Bond Avenue, Bletchley, Milton Keynes, Buckinghamshire MK1 1SW, England. *Tel*: (01908) 271660. *Fax*: (01908) 271332.
Category: Training and development consultancy.
Recruitment specialty: Technical training documentation personnel such as: technical authors, editors, technical clerks, copy writers, graphic designers, technical illustrators, tracers, CAD operators, desktop publishing (DTP) and word processing (WP) operators and proofreaders. Permanent and contract assignments.
Locations: Europe and United Kingdom.
Additional information: This division provides comprehensive analysis of client training requirements, all development stages through to solution. In consultation with client personnel, training programmes are devised and implemented and a comprehensive range of training material and equipment is produced. This can include: visual classroom material, documentation, computer based training programs, part-task simulators, videos etc.

Strongfield Aviation Ltd, 62 Marylebone High Street, London W1M 3AF, England. *Tel*: (0171) 224 1200. *Fax*: (0171) 224 0031.
Other offices: 2 in the United Kingdom and 11 overseas including 7 representative offices.
Category: Recruitment management consultancy.
Recruitment specialty: Maintenance and support personnel for the aviation industry, flight crew, cabin staff and maintenance engineers and technicians.
Locations: Asia, Canada, Europe, Far East, Ireland, Middle East, Near East, South America, United Kingdom and United States.

Strongfield Engineering Ltd, 62 Marylebone High Street, London W1M 3AF, England. *Tel*: (0171) 224 1200. *Fax*: (0171) 224 0031.
Other offices: 2 in the United Kingdom and 11 overseas including 7 representative offices.

Category: Recruitment management consultancy.

Recruitment specialty: Senior engineering and technical personnel within the aerospace, electronics, space, telecommunications, automotive, power, rail, civil and computing industries.

Locations: Asia, Canada, Europe, Far East, Ireland, Middle East, Near East, South America, United Kingdom and United States.

Strongfield International Plc, 62 Marylebone High Street, London W1M 3AF, England. *Tel*: (0171) 224 1200. *Fax*: (0171) 224 0031.

Other offices: 2 in the United Kingdom and 11 overseas including 7 representative offices.

Category: Recruitment management consultancy.

Recruitment consultancy: Senior engineering and technical personnel within the aerospace, electronics, space, telecommunications, automotive, power, rail, civil and computing industries. Also maintenance and support personnel for the aviation industry, flight crew, cabin staff and maintenance engineers and technicians.

Locations: Asia, Canada, Europe, Far East, Ireland, Middle East, Near East, South America, United Kingdom and United States.

T. N. Soong & Company, 12th Floor, Hung Tai Century Tower, 156 Min Sheng East Road, Section 3, Taipei, Taiwan, Republic of China.

Category: Accountancy practice and management consultancy.

Recruitment specialty: Most accountancy specialist areas including: auditing, taxation, accountancy, business services, insolvency and corporate advisory services.

Location: Asia.

TA Engineering Services Ltd, Badentoy Avenue, Portlethen, Aberdeen AB12 4YB, Scotland. *Tel*: (01224) 780790. *Fax*: (01224) 783078.

Category: Engineering consultancy.

Recruitment specialty: Management and technical personnel, senior engineers, consultants, specialist technicians and trades etc. in most engineering based industries.

Locations: Asia, Europe, Far East, Ireland, Middle East and United Kingdom.

Additional information: TA Engineering offer specialist consultancy services to their clients in reliability maintenance, criticality studies etc.

Tangent International, Shelduck House, 10/11 Woodbrook Crescent, Billericay, Essex CM12 0EQ, England. *Tel*: (01277) 630055. *Fax*: (01277) 633133.

Category: Recruitment consultancy.

Recruitment specialty: Most levels of personnel for the IT/computing industry on a permanent and contract basis. Skills in software engineering, real time software engineering, cellular and mobile communications etc.

Locations: Africa, Asia, Australia, Canada, Europe, Far East, Ireland, Middle East, Near East, New Zealand, Scandinavia, South America, United

Kingdom and United States.

Additional information: Tangent International offer professional advice and guidance to contractors seeking assignments overseas.

TASK Contracts Ltd, Monchelsea Farm, Heath Road, Boughton Monchelsea, Maidstone, Kent ME17 4JD, England. *Tel*: (01622) 746 277. *Fax*: (01622) 747 466.

Category: Recruitment consultancy.

Recruitment specialty: Engineering and technical personnel for the process control industry in a broad band of functional levels and across most specialty skill areas.

Locations: Africa, Asia, Europe, Far East, Ireland, Middle East and United Kingdom.

TDM Technical Services, 107 Delaware Avenue, Suite 500, Buffalo, New York, NY 14202, United States.

Category: Recruitment consultancy.

Recruitment specialty: Senior engineers and other technical personnel for the aerospace and telecommunictions industries, CNC programmers, software engineers, designers, project engineers, R/F designers, network planners etc.

Locations: Asia, Australia, Canada, Far East, Middle East, New Zealand and United States.

TDM Technical Services, 3 Church Street, Suite 300, Toronto, Ontario, Canada. *Tel*: 00 416 777 007. *Fax*: 00 416 777 1117.

Category: Recruitment consultancy.

Recruitment specialty: Senior engineers and other technical personnel for the aerospace and telecommunications industries, CNC programmers, software engineers, designers, project engineers, R/F designers, network planners etc.

Locations: Asia, Australia, Canada, Europe, Far East, Middle East, New Zealand and United States.

TDM Europe Ltd, Hunter House, Biggin Hill Airport, Biggin Hill, Kent TN16 3BN, England. *Tel*: (0195) 957 0707. *Fax*: (0195) 957 0606.

Category: Recruitment consultancy.

Recruitment specialty: Senior engineers and other technical personnel for the aerospace and telecommunications industries, CNC programmers, software engineers, designers, project engineers, R/F designers, network planners etc.

Locations: Asia, Australia, Canada, Europe, Far East, Ireland, Middle East, New Zealand, United Kingdom and United States.

TDM Technical Services, JL Griya Raya Utara #20, Bandung, Indonesia. *Tel*: 00 011 62 2221 2952. *Fax*: 00 011 62 2221 2952.

Category: Recruitment consultancy.

Recruitment specialty: Senior engineers and other technical personnel for the aerospace and telecommunications industries, CNC programmers, software

engineers, designers, project engineers, R/F designers, network planners etc.
Locations: Asia, Australia, Far East and New Zealand.

Technicon, 34 Coldharbour Lane, Harpenden, Hertfordshire AL5 4UN, England. *Tel*: (01582) 764422. *Fax*: (01582) 764777.
Category: Recruitment consultancy.
Recruitment specialty: Engineering design and styling personnel for the automotive industry, vehicles only.
Locations: Africa, Australia, Canada, Europe, New Zealand, South America, United Kingdom and United States.

Thomas Le C. Kuen & Company, 23rd Floor, Wing On Centre, 1111 Connaught Road Central, Hong Kong.
Category: Accountancy practice and management consultancy.
Recruitment specialty: Most accountancy specialist areas including: auditing, taxation, accountancy, business services, insolvency and corporate advisory services.
Location: Hong Kong.

Thomas Mining Associates, PO Box 2023, Bournemouth BH4 8YR, England. *Tel*: (01202) 751 658. *Fax*: (01202) 764 448.
Category: Recruitment consultancy.
Recruitment specialty: Engineering and technical personnel for the mining, quarrying and extractive industries, including most services and associated functions. Placements cover a wide band of levels and skills, ranging from main board to technical workforce, geologists, mining engineers, metallurgists, mechanical/electrical/civil/construction engineers, accountancy and most administrative functions.
Locations: Africa, Asia, Australia, Canada, Europe, Far East, Ireland, Middle East, Near East, New Zealand, Russia, South America, United Kingdom and United States.

Tilintarkastajien Oy-Ernst & Young, Kaivokatu 8, 00100 Helsinki, Finland.
Category: Accountancy practice and management consultancy.
Recruitment specialty: Most accountancy specialist areas including: auditing, taxation, accountancy, business services, insolvency and corporate advisory services.
Location: Europe.

Torres & Partners Ltd, Sandpiper Quay, 36 Modwen Road, Salford, Greater Manchester M5 3EZ, England. *Tel*: (0161) 876 5200. *Fax*: (0161) 876 5203.
Category: Recruitment consultancy.
Recruitment specialty: Senior management and technical personnel for the manufacturing, information technology (IT), telecommunications, networking, sales and marketing, FMCG, finance, construction, engineering industries and specialty areas.

Locations: Canada, Europe, Ireland, Middle East, United Kingdom and United States.

Towers Perrin, Castlewood House, 77/91 New Oxford Street, London WC1A 1PX, England. *Tel*: (0171) 872 0397/(0171) 379 4000. *Fax*: (0171) 836 9240/ (0171) 379 7478.
Category: Human resources and management consultancy.
Recruitment specialty: Human resource management and consultants with actuarial expertise, actuarial analysts in life, general insurance and pensions.
Location: United Kingdom.

TRG European, 21 Lovat Lane, London EC3R 8EB, England. *Tel*: (0171) 283 6794/(0171) 236 2661. *Fax*: (0171) 929 5706/(0171) 621 0286.
Category: Recruitment consultancy.
Recruitment specialty: Sales personnel, telephonists, engineers, communications support, technical support, network controllers etc.
Locations: Asia, Europe, Far East, Middle East, Near East, South America and United Kingdom.

Triage Ltd, King's House, 32/40 Widmore Road, Bromley, Kent BR1 1RY, England. *Tel*: (0181) 464 2881. *Fax*: (0181) 466 7891.
Category: Recruitment consultancy.
Recruitment specialty: Senior management and technical personnel for the IT/ computing industry, particularly in the mobile markets and most levels.
Locations: Asia, Australia, Canada, Europe, Far East, Middle East, New Zealand, United Kingdom and United States.

TSA Human Resources Ltd, Ertfstadt Court, Wokingham, Berkshire RG40 2AY, England. *Tel*: (01734) 791212. *Fax*: (01734) 794800.
Category: Management consultancy.
Recruitment specialty: Sales, marketing and technical support personnel in the telecommuncations, networking and document management specialty areas.
Locations: Europe, Ireland and United Kingdom.

UK Inspection Ltd, UK House, Station Road, Ellesfield, Sheffield, South Yorkshire S30 3YR, England. *Tel*: (0114) 246 6666. *Fax*: (0114) 246 3312.
Category: Engineering consultancy.
Recruitment specialty: Senior engineers and technical personnel, predominantly in the oil and gas and petrochemical industries. Specialist engineers in design, construction, installation, commissioning, inspection etc.
Locations: Africa, Asia, Canada, Europe, Far East, Middle East, United Kingdom and United States.

Vantage Management Consultants, 8 Prebendal Court, Aylesbury, Buckinghamshire HP19 3EY, England. *Tel*: (01296) 397184. *Fax*: (01296) 330816.

Category: Human resource and management consultancy.
Recruitment specialty: Senior executive, management and technical personnel in most industries and sectors.
Locations: Europe and United Kingdom.
Additional information: Vantage Management Consultants is the United Kingdom member of European Human Resource Consultants (EHRC). The services provided by the company include: human resources consultancy in all the known specialty areas, management development programmes, corporate strategy, executive recruitment, total staffing, performance programmes etc.

Varley Walker, St George's House, Adelaide Street, St Albans, Hertfordshire AL3 5EY, England. *Tel*: (01727) 866500. *Fax*: (01727) 865284.
Category: Engineering consultancy.
Recruitment specialty: Senior management, technical and support personnel in aerospace, automotive, chemical, construction, distribution, education, electronics, information technology (IT), packaging, pharmaceuticals and the general electrical and mechanical industries.
Locations: Africa, Asia, Australia, Canada, Europe, Far East, Ireland, Near East, New Zealand, South America, United Kingdom and United States.

VIP International, 17 Charing Cross Road, London WC2H 0EP, England. *Tel*: (0171) 930 0541. *Fax*: (0171) 930 2860.
Category: Recruitment consultancy.
Recruitment specialty: Management and support personnel for the hospitality industry.
Locations: Africa, Asia, Australia, Europe, Far East, Ireland, Middle East, Near East, New Zealand, South America and United Kingdom.

Wallace Hind Associates. 5 Duncan Close, Moulton Park, Northampton NN3 6WL, England. *Tel*: (01604) 671176. *Fax*: (01604) 642733.
Category: Recruitment consultancy.
Recruitment specialty: Senior and other levels of sales personnel in most industries including a specialist interest in engineering, packaging, print, export, chemical and general industrial and commercial sectors and markets.
Location: United Kingdom.
Additional information: Export positions, although based in the United Kingdom, cover countries worldwide.

WEL Technical Services Ltd, Romney House, Romney Place, Maidstone, Kent, ME15 6LG, England. *Tel*: (01622) 678031. *Fax*: (01622) 683813.
Category: Recruitment consultancy.
Recruitment specialty: Senior management and technical personnel for the petrochemical offshore industry. Structural design, in-house inspection, testing to BS EN ISO 9001 etc.

Locations: Europe, Far East (including Malaysia) and United Kingdom.

Weltec Ltd, Romney House, Romney Place, Maidstone, Kent, ME15 6LG, England. *Tel*: (01622) 678031. *Fax*: (01622) 683813.
Category: Structural design consultancy.
Recruitment specialty: Management, engineers, technical and support personnel for the petrochemical industries onshore and offshore, inspectors, engineers, project managers etc. Also datacommunications, installation technicians, engineers etc.
Locations: Europe, Far East (Kuala Lumpur) and United Kingdom.

Wetherby, Matthew Murray House, 87 Water Lane, Leeds, West Yorkshire LS11 5QN, England. *Tel*: (0113) 242 8558/0721/(0113) 233 9606. *Fax*: (0113) 242 8551.
Category: Recruitment consultancy.
Recruitment specialty: Senior to middle management levels in professional roles within the manufacturing, business development, human resources, design, quality assurance, information technology (IT), sales and marketing, logistics, finance etc. industries and specialist areas.
Locations: Australia, Canada, Europe, Far East, United Kingdom and United States.

Wey Personnel, 1 High Street, Godalming, Surrey GU7 1AZ, England. *Tel*: (01483) 414222. *Fax*: (01483) 425437.
Category: Recruitment consultancy.
Recruitment specialty: Senior engineers, technical and support personnel for the power generation, energy and chemical industries. Also most general office and administrative staff for the United Kingdom.
Locations: Africa, Asia, Europe, Far East, Middle East and United Kingdom.

Windows Resourcing Ltd, Shirley Lodge, 470 London Road, Slough, Berkshire SL3 8QY, England. *Tel*: (01753) 710439. *Fax*: (01753) 540873.
Category: Recruitment consultancy.
Recruitment specialty: Senior management, technical and support personnel for the IT/computing industry, training, support and development roles, project management, for permanent and contract assignments. Skills include: PC environments, WINDOWS, UNIX, ORACLE, LOTUS etc.
Locations: Europe, Ireland and United Kingdom.

World Crews, 52 York Place, Bournemouth BH7 6JN, England. *Tel/Fax*: (01202) 431520.
Category: Recruitment consultancy.
Recruitment specialty: Crews for private and chartered yachts including: skippers, engineers, chefs, cooks, hostesses, sailing school instructors, deckhands and boat minders.
Locations: Australia, Canada, Caribbean, Europe, Far East, Ireland,

Mediterranean, New Zealand, United Kingdom and United States.

Wray Partnership, The, 150 Regent Street, London W1R 5FA, England. *Tel*: (0171) 734 9571. *Fax*: (0171) 494 3634.
Category: Recruitment consultancy.
Recruitment specialty: Senior management and technical personnel within the IT/computing industry, in banking, financial services and insurance and retail specialist areas for permanent and contract assignments.
Locations: Far East and United Kingdom.

Wright Matsui Association Japan, 8/16 Mirokuji, 3 Chome, Fujisawa-Shi, Kanagawa, 251 Japan. *Tel/Fax*: 00 81 466 28 0023.
Category: Recruitment consultancy.
Recruitment specialty: Management personnel for the construction industry in most specialty areas, civil engineering, building, building services, quantity surveying etc. for consulting engineers, international contractors and professional quantity surveying firms.
Locations: Africa, Asia, Europe, Far East, Middle East, Near East and South America.

WS Recruitment, Cottrell House, High Street, Angmering, West Sussex BN16 4AE, England. *Tel*: (01903) 786199. *Fax*: (01903) 787616.
Category: Recruitment consultancy.
Recruitment specialty: Senior management and technical personnel for the oil and gas, petrochemical industries. Specialty areas include: design, construction, production, drilling safety etc.
Locations: Africa, Far East, Middle East and South America.

Wynnwith Engineering Co Ltd, Aviation Division, Commercial House, Chapel Street, Woking, Surrey GU21 1BY, England. *Tel*: (01483) 748201. *Fax*: (01483) 772222.
Category: Recruitment consultancy.
Recruitment specialty: Management, technical and support personnel for the aviation industry.
Locations: Asia, Caribbean, Europe, Middle East and United Kingdom.

Wynnwith Engineering Co Ltd, Electrical and Building Services Division, Commercial House, Chapel Street, Woking, Surrey GU21 1BY, England. *Tel*: (01483) 748202. *Fax*: (01483) 772222.
Category: Recruitment consultancy.
Recruitment specialty: Management, technical and support personnel for the building, electrical, mechanical and petrochemical industries and specialist areas.
Locations: Asia, Caribbean, Europe, Middle East and United Kingdom.

Wynnwith Engineering Co Ltd, IT & Telecommunications Division, Commercial House, Chapel Street, Woking, Surrey GU21 1BY, England. *Tel*: (01483) 748203. *Fax*: (01483) 772222.
Category: Recruitment consultancy.
Recruitment specialty: Management, technical and support personnel for the IT/computing industry, telecommunications etc.
Locations: Asia, Caribbean, Europe, Middle East and United Kingdom.

Part Two Section 2
Agencies and Employers

AAD Executive Selection, 7 Curzon Street, London W1Y 7FL, England. *Tel*: (0171) 499 8811. *Fax*: (0171) 499 6725.

Category: Recruitment agency.

Recruitment specialty: Middle and senior executives in commerce and industry for all business functions, general management, sales and marketing, finance, IT, human resources, manufacturing, engineering, research and development, corporate communications.

Location: United Kingdom.

ABB Higrade Resources Ltd, South Point, Sutton Court Road, Sutton, Surrey SM1 4TZ, England. *Tel*: (0181) 288 0920. *Fax*: (0181) 288 0921.

Category: Recruitment agency and employer.

Recruitment specialty: Engineering disciplines in design, construction, general management, project management in oil and gas, petrochemical, energy and transportation sectors including: IT specialists in PC support, desk, help desk and operations.

Locations: Africa, Asia, Canada, Europe (Scandinavia), Far East, Middle East, Near East, United Kingdom and United States.

ABB Higrade Resources Ltd, South Point, Sutton Court Road, Sutton, Surrey SM1 4TZ, England. *Tel*: (0181) 395 8100. *Fax*: (0181) 395 8990,.

Category: Recruitment agency.

Recruitment specialty: Engineering and technical support for the oil and gas, petrochemical, power, water, HVAC, civil, construction, design engineering, commissioning, project management, planning, costing specialty areas and industries. Also IT/computing analyst programmers etc.

Locations: Africa, Asia, Europe, Far East, Middle East, Near East, Scandinavia and United Kingdom.

Abu Dhabi Gas Liquefaction Co Ltd, (Recruitment Office), PO Box 3500, Abu Dhabi, United Arab Emirates. *Tel*: 00 971 2 606 5765. *Fax*: 00 971 2 606 5500.

Category: Employer.

Recruitment specialty: Most engineering and technical support personnel in the oil and gas and petrochemical industries.

Location: Middle East.

Acetech Personnel Ltd, Clive House, Langley Business Centre, Langley, Slough, Buckinghamshire SL3 8DS, England. *Tel*: (01753) 580028/211230. *Fax*: (01753) 211248.

Category: Recruitment agency.

Recruitment specialty: Most levels of personnel for the IT/computing industry, telecommunictions, design, installation, commissioning and testing, maintenance, GSM, PCN, local loop, LAN, WAN, switching, transmission, microwave technology etc.

Locations: Africa, Asia, Europe, Far East, Middle East, South America and United Kingdom.

Action Health, The Gate House, 25 Gwydir Street, Cambridge, Cambridgeshire CB1 2LG, England. *Tel*: (01223) 460853. *Fax*: (01223) 461787.

Category: Charity recruitment agency.

Recruitment specialty: Medical and nursing staff in most specialty areas, GPs, specialists, dentists, midwives, health visitors, physiotherapists, occupational therapists, speech therapists etc.

Locations: Africa (Tanzania and Uganda), Asia (India) and Far East.

Additional information: Action Health is a Cambridge based charity which develops primary healthcare and training programmes with communities in developing countries. The programmes are long term with focus on skills transfer and ultimate self reliance. Voluntary work, 6 month to 2 year contracts.

Action Recruitment, St Andrews House, 28/30 Exchequer Street, Dublin 2, Republic of Ireland. *Tel*: 00 353 1 677 8544. *Fax*: 00 353 1 679 6830.

Category: Recruitment agency.

Recruitment specialty: Management, technical and support personnel for the hotel and catering industry. Hotel and catering managers, bar managers, chefs, cooks, bar and waiting staff, receptionists, sales and marketing, human resources/personnel etc.

Locations: Asia, Europe, Far East, Ireland and United Kingdom.

Aeroquip EID, Status Park Four, 3 Nobel Drive, Hayes, Middlesex UB3 5EY, England.

Other offices: 1 other plant in Italy.

Category: Employer

Recruitment specialty: Manufacturer and distributor of fluid connectors and systems for the industrial, automotive and aerospace sectors.

Locations: Europe (Italy) and United Kingdom.

AIL International Ltd, 57 London Road, St Albans, Hertfordshire AL1 1LJ, England. *Tel*: (01727) 630123. *Fax*: (01727) 810520.

Category: Recruitment agency and employer.

Recruitment specialty: Serves Japanese companies and recruits personnel to work on Japanese projects internationally. All projects are related to the building industry such as design, procurement, construction, commissioning etc.

Locations: Africa, Asia, Europe, Far East, Middle East, South America and United Kingdom.

Aker Oil & Gas Technology (UK) Plc, Aker House, Blackness Road, Altens, Aberdeen AB1 4LH, Scotland. *Tel*: (01224) 403100. *Fax*: (01224) 890662.

Category: Recruitment agency.

Recruitment specialty: Professionals in design engineering, technical, procurement, safety, subsea petroleum drilling, petroleum processing and operational support personnel.

Locations: Asia, Australia, Canada, Europe, Far East, Ireland, Middle East, Near East, New Zealand, South America, United Kingdom and United States.

Alan Davis & Associates, 455 Main Road, Suite 201, Hudson, Québec, Canada JOP 1HO. *Tel*: 00 514 458 3535. *Fax*: 00 514 458 3530.

Category: Recruitment agency.

Recruitment specialty: Management and technical personnel for the aerospace, electronics, telecommunications, pharmaceutical, engineering and information technology (IT) industries.

Locations: Canada and United States.

Alasdair Graham Associates Ltd, 97 Ayr Road, Newton Mearns, Glasgow GL77 6RA, Scotland. *Tel*: (0141) 639 3345. *Fax*: (0141) 639 2918.

Category: Recruitment agency.

Recruitment specialty: Senior executive, management and technical personnel for the oil and gas, petrochemical, rail, construction, power, marine and water industries. Permanent and contract assignments.

Locations: Africa, Asia, Canada, Europe, Far East, Middle East, Near East, South America, United Kingdom and United States.

Alba International (IOM) Ltd, Alba House, Princes Street, Douglas, Isle of Man, United Kingdom. *Tel*: (01624) 621293. *Fax*: (01624) 626177.

Category: Recruitment agency and employer.

Recruitment specialty: Personnel for the petrochemical industry, oil and gas, associated project management. Consultants for computing (check out – mainframes, PCs, networks, hardware, software, IT etc.) and construction industries.

Locations: Asia, Far East, Middle East, Near East and South America.

Alexander Mann Associates Plc, Alexander House, 9/11 Fulwood Place, London WC1V 6HG, England. *Tel*: (0171) 242 9000. *Fax*: (0171) 242 9001.

Category: Recruitment agency.

Recruitment specialty: Senior management and technical personnel for the financial and investment banking sectors.

Locations: Asia, Canada, Europe, Middle East, United Kingdom and United States.

Anders Glaser Wills, Capital House, Houndwell Place, Southampton, Hampshire SO14 1HU, England. *Tel*: (01703) 223511. *Fax*: (01703) 227911.
Other offices: 5 in the United Kingdom.
Category: Recruitment agency.
Recruitment specialty: Technical personnel for the building and civil engineering disciplines.
Locations: Africa, Asia, Canada, Europe, Far East, Ireland, Middle East, Near East, South America, United Kingdom and United States.
Additional information: Specialist work undertaken for contracting organisations, consulting engineers and project management companies.

Angel International Recruitment, 50 Fleet Street, London EC4Y 1BE, England.*Tel*: (0171) 583 1661. *Fax*: (0171) 353 8538/(0171) 454 9608.
Category: Recruitment agency.
Recruitment specialty: Healthcare – medical and nursing staff for overseas and nationally: locums, medical and temporary nursing staff. Also nationally: hotel/catering, secretarial, VDU operators etc, temporary staff, IT/computing contract staff.
Locations: Asia. Australia, Far East, Middle East, New Zealand and United Kingdom.

ARA International Ltd, Scottish Union House, 26/28 Addiscombe Road, Croydon, Surrey CRO 5PE, England. *Tel*: (0181) 686 9511. *Fax*: (0181) 686 9488.
Category: Recruitment agency.
Recruitment specialty: Professional and technical engineering personnel for the oil, gas, petrochemical and process industries. Most engineering disciplines, medical, financial and IT specialists.
Location: Middle East.

ASA International, 498 Union Street, Aberdeen AB1 1TS, Scotland. *Tel*: (01224) 648062. *Fax*: (0131) 226 5110.
Category: Recruitment agency.
Recruitment specialty: Senior executive, management and technical personnel for the legal and financial services specialty areas, including: legal practitioners, accountants, accountancy technicians, secretarial, administrative, clerical etc.
Locations: Africa, Australia, Canada, Europe, Far East, Middle East, Near East, New Zealand, South America, United Kingdom and United States.

ASA International, 63 George Street, Edinburgh EH2 2JG, Scotland. *Tel*: (0131) 226 6222. *Fax*: (0131) 226 5110.

Category: Recruitment agency.

Recruitment specialty: Senior executive, management and technical personnel for the legal and financial services specialty areas, including: legal practitioners, accountants, accountancy technicians, secretarial, administrative, clerical etc.

Locations: Africa, Australia, Canada, Europe, Far East, Middle East, Near East, New Zealand, South America, United Kingdom and United States.

ASA International, 69 St Vincent Street, Glasgow G2 5TF, Scotland. *Tel*: (0141) 221 4166. *Fax*: (0131) 226 5110.

Category: Recruitment agency.

Recruitment specialty: Senior executive, management and technical personnel for the legal and financial services specialty areas, including: legal practitioners, accountants, accountancy technicians, secretarial, administrative, clerical etc.

Locations: Africa, Australia, Canada, Europe, Far East, Middle East, Near East, New Zealand, South America, United Kingdom and United States.

ASA International, Glenrothes House, North Street, Glenrothes KY2 5PB, Scotland. *Tel*: (01592) 752312. *Fax*: (0131) 226 5110.

Category: Recruitment agency.

Recruitment specialty: Senior executive, management and technical personnel for the legal and financial services specialty areas, including: legal practitioners, accountants, accountancy technicians, secretarial, administrative, clerical etc.

Locations: Africa, Australia, Canada, Europe, Far East, Middle East, Near East, New Zealand, South America, United Kingdom and United States.

Ashbrittle Ltd, Ashbrittle House, Lower Dagnall Street, St Albans, Hertfordshire AL3 4PA, England. *Tel*: (01727) 854854. *Fax*: (01727) 865557.

Category: Recruitment agency.

Recruitment specialty: Management and technical personnel for the construction, building, civil engineering and process/oil industries etc.

Locations: Europe, Far East, Middle East, Near East and United Kingdom.

Astles Partnership, The, PO Box 243, Aylesbury, Buckinghamshire HP17 8RT, England. *Tel*: (01296) 747247. *Fax*: (01296) 747234.

Category: Recruitment agency.

Recruitment specialty: Sales and marketing executives.

Location: Eastern Europe.

Aston Zoraster Ltd, Westminster House, 58 London Street, Reading, Berkshire RG1 4SQ, England. *Tel*: (01734) 566123. *Fax*: (01734) 596222.

Category: Recruitment agency.

Recruitment specialty: Senior executive, management and technical personnel for the banking and finance, IT/computing, datacommunications, electro-

nics, FMCG, food, high technology logistics, manufacturing, retail, telecommunications, transportation and distribution industries, public sector. Also non-executive directors.
Location: United Kingdom.
Additional information: Aston Zoraster Ltd has expertise in all the following functional disciplines: engineering, general management, finance, facilities management, human resources, information technology (IT), management consulting, market research, production, quality assurance, sales and marketing. Also: management development, training, team building, management audit, competency based assessment and psychometric assessments.

Au Pair In America, 37 Queen's Gate, London SW7 5HR, England. *Tel*: (0171) 581 7322/7311/7355. *Fax*: (0171) 581 7345.
Category: Employer.
Recruitment specialty: Au pairs.
Location: United States.
Additional information: Au Pair In America sends around 4,000 individuals to the United States each year to many destinations including: New York, Boston, Detroit, Atlanta, San Francisco and almost 170 other locations throughout the country. Employees normally work a 45-hour week and some of the company benefits include: legal J-1 exchange visitor's visa, free return flight to Europe, 4 day orientation in New York City, free room and board, up to $135 weekly payment, private room and meals, $500 study allowance, free 12 month medical insurance, $500 assignment bonus etc. Applicants must be aged between 18–26 years, possess childcare experience, NNEB qualified, full driving licence, a minimum of a secondary school education, no criminal record and agree to a full 12 month contract. The Au Pair In America programme is regulated by the Goverment of the United States. Extensive support and back-up include local community counselling facility and a 24-hour toll-free telephone number to the firm's office in Greenwich, Connecticut.

Audiobyte Business Consultants, The Blackfriars Foundry, 156 Blackfriars Road, London SE1 8EN, England. *Tel*: (0181) 721 7117. *Fax*: (0181) 721 7107.
Category: Recruitment agency.
Recruitment specialty: IT contract and permanent personnel in connectivity, communications, database development, front end developers especially in banking and associated markets, AS/400 operations and RPC.
Locations: Asia, Australia, Canada, Europe, New Zealand, United Kingdom and United States.

Austin Harrison Worldwide Ltd, St Nicholas House, 40 High Street, Seven Oaks, Kent TN13 1JG, England. *Tel*: (01732) 465680.
Category: Recruitment agency.

Recruitment specialty: IT and computing most areas.
Locations: Europe and United Kingdom.

Avalon Au Pairs, 7 Highway, Edgcumbe Park, Crowthorne, Berkshire RG45 6HE, England. *Tel*: (01344) 778246. *Fax*: (01344) 778246.
Category: Recruitment agency.
Recruitment specialty: Au pairs.
Locations: Europe and United Kingdom.

Bartwell International (UK) Ltd, Bradford Court, Bradford Street, Birmingham B12 0NS, England. *Tel*: (0121) 773 1770. *Fax*: (0121) 773 9998.
Category: Recruitment agency.
Recruitment specialty: Senior executive and management levels in most sectors.
Locations: Africa, Canada, Europe, Middle East, United Kingdom and United States.
Additional information: The firm applies a team approach and two senior recruitment consultants have functional and industry experience.

Beament Leslie Thomas, Quality House, 5/9 Quality Court, Chancery Lane, London WC2B 1HP, England. *Tel*: (0171) 405 3404. *Fax*: (0171) 405 3310.
Category: Recruitment agency.
Recruitment specialty: Specialists with experience in corporate and personal taxation, customs and duties, for large international firms of accountants, lawyers and multinational corporations.
Locations: Europe and United Kingdom.

Beechwood Recruitment Ltd, 221 High Street, London W3 9BY, England. *Tel*: (0181) 992 8647. *Fax*: (0181) 992 5658.
Category: Recruitment agency.
Recruitment specialty: Most levels of personnel in the following specialist areas and industries: electronics, telecommunications, automotive, aerospace, computing, purchasing, pharmaceutical, oil and gas, research and development, sales and marketing, defence, civil engineering etc.
Locations: Africa, Asia, Australia, Canada, Europe, Far East, Ireland, Middle East, Near East, New Zealand, South America, United Kingdom and United States.
Additional information: The Beechwood appointments register gives companies in the United Kingdom and worldwide the opportunity of contacting job seekers directly from a candidate bank (database) and does not charge fees on appointment. The register is updated daily and consists of experienced engineers, scientists, technologists, sales, marketing and computing engineers.

Bees Knees Agency, 53 Church Avenue, East Sheen, London SW14 8NL, England. *Tel/Fax*: (0181) 867 7039.
Category: Recruitment agency.

Recruitment specialty: Au pairs, nannies, housekeepers and companions. Also secretaries, carers of the elderly etc.
Locations: Europe and United Kingdom.

BePos, PO Box 1413, London W6 7PW, England. *Tel*: (0181) 846 6910. *Fax*: (0181) 741 2001.
Category: Recruitment agency.
Recruitment specialty: Engineers and other technical personnel. Specialty areas include: process, power, civil engineering, piping, quality assurance, structural/mechanical/electrical engineering and administrative support staff.
Locations: Europe, Far East, Middle East and United Kingdom.

BJD Logistics, St Marys House, 1/7 St Marys Road, Market Harborough, Leicestershire LE16 7DS, England. *Tel*: (01858) 433071. *Fax*: (01858) 463269.
Category: Recruitment agency.
Recruitment specialty: Management personnel in logistics, distribution, transportation and related areas.
Locations: Europe and United Kingdom.

Boyce Agency Ltd, Liberty House, 22 Regent Street, London W1R 5DE, England. *Tel*: (0171) 287 6060. *Fax*: (0171) 494 4652.
Category: Recruitment agency.
Recruitment specialty: Administrative and secretarial bilingual personnel including: translators, interpreters etc across most sectors, including banking etc.
Locations: Europe and United Kingdom.

Brunel Recruitment, 80 Prospect Hill, Redditch, B97 4BY, England. *Tel*: (01527) 584430. *Fax*: (01527) 584173.
Category: Recruitment agency.
Recruitment specialty: Senior and managerial engineers such as: civil, design and project and senior executive engineers within most industries and sectors.
Locations: Asia, Canada, Europe, Ireland, United Kingdom and United States.

Butler International, (European Head Office), Kings Mill, Kings Mill Lane, South Nutfield, Redhill, Surrey RH1 5NE, England. *Tel*: (01737) 822000. *Fax*: (01737) 823031.
Other offices: 3 in the United Kingdom.
Category: Recruitment agency.
Recruitment specialty: Contract technical personnel for the aerospace, aircraft maintenance, cable TV, telecommunications, utilities, process, civil engineering, rail manufacturing, CAD/IT, marine, petrochemical and electronics industries.

Locations: Africa, Asia, Australia, Canada, Europe, Far East, Ireland, Middle East, Near East, New Zealand, South America, United Kingdom and United States.

Cambridge Collocation, 6 Ross Street, Cambridge, Cambridgeshire CB1 3BX, England. *Tel*: (01223) 249606. *Fax*: (01223) 414474.
Category: Recruitment agency.
Recruitment specialty: Registered nurses.
Location: United Kingdom.

Camco Drilling Group Ltd, Oldends Lane Industrial Estate, Stonehouse, Gloucester, Gloucestershire GL10 3RQ, England.
Category: Employer.
Recruitment specialty: Oil and gas exploration and production personnel, most skills.
Locations: United Kingdom and worldwide.
Additional information: There are two divisions, Drilling & Service (D&S) specialising in the developing of steerable drilling systems and Hycalog specialising in the development and manufacture of cutter and drill bits. Suitably qualified and experienced candidates are welcome to forward their detailed CVs.

Cannon Persona International Recruitment, Aldermary House, 10/15 Queen Street, London EC4N 1TX. *Tel*: (0171) 489 8141. *Fax*: (0171) 236 5785.
Category: Recruitment agency.
Recruitment specialty: Senior executive, management and technical personnel for most industries and sectors.
Locations: Europe and United Kingdom.
Additional information: Placements for Japanese speaking candidates.

Capita Recruitment Services, Great West House, Great West Road, Brentford, Middlesex TW8 9DF, England. *Tel*: (0181) 560 9997. *Fax*: (0181) 560 9788.
Category: Recruitment and management consultancy.
Recruitment specialty: Senior to middle management within the finance, IT, and project management industries to both interim management assignments and in search and selection campaigns in public and utility sectors.
Locations: Africa, Europe, Ireland and United Kingdom.

Capital Group, The, Broadway House, 112/134 The Broadway, Wimbledon, London SW19 1RL, England. *Tel*: (0181) 542 8131. *Fax*: (0181) 540 7385.
Category: Recruitment agency.
Recruitment specialty: Engineering, management and technical personnel for the aviation and general engineering industries.
Locations: Africa, Asia, Canada, Europe, Far East, Ireland, Middle East, Near East, South America, United Kingdom and United States.

Cappo International Ltd, Cappo House, 38/40 High Street, West Wickham, Kent BR4 0NJ, England. *Tel*: (0181) 776 1850. *Fax*: (0181) 777 9952.
Category: Recruitment agency.
Recruitment specialty: Senior and supervisory process, mechanical, instrumentation and electrical technical personnel within the chemical, oil and gas industries.
Locations: Asia, Europe, Far East, Middle East and United Kingdom.

Career International Recruitment Ltd, 9 Ashford Road, Maidstone, Kent ME14 5BJ, England. *Tel*: 01622 678555. *Fax*: (01622) 695140.
Category: Recruitment agency.
Recruitment specialty: Medical and nursing staff, paramedical and support personnel.
Location: Middle East.

Career Management International (CMI), 43 Fitzwilliam Square, Dublin D2, Republic of Ireland. *Tel*: 00 353 1 676 5722. *Fax*: 00 353 1 676 5774.
Category: Recruitment agency.
Recruitment specialty: Senior management, engineering and technical support personnel for the construction, design and project management industry specialty areas, including: design and construction teams, land and hydrographic survey teams, project managers for oil/construction and manufacturing projects, telecommunictions engineers, technical sales, buyers etc.
Locations: Africa, Asia, Canada, Europe, Far East, Ireland, Middle East, Near East, Philippines, South America, United Kingdom and United States.

Carlcrest Ltd, SGS House, 217/221 London Road, Camberley, Surrey GU15 3EY, England. *Tel*: (01276) 691144. *Fax*: (01276) 684849.
Category: Recruitment agency.
Recruitment specialty: Engineering and other technical personnel for the oil and gas, petrochemical, chemical, food, pharmaceutical, water, power generation and nuclear industries.
Locations: Asia, Europe, Far East, Ireland, Middle East and United Kingdom.

Castlebay, The APL Centre, Stevenston, Ayrshire KA20 3LR, Scotland. *Tel*: (01294) 605 466. *Fax*: (01294) 605 486.
Category: Recruitment agency.
Recruitment specialty: Management, engineering and other technical personnel for the oil, gas and petrochemical industries. Engineers, technical support and management etc.
Locations: Europe, Far East, Middle East and United Kingdom.

CCL Recruitment International Ltd, 298 High Street, Dovercourt, Harwich, Essex CO12 3PJ, England. *Tel*: (01255) 506001. *Fax*: (01255) 506002.
Category: Recruitment agency.

Recruitment specialty: Senior executive, management and technical personnel for the automotive industry.
Locations: Africa, Far East, Middle East, Near East and United Kingdom.

CDI International Ltd, Capital House, Houndwell Place, Southampton, Hampshire SO14 1HU, England. Tel: (01703) 223511. *Fax*: (01703) 227911.
Other offices: 5 in the United Kingdom.
Category: Recruitment agency.
Recruitment specialty: Technical personnel in the aerospace, automotive, information technology (IT), petrochemical and manufacturing industries.
Locations: Africa, Asia, Canada, Europe, Far East, Ireland, Middle East, United Kingdom and United States.

Certes Computing Ltd, Arthur House, Roman Way, Coleshill, Warwickshire B46 1HQ, England. *Tel*: (01675) 467475. *Fax*: (01675) 467314.
Category: Recruitment agency.
Recruitment specialty: Management, engineering and technical support personnel for the IT/computing industry. Permanent and contract assignments, most specialists across most sectors.
Locations: Canada, Europe, Far East, Middle East, United Kingdom and United States.

Charity People, Leeming House, Vicar Lane North, Leeds, West Yorkshire LS2 7JF, England. *Tel*: (0113) 234 6969. *Fax*: (0113) 245 8222.
Category: Recruitment agency.
Recruitment specialty: Senior executive, secretarial, clerical, administrative personnel in financial, personnel, IT, marketing and fund-raising areas/industries. Specialising in the 'not for profit' sector.
Locations: Asia, Australia, Canada, Europe, Middle East, New Zealand, United Kingdom and United States.

Charity People, Station House, 150 Waterloo Road, London SE1 8SB, England. *Tel*: (0171) 620 0062. *Fax*: (0171) 633 0331.
Category: Recruitment agency.
Recruitment specialty: Senior executive, secretarial, clerical, administrative personnel in financial, personnel, IT, marketing and fund-raising areas/industries. Specialising in the 'not for profit' sector.
Locations: Asia, Australia, Canada, Europe, Middle East, New Zealand, United Kingdom and United States.

Chiyoda International Ltd, 33 Cavendish Square, London W1M 0LX, England. *Tel*: (0171) 867 1221. *Fax*: (0171) 867 1414.
Category: Recruitment agency.
Recruitment specialty: Engineers, supervisors, coordinators, inspectors etc. for the engineering and petrochemical industries.
Locations: Africa, Asia, Far East, Middle East and United Kingdom.

Cliveden Technical Recruitment, Head Office, 92 Broadway, Bracknell, Berkshire RG12 1AR, England. *Tel*: (01344) 489489. *Fax*: (01344) 489505.
Other offices: 4 in the United Kingdom and 1 overseas.
Category: Recruitment agency.
Recruitment specialty: Technical personnel for the electronics, IT and engineering industries for permanent and temporary assignments.
Locations: Australia, Europe, New Zealand and United Kingdom.

Cole Henry Associates Ltd, Airport House, Purley Way, Croydon, Surrey CRO 0XZ, England. *Tel*: (0181) 781 6930. *Fax*: (0181) 781 6932.
Category: Recruitment agency.
Recruitment specialty: Senior to junior management levels in areas of support and human resources personnel. Retail sales and service industry including wholesale and distribution of a wide variety of product types.
Location: United Kingdom.

Commissioning & Technical Services Ltd, Design House, Butts Road, Thornton Cleveleys, Lancashire FY5 4HX, England. *Tel*: (01253) 864 509. *Fax*: (01253) 866 665.
Category: Recruitment agency.
Recruitment specialty: Senior management, engineering and technical personnel for the nuclear, petrochemical, water, construction, aerospace, defence and general engineering industries.
Locations: Canada, Europe, Far East, Ireland, Middle East, United Kingdom and United States.

Comms People, The Quadrangle, 180 Wardour Street, London W1Y 5AE, England. *Tel*: (0171) 734 0090. *Fax*: (0171) 734 3993.
Other offices: 4 in the United Kingdom and 8 overseas.
Category: Recruitment agency.
Recruitment specialty: IT/computing most skills for permanent and contract work.
Locations: Europe and United Kingdom.

Computec International Resources, 34 Francis Grove, Wimbledon, London SW19 4DY, England. *Tel*: (0181) 288 4880. *Fax*: (0181) 288 4882.
Category: Recruitment agency.
Recruitment specialty: IT/computing specialising in niche markets such as: SAP, Oracle financials, HOGAN, GSM, TELCON IMS.
Locations: United States.

Computer International Resources Ltd, 34 Francis Grove, Wimbledon, London SW19 4DY, England. *Tel*: (0181) 288 4880. *Fax*: (0181) 288 4882.
Other offices: 1 UK and 1 United States.
Category: Recruitment agency.
Recruitment specialty: Digital telecommunications, consultants and engineers

in system design, planning, engineering, networks etc.
Location: United States.
Additional information: Contracts offered for a minimum of 12 months. Suitably qualified and experienced candidates are welcome to forward their detailed CVs.

Computer People International, Victory House, 7 Selsdon Way, London E14 9GL, England. *Tel*: (0171) 510 2000. *Fax*: (0171) 510 2291.
Other offices: 9 in the United Kingdom and 5 in the United States, Switzerland and Japan.
Category: Recruitment agency.
Requirement specialty: IT/computing all areas especially rare skills.
Locations: Canada, Europe, United Kingdom and United States.

Computer People South, Quadrant House, Princess Way, Redhill, Surrey RH1 1NP, England. *Tel*: (01737) 770321. *Fax*: (01737) 772609.
Category: Recruitment agency.
Recruitment specialty: IT/computing personnel on a permanent and contract basis, most skills and sectors.
Location: United Kingdom.

Computer Team Group Ltd, 1 St Ann Street, Manchester, Greater Manchester M2 7LG, England. *Tel*: (0161) 834 7435. *Fax*: (0161) 834 7436.
Category: Recruitment agency.
Recruitment specialty: IT/computing personnel at most levels and with a wide band of skills. Specialist areas are: systems and programming, network and communications, operations, consultancy, PC support, helpdesk, voice and data, LAN and WAN, cabling systems engineers. Also personnel for the public finance and commercial sectors and industries such as manufacturing, oil and gas, chemicals etc.
Locations: Europe, Ireland and United Kingdom.

Computing Resource Centre Ltd, West Lodge, 407 Uxbridge Road, London W3 9SH, England. *Tel*: (0181) 896 3110. *Fax*: (0181) 896 2912.
Category: Recruitment agency.
Recruitment specialty: Technical personnel with SAP skills for the computing industry.
Locations: Africa, Australia, Canada, Europe, Far East, Ireland, New Zealand. United Kingdom and United States.

Compuvac, 66 Great Eastern Street, London EC2A 3PP, England. *Tel*: (0171) 613 7000. *Fax*: (0171) 613 7001.
Category: Recruitment agency.
Recruitment specialty: IT/computing most skills such as: analysts, software engineers, telecommunications, datacommunications etc.
Locations: Canada, United Kingdom and United States.

Connect Medical Recruitment, PO Box 110, Biceser, Oxfordshire OX6 3LH, England. *Tel*: (01869) 232262/232698. *Fax*: (01869) 232698.
Category: Recruitment agency.
Recruitment specialty: Senior executive, management and technical such as: sales and marketing personnel in healthcare markets, i.e. products in the medical field related to disposable and capital equipment.
Locations: Europe, Far East and United Kingdom.

Conrad Taylor Marketing, Gatsby Court, 170 Holliday Street, Birmingham B1 1FS, England. *Tel*: (0121) 634 1944. *Fax*: (0121) 631 3278.
Category: Recruitment agency.
Recruitment specialty: Executive and management experienced personnel for the plastics and packaging industry.
Locations: Asia, Canada, Europe, Far East, Ireland, United Kingdom and United States.

Contracts Consultancy (CCL) Ltd, London House, 68 Upper Richmond Road, London SW15 2RP, England. *Tel*: (0181) 871 2994, *Fax*: (0181) 871 9461.
Category: Recruitment agency.
Recruitment specialty: Senior and other technical personnel for the oil and gas, power, engineering, construction and high technology industries. Project managers and engineers and cost and planning/pipeline and subsea/ procurement and logistics etc.
Locations: Africa, Asia, Australia, Canada, Europe, Far East, Ireland, Middle East, Near East, New Zealand, South America, United Kingdom and United States.

CRC Direct, West Lodge, 407 Uxbridge Road, London W3 9SH, England. *Tel*: (0181) 896 3110. *Fax*: (0181) 896 2912.
Category: Recruitment agency.
Recruitment specialty: Most levels and across most sectors.
Locations: Africa, Australia, Canada, Europe, Far East, Ireland, New Zealand, United Kingdom and United States.
Additional information: CRC Direct offers an Internet recruitment service. Computer personnel and employers can be introduced directly. Employers pay a reduced fee for the service and it is free of charge to candidates.

Crone Corkill, Victory House, 99/101 Regent Street, London W1R 7HB. *Tel*: (0171) 434 4512. *Fax*: (0171) 437 9239.
Category: Recruitment agency.
Recruitment specialty: Most levels senior to junior, bilingual, trilingual secretaries and personal assistants (PAs), administrators, marketing assistants, customer services personnel, human resources officers, public relations, account directors and managers etc.
Locations: Europe and United Kingdom.
Additional information: Speculative candidate enquiries are not required.

CSL Recruitment, 44 Richmond Road, Kingston upon Thames, Surrey KT2 5EE, England. *Tel*: (0181) 547 3595. *Fax*: (0181) 547 3735.
Category: Recruitment agency.
Recruitment specialty: Engineers and technical personnel in oil/gas, petrochemical, power generation and transmission, water treatment and desalination, construction, telecommunications, marine and port operations, chemical and pharmaceutical industries.
Locations: Africa, Asia, Europe, Far East, Middle East, Near East, South America and United Kingdom.

CST Selection, Sardinia House, 52 Lincolns Inn Fields, London WC2A 3LZ, England. *Fax*: (0171) 242 0515.
Category: Recruitment agency.
Recruitment specialty: Executive, management and technical in most sectors including the oil and gas industries.
Location: Australia.

CTS International Inc, 11100 NE 8th Street, Suite 450 Bellvue, Washington, United States 98004. *Tel*: 00 1 206 451 0051. *Fax*: 00 1 206 451 0052.
Category: Recruitment agency.
Recruitment specialty: Engineers, designers and draughting personnel for the aircraft industry.
Location: United States.

Dalroth & Partners Ltd, Nightingale House, 46/48 East Street, Epsom, Surrey KT1 1HQ, England. *Tel*: (01872) 726299.*Fax*: (01872) 744020.
Category: Recruitment agency.
Recruitment specialty: Senior executive, management and technical personnel for the IT/computing industry such as: engineers, technical authors and other skills including programming, systems, software and hardware, sales, support and training.
Locations: Europe, Middle East and United Kingdom.

Dart Resourcing Group, MDA House, The Grove, Slough, Berkshire SL1 1RH, England. *Tel*: (01753) 534610/693633/693611.
Category: Recruitment agency.
Recruitment specialty: IT/computing specialists, IT multi-media industries, engineering programming, design analysis, telecommunications, CAD-CAM, PC and networking.
Locations: Europe, Ireland, Middle East and United Kingdom.

Datel Staff Contracting, Old Docks House, 90 Watery Lane, Preston, Lancashire PR2 1AU, England. *Tel*: (01772) 760600.
Category: Recruitment agency.
Recruitment specialty: Engineers for avionic systems, software, military equipment, control systems engineers, transit software and systems

engineers, telecommunications, network designers etc.

Locations: Africa, Asia, Australia, Canada, Europe, Far East, Middle East, Near East, New Zealand, United Kingdom and United States.

Daulton Construction Personnel Ltd, 2 Greycoat Place, London SW1P 1SB, England. *Tel*: (0171) 222 0816. *Fax*: (0171) 203 0734.

Category: Recruitment agency.

Recruitment specialty: Management and senior technical levels for the construction and building services industry, quantity surveyors, civil engineers, project and construction managers.

Locations: Africa, Asia, Australia, Canada, Europe, Far East, Ireland, Middle East, Near East, New Zealand, South America, United Kingdom and United States.

Dawood Consultants Plc, Dawood House, 28 Mayday Road, Thornton Heath, Surrey CR7 7HL, England. *Tel*: (0181) 683 2126 (10 lines). *Fax*: (0181) 683 4357.

Category: Recruitment agency.

Recruitment specialty: Executive, management, engineers and technical personnel for the IT/computing and general engineering industries.

Locations: Australia, Europe, Ireland, Middle East, New Zealand and United Kingdom.

DBM International, 7A South Gyle Broadway, South Gyle Industrial Estate, Edinburgh EH12 9EH, Scotland. *Tel*: (0131) 316 4088. *Fax*: (0131) 316 4755.

Category: Recruitment agency.

Recruitment specialty: Computing, telecommunications and specialist engineers such as: hardware, software, production, quality, mechanical, electrical, C&I and manufacturing. In addition, technical authors, draughting technicians etc.

Locations: Europe and United Kingdom.

DH Associates, Wrights House, 102/104 High Street, Great Missenden, Buckinghamshire HP16 0BE, England. *Tel*: (01494) 862007. *Fax*: (01494) 862009.

Category: Recruitment agency.

Recruitment specialty: Senior to middle management in the catering industry overseas. In addition, similar personnel in maintenance, logistics and purchasing, retail (supermarkets) and catering (hotels) appointments in the United Kingdom.

Locations: Africa, Asia, Europe (CIS), Far East, Ireland, Middle East, Near East, South America and United Kingdom.

Additional information: Overseas appointments are often in hardship areas, in jungles, swamps, deserts, offshore rigs, war zones, mines etc.

DJ Mills Management, 15/17 Church Street, Epsom, Surrey KT17 4PF, England. *Tel*: (01372) 728911. *Fax*: (01372) 722826.
Category: Specialist technical recruitment and contract agency.
Recruitment specialty: Technical personnel within the engineering industry including: building services, civil engineering, architectural, maintenance, electromechanical and manual building trades.
Locations: Europe, Middle East and United Kingdom.

Douglas Llambias, 410 Strand, London WC2R 0NS, England. *Tel*: (0171) 836 9501.
Category: Recruitment agency.
Recruitment specialty: Executive and management personnel for the finance, accountancy, banking and general management specialty areas.
Locations: Africa, Asia, Australia, Eastern Europe, Far East, Middle East, Near East, New Zealand and United Kingdom.

DP Group, The, 6th Floor, Berkley House, 73 Upper Richmond Road, London SW15 2SZ, England. *Tel*: (0181) 877 1121. *Fax*: (0181) 877 1104.
Category: Recruitment agency.
Recruitment specialty: Senior executive, management and engineering personnel for the IT/computing industry, project managers, senior consultants, senior computer audit and senior communications specialists.
Locations: Europe, Ireland and United Kingdom.
Additional information: The DP Group's clients include management consultancies and international finance organisations. Salary range: £20,000–£150,000.

DS Group, 349 Edinburgh Avenue, Slough, Berkshire SL1 4TH, England. *Tel*: (01753) 820004. *Fax*: (01753) 576229.
Category: Recruitment agency.
Recruitment specialty: IT/computing skills within the desktop environment specialist areas in Microsoft applications, NT and NOVELL.
Locations: Australia, New Zealand and United Kingdom.

EAE Manpower Ltd, Offshore House, 3 Wellheads Way, Dyce, Aberdeen AB2 0GD, Scotland. *Tel*: (01224) 725551. *Fax*: (01224) 722874.
Category: Recruitment agency.
Recruitment specialty: IT/computing and telecommunications within satellite communications, radio, networking, datacommunications installation/ commissioning and maintenance and most areas of communications design.
Locations: Far East, Middle East and United Kingdom.

Eagling Computer Services Ltd, 4 Cromwell Road, Stevenage, Hertfordshire SG2 9HT, England. *Tel*: (01438) 353262. *Fax*: (01438) 314619.
Category: Recruitment agency.
Recruitment specialty: IT/computing including most hardware and software platforms, placement levels from IT directors to trainees for permanent and

contract assignments and for fixed term employees, interim managers and
management consultants.

Locations: Africa, Australia, Canada, Europe, New Zealand, United Kingdom
and United States.

Additional information: Provides additional services, search and selection,
outsourcing, outplacement and competency psychometric testing.

Earl Associates, Lakeside, Common Road, Weston Colville, Cambridge, CB1
5NS, England. *Tel*: (01223) 290343. *Fax*: (01223) 290090.

Category: Recruitment agency.

Recruitment specialty: Executive, management and technical personnel such as:
general managers, sales and marketing management, hardware and
software engineers and engineering managers.

Location: United Kingdom.

EC Consultants Plc, 329/331 London Road, Camberley, Surrey GU15 3HQ,
England. *Tel*: (01276) 676969. *Fax*: (01276) 676755.

Category: Recruitment agency.

Recruitment specialty: IT/computing, datacommunications, transportation,
utilities and electronics.

Locations: Africa, Asia, Australia, Canada, Eastern Europe, Far East, Ireland,
Middle East, Near East, New Zealand, South America, United Kingdom,
United States and Western Europe.

Additional information: Additional services provided to clients: EC Consultants
Plc is experienced in both the private and public sectors. It offers speciality
recruitment services such as: psychometric testing, advertising, campaign
management, salary surveys and human resources newsletter.

Eden Brown Recruitment Ltd, 2 Plough Yard, London EC2A 3PL, England.
Tel: (0171) 377 6222. *Fax*: (0171) 377 1313.

Category: Recruitment agency.

Recruitment specialty: Senior engineers and most technical personnel in the
construction industry such as: quantity surveyors, project/civil/structural/
design engineers and managers, architects, estimators, buyers etc.

Locations: Africa, Asia, Europe, Far East, Middle East, Near East and United
Kingdom.

Elan Communications Ltd, 93 Newman Street, London W1P 4DS, England.
Tel: (0171) 830 1500. *Fax*: (0171) 830 1333.

Other offices: 5 in the United Kingdom and 3 overseas.

Category: Recruitment agency.

Recruitment specialty: IT/computing permanent and contract in most skills.

Locations: Europe, Far East and United Kingdom.

Ellis Employment, 15 College Green, Dublin 2, Republic of Ireland. *Tel*: 00 353
1 679 3561. *Fax*: 00 353 1 679 3717.

Category: Recruitment agency.

Recruitment specialty: Senior executive, management and technical personnel in IT/computing, financial services, hospitality, legal, healthcare, sales and marketing, accountancy industries and specialist areas. Permanent or temporary assignments.

Locations: Far East, Ireland and Near East.

EM Engineering Ltd, Damson House, Broad Oak, Odiham, Hampshire RG29 1AQ, England. *Tel*: (01256) 701177. *Fax*: (01256) 702277.

Category: Recruitment agency.

Recruitment specialty: Professional engineers, permanent and short term placements in the oil and gas, water and utility sectors.

Locations: Africa and Middle East.

Encounter Overland Expeditions Ltd, 267 Old Brompton Road, London SW5 9JA, England. *Tel*: (0171) 370 6951. *Fax*: (0171) 244 9737.

Category: Employer.

Recruitment specialty: Custom travel/expedition leaders and drivers.

Locations: Africa, Asia and South America.

Additional information: Leader/drivers are required to lead groups on expeditions of up to 7 months duration and for shorter periods, adventure holiday projects. Only the most responsible, reliable, sociable and people orientated need apply. They must be capable of driving and maintaining vehicles such as Bedford and Ford cargo trucks over tough terrain and in inhospitable regions of the world.

Enterprise Oil Plc, Grand Buildings, Trafalgar Square, London WC2N 5EJ, England.

Category: Employer.

Recruitment specialty: Oil exploration and production – all related skills.

Locations: United Kingdom and worldwide.

Additional information: Interests in 13 countries worldwide and in the North Sea.

ESDU International Plc, 27 Corsham Street, London N1 6UQ, England. *Tel*: (0171) 490 5151. *Fax*: (0171) 490 2701.

Category: Employer.

Recruitment specialty: Technical personnel in computing and mathematical sciences, aerospace engineering in mechanical, chemical and structural disciplines.

Location: United Kingdom.

Additional information: Additional services provided to clients are: engineering design data and methodology in looseleaf binders and software for use in the aerospace, process and mechanical engineering industries.

Eskal Strategic Resources Ltd, 174c Queenstown Road, London SW8 3NR, England. *Tel*: (0171) 207 1648/1970/(0171) 498 0374. *Fax*: (0171) 498 9839/ (0171) 627 0952.
Category: Recruitment agency.
Recruitment specialty: Engineers for the petrochemical, oil, gas and construction industries.
Locations: Far East, Middle East and United Kingdom.
Additional information: Minimum qualification to BSc with at least 15 years' post-graduate experience.

Euro Pair Agency, 28 Derwent Avenue, Pinner, Middlesex HA5 4QJ, England. *Tel*: (0181) 421 2100. *Fax*: (0181) 428 6416.
Category: Recruitment agency.
Recruitment specialty: Au pairs.
Locations: Europe and United Kingdom.
Additional information: Applicants must be aged between 18–27 years, be child orientated, competent in basic domestic duties, and preferably with good conversational knowledge of another language. Full board, pocket money and lodging applies to each assignment. Language classes are usually available from September for one year.

Euro Secretaries, 2 Beechworth Close, London NW3 7UT, England. *Tel*: (0171) 435 0718/(0374) 920790. *Fax*: (0171) 794 0249.
Category: Recruitment agency.
Recruitment specialty: Monolingual and multilingual secretarial personnel with recognised qualifications and appropriate experience.
Locations: Europe and United Kingdom.

Eurolink Group, 56 Old Steine, Brighton BN1 1NH, England. *Tel*: (01273) 202316. *Fax*: (01273) 723078.
Other offices: 7 in the United Kingdom and 9 overseas.
Category: Recruitment agency and management consultancy.
Recruitment specialty: IT/computing both permanent and contract personnel.
Locations: Europe and United Kingdom.

European Project Consultants, Tower House, Fishergate, York YO1 4UA, England. *Tel*: (01904) 624442. *Fax*: (01904) 624187.
Category: Recruitment agency.
Recruitment specialty: Project, commercial and construction management in oil and gas, chemicals/pharmaceuticals, cryogenics, telecommunications, transportation and infrastructure projects.
Locations: Africa, Asia, Europe (Scandinavia), Far East, Middle East and United Kingdom.

Eurosoft Services Ltd, Orchard Fields, Maylands Avenue, Hemel Hempstead, Hertfordshire HP2 7DF, England.

Other offices: 5 overseas.
Category: Employer.
Recruitment specialty: IT/computing software and hardware engineers, service sales consultants etc.
Locations: Europe and United Kingdom.
Additional information: Suitably qualified and experienced candidates may forward CVs to the human resources department.

Executive Choice, Mead Cottage, Memorial Avenue, Shiplake, Oxfordshire RG9 4DF, England. *Tel/Fax*: (01734) 403095.
Category: Recruitment agency.
Recruitment specialty: Banking systems both retail and wholesale, including dealing room systems and investment job categories in roles such as: senior management, sales and marketing executives, client consultants, project managers and client service personnel.
Locations: Africa, Asia, Europe, Far East, Middle East and United Kingdom.

Executive Facilities (Maidenhead) Ltd, St Ives House, St Ives Road, Maidenhead, Berkshire SL6 1QS, England. *Tel*: (01628) 29333. *Fax*: (01628) 770398.
Category: Recruitment agency.
Recruitment specialty: Senior personnel for the IT/computing and healthcare industries. Medical consultants, clinical research associates, medical representatives, nursing staff, paramedical and support. Permanent and contract assignments for analyst programmers, computer sales, electronic component sales, data analysts, software and hardware engineers.
Locations: Canada, Europe, Ireland, United Kingdom and United States.

Executive Recruitment Services, Boundary Way, Hemel Hempstead, Hertfordshire HP2 7RX, England. *Tel*: (01442) 231691. *Fax*: (01442) 230063.
Category: Recruitment agency.
Recruitment specialty: Computing, electronics and high technology industries. Also legal professions predominantly from graduate level upwards.
Locations: Canada, Europe, Middle East, United Kingdom and United States.

Fairstaff Agency Ltd, 29/31 Oxford Street, London W1R 1RE, England. *Tel*: (0171) 439 2051. *Fax*: (0171) 287 0850.
Category: Recruitment agency.
Recruitment specialty: Specialists to the healthcare and commercial sectors at most levels and specialist area placements such as: medical secretaries and receptionists, ward and clinic clerks for the private sector and the National Health Service (NHS) and most administrative placements both permanent and temporary assignments.
Location: United Kingdom.

Fasttrack Recruitment Ltd, Fasttrack House, 262 Grane Road, Haslingden, Lancashire BB4 4PB, England. *Tel*: (01706) 223211/223204. *Fax*: (01706) 223212.

Category: Recruitment agency.

Recruitment specialty: Industrial and technical personnel such as: senior management, designers, engineers, craftsmen and ancillary.

Locations: Africa, Asia, Australia, Canada, Europe, Far East, Ireland, Middle East, Near East, New Zealand, South America, United Kingdom and United States.

Federal Resources Europe Ltd, 1st Floor, Celcon House, 289/293 High Holborn, London WC1V 2HU, England. *Tel*: (0171) 729 0929. *Fax*: (0171) 316 7700.

Other offices: 6 in the United Kingdom and 3 overseas.

Category: Executive search and selection.

Recruitment specialty: Senior executive and management across most industries and sectors.

Locations: Europe, Ireland, Middle East and United Kingdom.

Additional information: All assignments undertaken are underpinned with psychometric assessment by occupational and/or chartered psychologist, from associate company.

FHELP Marketing, Henriette Villa, Common Mead Avenue, Gillingham, Dorset, SP8 4NB, England. *Tel*: (01747) 822651. *Fax*: (01747) 825845.

Category: Recruitment agency.

Recruitment specialty: Petrochemical engineers and technicians in the processing, refining and chemical industries etc. Healthcare personnel including: doctors, dentists, paramedics, nursing staff and recreactional support especially diving.

Locations: Africa, Canada, Europe, Middle East, Near East, United Kingdom and United States.

Finlayson Wagner & Black Ltd, 19 Alva Street, Edinburgh EH2 4PH, Scotland. *Tel*: (0131) 539 7087. *Fax*: (0131) 539 7086.

Category: Recruitment agency.

Recruitment specialty: Senior executive and management levels for Scottish based organisations and companies in most sectors.

Location: United Kingdom.

First (1st) Future, 175 High Street, Banstead, Surrey SM7 2NT, England. *Tel*: (01737) 370037. *Fax*: (01737) 370009.

Category: Recruitment agency.

Recruitment specialty: IT/computing sales and marketing and support personnel, most levels.

Locations: Europe and United Kingdom.

Firstaff Personnel Consultants Ltd, 85/86 Grafton Street, Dublin 2, Republic of Ireland. *Tel*: 00 353 1 679 7766. *Fax*: 00 353 1 679 6281.
Category: Recruitment agency.
Recruitment specialty: Financial, accounting, manufacturing, sales and marketing, logistics, secretarial, information technology (IT) and computing such as: analysts, programmers, software engineers, IT specialists, mechanical/electrical and electronic engineers, production supervisors, buyer planners, financial and accounting personnel, account executives (representatives, managers etc.), merchandisers, secretaries and word-processing operators, receptionists and credit controllers.
Locations: Europe, Ireland and United Kingdom.

Firth & Associates, 67 High Street, Hemel Hempstead, Hertfordshire HP1 3AF, England. *Tel*: (01442) 219210. *Fax*: (01442) 243610.
Category: Recruitment agency.
Recruitment specialty: Senior executive to middle management levels involved in management buy-ins/outs, in the general management, financial, sales and marketing and manufacturing areas.
Locations: Canada, Europe, Far East, Middle East, United Kingdom and United States.
Additional information: Salary ranges £30,000–£200,000 working for clients on a retained basis only.

FM Recruitment, Greencoat House, Francis Street, London SW1P 1DH, England. *Tel*: (0171) 828 3344. *Fax*: (0171) 828 3355.
Category: Recruitment agency.
Recruitment specialty: Management and technical personnel for the hotel, catering and leisure industries. Specialist areas: accounting, finance and systems for long and short term assignments.
Locations: Africa, Asia, Caribbean, Europe, Far East, Ireland, Middle East, Near East and United Kingdom.
Additional information: Applicants must possess appropriate industry experience. Salary ranges £15,000–£100,000.

Foodjobs, Grovemere House, Lancaster Way, Ely, Cambridgeshire CB6 3NP, England. *Tel*: (01353) 669 229. *Fax*: (01353) 667 740.
Category: Recruitment agency.
Recruitment specialty: Management and technical personnel for the food processing industry, technical sales, product development, marketing, laboratory, hygiene, purchasing, stores, warehousing, microbiology, engineering etc.
Location: United Kingdom and overseas.

Footprint Computer, 42 Alfred Place, Kingsdown, Bristol, Avon BS2 8HD, England. *Tel*: (0117) 944 1050. *Fax*: (0117) 944 1055.
Category: Recruitment agency.

Recruitment specialty: IT/computing specialist skills, permanent and contract placements.
Location: United Kingdom.

FSS Financial Selection Services, 4a The High Street, Windsor, Berkshire SL4 1LD, England. *Tel*: (01753) 621866. *Fax*: (01753) 621877.
Category: Recruitment agency.
Recruitment specialty: Executive, qualified and non-qualified finance personnel for financial services and associated areas.
Location: United Kingdom.

FSS Group, Charlotte House, 14 Windmill Street, London W1P 2DY, England. *Tel*: (0171) 209 1000. *Fax*: (0171) 209 0001.
Category: Recruitment agency.
Recruitment specialty: Senior management and technical personnel for the finance and accountancy specialties, qualified and part-qualified accountants etc.
Locations: Asia, Central and Eastern Europe, Far East, Ireland, Middle East, United Kingdom and United States.

Gatton Consulting Group Ltd, Gatton Place, St Matthew's Road, Redhill, Surrey RH1 1TA, England. *Tel*: (01737) 774100. *Fax*: (01737) 772949.
Category: Recruitment agency.
Recruitment specialty: IT/computing contract personnel most skills and levels such as: senior project managers, consultants, programmers etc.
Locations: Europe, Ireland and United Kingdom.

Global Reflex Corporation (GRC) Ltd, 28 Parnell Street, Clonmel, County Tipperary, Republic of Ireland. *Tel*: 00 353 52 27177/25646. *Fax*: 00 353 52 24787.
Category: Recruitment agency.
Recruitment specialty: Management and technical personnel within the oil and gas, power generation, water and civil engineering specialist areas. Project managers, QS, quality assurance and control (QA/QC), planning/design/installation/electrical and mechanical engineers and technicians.
Locations: Africa, Asia, Europe, Far East, Ireland, Middle East and United Kingdom.

GPW Search & Selection, Worsley House, North Road, St Helens, Isle of Wight WA10 2BL. *Tel*: (01744) 23454. *Fax*: (01744) 451766.
Category: Recruitment agency.
Recruitment specialty: Senior executive, management, technical and trades personnel predominantly for the engineering and automotive industries.
Locations: Canada, Europe, United Kingdom and United States.

Grafton Recruitment, 35/37 Queens Square, Belfast BT1 3FG, Northern Ireland. *Tel*: (01232) 242824. *Fax*: (01232) 242897.
Category: Employment agency.
Recruitment specialty: Senior executive, management and technical personnel for most sectors.
Locations: Canada, Central and Eastern Europe, Ireland, Middle East, United Kingdom and United States.

Grafton Recruitment, 94 High Street, Belfast BT1 2BG, Northern Ireland. *Tel*: (01232) 242824. *Fax*: (01232) 242897.
Category: Recruitment agency.
Recruitment specialty: In Northern Ireland, recruit both permanent and temporary staff in accountancy, computers, administration, industrial catering, construction, aviation and nursing.
Locations: Europe (Czech Republic) and Northern Ireland.
Additional information: Specialist recruiters for the Czech Republic in Eastern Europe.

Hamilton Parker Associates, Lyons House, 2 Station Road, Frimley, Surrey GU16 5HF, England. *Tel*: (01276) 418208. *Fax*: (01276) 418209.
Category: Recruitment agency and human resources consultancy.
Recruitment specialty: Information technology (IT), electronics, datacommunications and telecommunications specialist areas. Also general and line management, sales and marketing, projection management, technical support, design engineering, research and development etc.
Locations: Canada, Europe, United Kingdom and United States.
Additional information: Hamilton Parker Associates provides human resource consultancy services in all of the above areas.

Harriet Gabb Recruitment Ltd, Suite 3, 78 Buckingham Gate, London SW8 6PE, England. *Tel*: (0171) 222 3838. *Fax*: (0171) 222 2838.
Category: Recruitment agency.
Recruitment specialty: Personal assistants/secretaries, secretarial, administrative, desktop publishing (DTP) for permanent and temporary assignments.
Location: United Kingdom.

Harrison Jones Associates, 34 High Road, Watford, Hertfordshire WD2 3JG, England. *Tel*: (0181) 920 4401. *Fax*: (0181) 420 4402.
Category: Recruitment agency.
Recruitment specialty: Engineering and technical personnel for the oil and gas, general engineering and construction industries. Also retail managers, human resources/personnel, advertising agency staff etc.
Locations: Africa and Middle East.

Hartley Services Ltd, 46 Victoria Street, Manchester, Greater Manchester M3 1ST, England. *Tel*: (0161) 907 2050. *Fax*: (0161) 839 0306.

Category: Recruitment agency.
Recruitment specialty: Engineering and technical personnel on a permanent and contract basis, most sectors and levels.
Locations: Africa, Asia, Canada, Europe, Middle East, United Kingdom and United States.

Hawtal Whiting Holdings Plc, Phoenix House, Christopher Martin Road, Basildon, Essex SS14 3EZ, England. *Tel*: (01268) 531155. *Fax*: (01268) 531140.
Category: Recruitment agency.
Recruitment specialty: Engineering and support personnel for the transportation, automotive and associated industries including styling, computing, structural analysis, quality control and manufacturing.
Locations: Asia, Australia, Canada, Europe, Far East, Ireland, New Zealand, South America, United Kingdom and United States.

Haztek Executive Search, Premier House, 10 Greycoat Place, London SW1P 1SB, England. *Tel*: (0171) 222 8866. *Fax*: (0171) 223 2847.
Category: Recruitment agency.
Recruitment specialty: Specialist and chartered engineers, such as chemical engineers, process and safety on/off shore. Aeronautical engineers, railway design engineers, safety/reliability/risk and assessment engineers, pharmaceutical process engineers. All placements up to director level.
Locations: Australia, Europe, Far East, Middle East, New Zealand and United Kingdom.

HB Associates, 101 High Street, Evesham, Worcestershire WR11 4DN, England. *Tel*: (01386) 49856. *Fax*: (01386) 41925.
Category: Recruitment agency.
Recruitment specialty: Senior executive, management and technical personnel in sales and marketing, support, presales support consultants and sales managers within the information technology (IT) industry.
Locations: Canada, Europe, United Kingdom and United States.

Heads Employment Ltd, Kimada House, Flixton Road, Flixton, Manchester, Greater Mancheser M41 6EY, England. *Tel*: (0161) 746 8811. *Fax*: (0161) 747 0011.
Category: Recruitment agency.
Recruitment specialty: Professional and technical personnel within most specialist areas. Mechanical, piping, electrical, instrumentation, civil, structural engineers. A wide band of levels within the project engineering specialist areas, designers, operational staff, commissioning, construction support, planning, cost/QS, quality assurance/control (QA/QC), safety management etc.
Locations: Africa, Asia, Australia, Canada, Europe, Far East, Ireland, Middle East, Near East, New Zealand, South America, United Kingdom and

United States.

Healthcall Euromed, 6 Heddon Street, London W1R 7LH, England. *Tel*: (0171) 287 0880. *Fax*: (0171) 734 6723.
Category: Recruitment agency.
Recruitment specialty: Healthcare professionals in public and private sector hospitals, medical consultants, general practitioners, community nurses and carers, physiotherapists, occupational therapists, speech and language therapists, audiologists, clinical psychologists, cardiac technicians, radiographers, dieticians, MLSOs etc.
Location: United Kingdom.

Helix Recruitment, Wentworth House, George Street, Hailsham, East Sussex BN27 1AD, England. *Tel*: (01323) 440 842. *Fax*: (01323) 440 814.
Category: Recruitment agency.
Recruitment specialty: Senior management and technical personnel for the medical devices and scientific/laboratory equipment industries. Sales and marketing and support staff, technical development and production roles for the food industry.
Locations: Europe, Far East, Middle East and United Kingdom.

Hill McGlynn, Prospect House, Meridians Cross, Ocean Village, Southampton, Hampshire SO14 3TJ, England. *Tel*: (01703) 221 122.
Category: Recruitment agency.
Recruitment specialty: Engineers for building and civil engineering, geotechnical and materials, quantity surveying, project management, both mainstream contracting and consulting engineers etc.
Locations: Africa, Asia, Europe, Far East, Indian sub-continent, Middle East, Near East and United Kingdom.

Hoggett Bowers, 7/9 Breams Building, off Chancery Lane, London EC4A 1DY, England. *Tel*: (0171) 430 9000. *Fax*: (0171) 405 5995.
Category: Recruitment agency.
Recruitment specialty: Senior executive and management personnel for the financial, accountancy, information technology (IT), defence, aerospace, oil, gas and petrochemical industries.
Locations: Africa, Asia, Australia, Canada, Europe, Far East, Ireland, Middle East, Near East, New Zealand, United Kingdom and United States.

Horton International, 10 Tower Lane, Avon, CT 06001, United States. Tel: 00 1 860 674 8701. *Fax*: 00 1 860 676 9735.
Other offices: 2 in the United Kingdom and 28 overseas.
Category: Recruitment agency.
Recruitment specialty: General management in the financial services, construction, information technology (IT), aerospace and automotive industries; energy – electricity, oil, gas; utilities – electricity, gas, water, telecommunica-

tions including high tech electronics software engineering etc.
Locations: Asia, Australia, Canada, Europe, Far East, Ireland, Middle East, Near East, New Zealand, South America, United Kingdom and United States.

Horton International, 11th Floor, City Centre House, Union Street, Birmingham B2 4SR, England. *Tel*: (0121) 631 4555. *Fax*: (0121) 631 2306.
Other offices: 1 in the United Kingdom and 29 overseas.
Category: Recruitment agency.
Recruitment specialty: General management in the financial services, construction, information technology (IT), aerospace and automotive industries; energy – electricity, oil, gas; utilities – electricity, gas, water, telecommunications including high tech electronics software engineering etc.
Locations: Asia, Australia, Canada, Europe, Far East, Ireland, Middle East, Near East, New Zealand, South America, United Kingdom and United States.

Horton International, 15 Scotts Road, #05-05 Thong Teck Building, Singapore 228218. *Tel*: 00 65 738 6511. *Fax*: 00 65 738 6860.
Other offices: 2 in the United Kingdom and 28 overseas.
Category: Recruitment agency.
Recruitment specialty: General management in the financial services, construction, information technology (IT), aerospace and automotive industries; energy – electricity, oil, gas; utilities – electricity, gas, water, telecommunications including high tech electronics software engineering etc.
Locations: Asia, Australia, Canada, Europe, Far East, Ireland, Middle East, Near East, New Zealand, South America, United Kingdom and United States.

Horton International, 21/F Silom Complex Building, 191 Silom Road, Bangkok 10500, Thailand. *Tel*: 00 66 2 231 3940. *Fax*: 00 66 2 231 3662.
Other offices: 2 in the United Kingdom and 28 overseas.
Category: Recruitment agency.
Recruitment specialty: General management in the financial services, construction, information technology (IT), aerospace and automotive industries; energy – electricity, oil, gas; utilities – electricity, gas, water, telecommunications including high tech electronics software engineering etc.
Locations: Asia, Australia, Canada, Europe, Far East, Ireland, Middle East, Near East, New Zealand, South America, United Kingdom and United States.

Horton International, 3 rue Troyon, 75017 Paris, France. *Tel*: 00 33 1 4766 4318. *Fax*: 00 33 1 4380 2993.
Other offices: 2 in the United Kingdom and 28 overseas.
Category: Recruitment agency.
Recruitment specialty: General management in the financial services, construc-

tion, information technology (IT), aerospace and automotive industries; energy – electricity, oil, gas; utilities – electricity, gas, water, telecommunications including high tech electronics software engineering etc.

Locations: Asia, Australia, Canada, Europe, Far East, Ireland, Middle East, Near East, New Zealand, South America, United Kingdom and United States.

Horton International, 3/22 Prabhaderi Industrial Estate, Veer Savarkar Marg, Bombay 400 025, India. *Tel*: 00 91 22 4362341. *Fax*: 00 91 22 4300127.
Other offices: 2 in the United Kingdom and 28 overseas.
Category: Recruitment agency.
Recruitment specialty: General management in the financial services, construction, information technology (IT), aerospace and automotive industries; energy – electricity, oil, gas; utilities – electricity, gas, water, telecommunications including high tech electronics software engineering etc.
Locations: Asia, Australia, Canada, Europe, Far East, Ireland, Middle East, Near East, New Zealand, South America, United Kingdom and United States.

Horton International, 33 Sloan Street, Roswell, GA 30075, United States. *Tel*: 00 1 770 640 1533. *Fax*: 00 1 770 640 6242.
Other offices: 2 in the United Kingdom and 28 overseas.
Category: Recruitment agency.
Recruitment specialty: General management in the financial services, construction, information technology (IT), aerospace and automotive industries; energy – electricity, oil, gas; utilities – electricity, gas, water, telecommunications including high tech electronics software engineering etc.
Locations: Asia, Australia, Canada, Europe, Far East, Ireland, Middle East, Near East, New Zealand, South America, United Kingdom and United States.

Horton International, 333 So Grand Avenue, Suite #2980, Los Angeles, CA 90071, United States. *Tel*: 00 1 213 628 2580. *Fax*: 00 1 213 628 2581.
Other offices: 2 in the United Kingdom and 28 overseas.
Category: Recruitment agency.
Recruitment specialty: General management in the financial services, construction, information technology (IT), aerospace and automotive industries; energy – electricity, oil, gas; utilities – electricity, gas, water, telecommunications including high tech electronics software engineering etc.
Locations: Asia, Australia, Canada, Europe, Far East, Ireland, Middle East, Near East, New Zealand, South America, United Kingdom and United States.

Horton International, 38 Grosvenor Gardens, London SW1W 0EB, England. *Tel*: (0171) 730 2122. *Fax*: (0171) 730 0261.
Other offices: 1 in the United Kingdom and 29 overseas.

Category: Recruitment agency.
Recruitment specialty: General management in the financial services, construction, information technology (IT), aerospace and automotive industries; energy – electricity, oil, gas; utilities – electricity, gas, water, telecommunications including high tech electronics software engineering etc.
Locations: Asia, Australia, Canada, Europe, Far East, Ireland, Middle East, Near East, New Zealand, South America, United Kingdom and United States.

Horton International, 666 Fifth Avenue, 37th Floor, New York NY 10103, United States. *Tel*: 00 1 212 541 3900. *Fax*: 00 1 212 541 3902.
Other offices: 2 in the United Kingdom and 28 overseas.
Category: Recruitment agency.
Recruitment specialty: General management in the financial services, construction, information technology (IT), aerospace and automotive industries; energy – electricity, oil, gas; utilities – electricity, gas, water, telecommunications including high tech electronics software engineering etc.
Locations: Asia, Australia, Canada, Europe, Far East, Ireland, Middle East, Near East, New Zealand, South America, United Kingdom and United States.

Horton International, 6th Floor, The Valero Tower, 122 Valero Street, Salcedo Village, Makati, Metro Manila, Philippines. *Tel*: 00 63 2 893 7891/7985. *Fax*: 00 63 2 893 8031.
Other offices: 2 in the United Kingdom and 28 overseas.
Category: Recruitment agency.
Recruitment specialty: General management in the financial services, construction, information technology (IT), aerospace and automotive industries; energy – electricity, oil, gas; utilities – electricity, gas, water, telecommunications including high tech electronics software engineering etc.
Locations: Asia, Australia, Canada, Europe, Far East, Ireland, Middle East, Near East, New Zealand, South America, United Kingdom and United States.

Horton International, 814 Gordon Woods Road, Wilmington, NC 28405, United States. *Tel*: 00 1 910 792 1103. *Fax*: 00 1 910 792 1105.
Other offices: 2 in the United Kingdom and 28 overseas.
Category: Recruitment agency.
Recruitment specialty: General management in the financial services, construction, information technology (IT), aerospace and automotive industries; energy – electricity, oil, gas; utilities – electricity, gas, water, telecommunications including high tech electronics software engineering etc.
Locations: Asia, Australia, Canada, Europe, Far East, Ireland, Middle East, Near East, New Zealand, South America, United Kingdom and United States.

Horton International, Av. Ibirapuera 2064-10°, 04028-001 São Paulo, Brazil. *Tel/Fax*: 00 55 11 575 5551.
Other offices: 2 in the United Kingdom and 28 overseas.
Category: Recruitment agency.
Recruitment specialty: General management in the financial services, construction, information technology (IT), aerospace and automotive industries; energy – electricity, oil, gas; utilities – electricity, gas, water, telecommunications including high tech electronics software engineering etc.
Locations: Asia, Australia, Canada, Europe, Far East, Ireland, Middle East, Near East, New Zealand, South America, United Kingdom and United States.

Horton International, Barranca del Muerto, No 472 Col Alpes, Mexico DF 01010. *Tel*: 00 525 593 8766. *Fax*: 00 525 593 8969.
Other offices: 2 in the United Kingdom and 28 overseas.
Category: Recruitment agency.
Recruitment specialty: General management in the financial services, construction, information technology (IT), aerospace and automotive industries; energy – electricity, oil, gas; utilities – electricity, gas, water, telecommunications including high tech electronics software engineering etc.
Locations: Asia, Australia, Canada, Europe, Far East, Ireland, Middle East, Near East, New Zealand, South America, United Kingdom and United States.

Horton International, Box 7026, S-103 86 Stockholm, Sweden. *Tel*: 00 46 8 613 1660. *Fax*: 00 46 8 791 8121.
Other offices: 2 in the United Kingdom and 28 overseas.
Category: Recruitment agency.
Recruitment specialty: General management in the financial services, construction, information technology (IT), aerospace and automotive industries; energy – electricity, oil, gas; utilities – electricity, gas, water, telecommunications including high tech electronics software engineering etc.
Locations: Asia, Australia, Canada, Europe, Far East, Ireland, Middle East, Near East, New Zealand, South America, United Kingdom and United States.

Horton International, Katona Jozsef u. 3.11/18, 1137 Budapest, Hungary. *Tel/Fax*: 00 361 269 3737.
Other offices: 2 in the United Kingdom and 28 overseas.
Category: Recruitment agency.
Recruitment specialty: General management in the financial services, construction, information technology (IT), aerospace and automotive industries; energy – electricity, oil, gas; utilities – electricity, gas, water, telecommunications including high tech electronics software engineering etc.
Locations: Asia, Australia, Canada, Europe, Far East, Ireland, Middle East, Near East, New Zealand, South America, United Kingdom and United States.

Horton International, Lagerstrasse 14, CH-8600 Dubendorf, Switzerland. *Tel*: 00 411 821 0515. *Fax*: 00 411 821 0517.
Other offices: 2 in the United Kingdom and 28 overseas.
Category: Recruitment agency.
Recruitment specialty: General management in the financial services, construction, information technology (IT), aerospace and automotive industries; energy – electricity, oil, gas; utilities – electricity, gas, water, telecommunications including high tech electronics software engineering etc.
Locations: Asia, Australia, Canada, Europe, Far East, Ireland, Middle East, Near East, New Zealand, South America, United Kingdom and United States.

Horton International, Level 2, 36 Albert Road, South Melbourne, Vic 3205, Australia. *Tel*: 00 61 3 9696 0800. *Fax*: 00 61 3 9682 1000.
Other offices: 2 in the United Kingdom and 28 overseas.
Category: Recruitment agency.
Recruitment specialty: General management in the financial services, construction, information technology (IT), aerospace and automotive industries; energy – electricity, oil, gas; utilities – electricity, gas, water, telecommunications including high tech electronics software engineering etc.
Locations: Asia, Australia, Canada, Europe, Far East, Ireland, Middle East, Near East, New Zealand, South America, United Kingdom and United States.

Horton International, Malesingel 27 A 3581 BH, Utrecht, Netherlands. *Tel*: 00 31 3 0236 9136. *Fax*: 00 31 3 0236 9199.
Other offices: 2 in the United Kingdom and 28 overseas.
Category: Recruitment agency.
Recruitment specialty: General management in the financial services, construction, information technology (IT), aerospace and automotive industries; energy – electricity, oil, gas; utilities – electricity, gas, water, telecommunications including high tech electronics software engineering etc. ·
Locations: Asia, Australia, Canada, Europe, Far East, Ireland, Middle East, Near East, New Zealand, South America, United Kingdom and United States.

Horton International, Monte Esquinza, 44 3° B 28010, Madrid, Spain. *Tel*: 00 34 1 319 2122/9091. *Fax*: 00 34 1 319 8942.
Other offices: 2 in the United Kingdom and 28 overseas.
Category: Recruitment agency.
Recruitment specialty: General management in the financial services, construction, information technology (IT), aerospace and automotive industries; energy – electricity, oil, gas; utilities – electricity, gas, water, telecommunications including high tech electronics software engineering etc.
Locations: Asia, Australia, Canada, Europe, Far East, Ireland, Middle East, Near East, New Zealand, South America, United Kingdom and United States.

Horton International, Plaza PP, Lantai 11, Jalan Raga Gedong 57, Jakarta, Timur, Indonesia. *Tel*: 00 62 21 840 3990. *Fax*: 00 62 21 840 3991.
Other offices: 2 in the United Kingdom and 28 overseas.
Category: Recruitment agency.
Recruitment specialty: General management in the financial services, construction, information technology (IT), aerospace and automotive industries; energy – electricity, oil, gas; utilities – electricity, gas, water, telecommunications including high tech electronics software engineering etc.
Locations: Asia, Australia, Canada, Europe, Far East, Ireland, Middle East, Near East, New Zealand, South America, United Kingdom and United States.

Horton International, Presnienski val 24-16, 123557 Moscow, Russia. *Tel*: 00 07 7 095 253 4586. *Fax*: 00 07 7 095 253 4442.
Other offices: 2 in the United Kingdom and 28 overseas.
Category: Recruitment agency.
Recruitment specialty: General management in the financial services, construction, information technology (IT), aerospace and automotive industries; energy – electricity, oil, gas; utilities – electricity, gas, water, telecommunications including high tech electronics software engineering etc.
Locations: Asia, Australia, Canada, Europe, Far East, Ireland, Middle East, Near East, New Zealand, South America, United Kingdom and United States.

Horton International, Rambla de Cataluna, 121. 1° 08008, Barcelona, Spain.
Other offices: 2 in the United Kingdom and 28 overseas.
Category: Recruitment agency.
Recruitment specialty: General management in the financial services, construction, information technology (IT), aerospace and automotive industries; energy – electricity, oil, gas; utilities – electricity, gas, water, telecommunications including high tech electronics software engineering etc.
Locations: Asia, Australia, Canada, Europe, Far East, Ireland, Middle East, Near East, New Zealand, South America, United Kingdom and United States.

Horton International, Room 1901, 19/F Queen's Place, 74 Queen's Road, Central Hong Kong. *Tel*: 00 852 2525 9127. *Fax*: 00 852 2521 6056.
Other offices: 2 in the United Kingdom and 28 overseas.
Category: Recruitment agency.
Recruitment specialty: General management in the financial services, construction, information technology (IT), aerospace and automotive industries; energy – electricity, oil, gas; utilities – electricity, gas, water, telecommunications including high tech electronics software engineering etc.
Locations: Asia, Australia, Canada, Europe, Far East, Ireland, Middle East, Near East, New Zealand, South America, United Kingdom and United States.

Horton International, Room 1218, Block B, Lucky Tower, 3 Dong Shan Huan, Bei Lu Chao,Yang District, Beijing, People's Republic of China. *Tel*: 00 86 10 461 6391. *Fax*: 00 86 10 461 6392.
Other offices: 2 in the United Kingdom and 28 overseas.
Category: Recruitment agency.
Recruitment specialty: General management in the financial services, construction, information technology (IT), aerospace and automotive industries; energy – electricity, oil, gas; utilities – electricity, gas, water, telecommunications including high tech electronics software engineering etc.
Locations: Asia, Australia, Canada, Europe, Far East, Ireland, Middle East, Near East, New Zealand, South America, United Kingdom and United States.

Horton International, Rue Copermic 6A, 1180 Brussels, Belgium. *Tel/Fax*: 00 32 2 374 0860.
Other offices: 2 in the United Kingdom and 28 overseas.
Category: Recruitment agency.
Recruitment specialty: General management in the financial services, construction, information technology (IT), aerospace and automotive industries; energy – electricity, oil, gas; utilities – electricity, gas, water, telecommunications including high tech electronics software engineering etc.
Locations: Asia, Australia, Canada, Europe, Far East, Ireland, Middle East, Near East, New Zealand, South America, United Kingdom and United States.

Horton International, Rusterstrasse, 1 PO Box 170250, 60325 Frankfurt, Germany. *Tel*: 00 49 6 9714 0060. *Fax*: 00 49 6 9714 00625.
Other offices: 2 in the United Kingdom and 28 overseas.
Category: Recruitment agency.
Recruitment specialty: General management in the financial services, construction, information technology (IT), aerospace and automotive industries; energy – electricity, oil, gas; utilities – electricity, gas, water, telecommunications including high tech electronics software engineering etc.
Locations: Asia, Australia, Canada, Europe, Far East, Ireland, Middle East, Near East, New Zealand, South America, United Kingdom and United States.

Horton International, Shugetsu, Building 6F, 3-12-7 Kita Aoyama, Minato-ku, Tokyo 107, Japan. *Tel*: 00 813 3486 2711. *Fax*: 00 813 3486 2722.
Other offices: 2 in the United Kingdom and 28 overseas.
Category: Recruitment agency.
Recruitment specialty: General management in the financial services, construction, information technology (IT), aerospace and automotive industries; energy – electricity, oil, gas; utilities – electricity, gas, water, telecommunications including high tech electronics software engineering etc.
Locations: Asia, Australia, Canada, Europe, Far East, Ireland, Middle East,

Near East, New Zealand, South America, United Kingdom and United States.

Horton International, Suite B & C, 10th Floor, 629 Ling Ling Road, Shanghai 200030, People's Republic of China. *Tel*: 00 86 21 486 4796. *Fax*: 00 86 21 486 4797.
Other offices: 2 in the United Kingdom and 28 overseas.
Category: Recruitment agency.
Recruitment specialty: General management in the financial services, construction, information technology (IT), aerospace and automotive industries; energy – electricity, oil, gas; utilities – electricity, gas, water, telecommunications including high tech electronics software engineering etc.
Locations: Asia, Australia, Canada, Europe, Far East, Ireland, Middle East, Near East, New Zealand, South America, United Kingdom and United States.

Horton International, ul. Koszykowa 60/62, 00-673 Warsaw, Poland. *Tel*: 00 482 628 4836. *Fax*: 00 482 622 0124.
Other offices: 2 in the United Kingdom and 28 overseas.
Category: Recruitment agency.
Recruitment specialty: General management in the financial services, construction, information technology (IT), aerospace and automotive industries; energy – electricity, oil, gas; utilities – electricity, gas, water, telecommunications including high tech electronics software engineering etc.
Locations: Asia, Australia, Canada, Europe, Far East, Ireland, Middle East, Near East, New Zealand, South America, United Kingdom and United States.

Horton International, Via Paolo da Cannobio, 8 20122 Milano, Italy. *Tel*: 00 39 2 8645 5500. *Fax*: 00 39 2 8645 6000.
Other offices: 2 in the United Kingdom and 28 overseas.
Category: Recruitment agency.
Recruitment specialty: General management in the financial services, construction, information technology (IT), aerospace and automotive industries; energy – electricity, oil, gas; utilities – electricity, gas, water, telecommunications including high tech electronics software engineering etc.
Locations: Asia, Australia, Canada, Europe, Far East, Ireland, Middle East, Near East, New Zealand, South America, United Kingdom and United States.

Hospitality Group Worldwide, The, 4 Cavendish Square, London W1M 0BX, England. *Tel*: (0171) 499 0900.
Other offices: 5 overseas.
Category: Employer.
Recruitment specialty: Hospitality personnel, conferences, entertainment facilities at recreational events, sales and support personnel.

Location: Worldwide.

Human Engineering Ltd, Shore House, 68 Westbury Hill, Bristol, Avon BS9 3AA, England. Tel: (0117) 962 0888. *Fax*: (0117) 962 9888.
Category: Recruitment agency.
Recruitment specialty: Executive and management personnel in sales roles within the engineering and FMCG areas and engineers within sales, design, software, hardware and reliability specialist areas.
Locations: Europe and United Kingdom.

Humana International Group Plc, The, 231 Tottenham Court Road, London W1P 9AE, England. *Tel*: (0171) 636 7636. *Fax*: (0171) 636 7666.
Other offices: 70 in the United Kingdom and 30 overseas.
Category: Recruitment agency.
Recruitment specialty: Executive, management and technical personnel in a wide band of levels in most business, banking and commercial sectors.
Locations: Asia, Canada, Europe, Far East, Ireland, Middle East, Near East, United Kingdom and United States.

Hunter Personnel Contracts Ltd, 24 St Peters Road, Bournemouth, Dorset BH1 2LN, England. *Tel*: (01202) 298322. *Fax*: (01202) 298383.
Category: Recruitment agency.
Recruitment specialty: Senior executive, management and technical placements specialising in tunnelling, mining and heavy civil engineering. Personnel placed in permanent or contract assignments. Specialist skills areas are: engineers, administration, consultants, ground personnel, production mining/tunnelling/structural engineers, quantity surveyors, quality control, electrical and mechanical engineers.
Locations: Africa, Asia, Australia, Canada, Europe, Far East, Ireland, Middle East, New Zealand, United Kingdom and United States.

IBNIX Ltd, 12/18 Paul Street, London EC2A 4NX, England. *Tel*: (0171) 377 9995. *Fax*: (0171) 247 5471.
Category: Recruitment agency.
Recruitment specialty: IT/computing contract personnel in communications, PC networks, skill in OOD, relational databases, client server development etc.
Locations: Europe, Ireland, Middle East and United Kingdom.

Ingineur Software Solutions Ltd, Draycote, Rugby, Warwickshire CV23 9RB, England. *Tel*: (01926) 633006. *Fax*: (01926) 633003.
Category: Recruitment agency.
Recruitment specialty: IT/computing most skills, including data processing, software engineers (real time etc.), analyst/programmers on permanent and contract assignments.
Locations: Europe, Ireland and United Kingdom.

Inlingua Teacher Training & Recruitment, Rodney Lodge, Rodney Road, Cheltenham, Gloucestershire GL50 1JF, England. *Tel*: (01242) 253171. *Fax*: (01242) 253181.

Category: Recruitment agency.

Recruitment specialty: Teachers of English as a foreign language as well as English for special purposes (ESP).

Locations: Europe and Far East.

Additional information: Usual minimum qualifications are a degree with a certificate TESOL/CTEFLA, some senior posts for candidates with Diploma TESOL/TEFLA.

Insurance Personnel Services, Lloyd's Avenue House, 6 Lloyd's Avenue, London EC3N 3ES, England. *Tel*: (0171) 481 8111. *Fax*: (0171) 481 0994.

Category: Recruitment agency.

Recruitment specialty: Management and technical personnel in most speciality areas within the insurance industry.

Locations: Africa, Asia, Australia, Canada, Europe, Far East, Ireland, Middle East, Near East, New Zealand, South America, United Kingdom and United States.

INTEC UK Ltd, Rhodes House, 114 St Leonard Gate, Lancaster, Lancashire LA1 1NN, England. *Tel*: (01524) 62324. *Fax*: (01524) 33085.

Category: Recruitment agency.

Recruitment specialty: Senior management and technical personnel, project management, quality consultants, inspectors, engineers, safety and environmental specialists.

Locations: Africa, Asia, Europe, Far East, Ireland, Middle East, Near East, South America and United Kingdom.

Interacto Services Ltd, Crown House, North Circular Road, Park Royal, London NW10 7PN, England.

Category: Recruitment agency.

Recruitment specialty: Mining – most skills including production management, technical and support.

Location: Africa.

Intereurope Recruitment Ltd, 21/23 East Street, Fareham, Hampshire PO16 0BZ, England. *Tel*: (01329) 220488. *Fax*: (01329) 220788.

Category: Recruitment agency.

Recruitment specialty: Engineers and technical personnel for most engineering based industries, contract and permanent assignments, design, IT/computing, development, installation, commissioning and documentation. Engineers in most disciplines, technical authors, technical illustrators, draughting technicians, programmers, IT administrators etc.

Locations: Europe, Middle East and United Kingdom.

Intermanagement Group, Head Office, 159 High Street, Huntingdon, Cambridgeshire PE18 6TF, England. *Tel*: (01480) 455455. *Fax*: 01480 52201.
Category: Recruitment agency.
Recruitment specialty: IT/computing, software engineering, electronics and telecommunications engineering, operations, business development, sales and marketing, electrical and mechanical engineering, banking, insurance and finance. Permanent, contract and consultancy assignments.
Locations: Africa, Europe, Far East, Middle East and United Kingdom.

International House, 106 Piccadilly, London W1V 9FL, England. *Tel*: (0171) 491 2410. *Fax*: (0171) 491 2679.
Category: Recruitment agency (for their own affiliated/client schools only).
Recruitment specialty: Language teaching staff, RSA CTEFLA qualified EFL teachers and senior staff for schools.
Locations: Asia, Europe, South America, United Kingdom and United States.
Additional information: This firm recruits up to 450 personnel annually for over 95 affiliated schools in 24 countries throughout the world. Nine month contracts are normally offered within Europe and two year contracts outside Europe.

International Voluntary Service, Castle Hill House, 21 Otley Road, Leeds, West Yorkshire LS6 3AA, England. *Tel*: (0113) 230 4600. *Fax*: (0113) 230 4610.
Category: Registered charity (No. 275424).
Recruitment specialty: Semi-skilled and unskilled personnel in various voluntary projects of 2 to 4 weeks duration.
Locations: Australia, Eastern Europe, Ireland, New Zealand, North Africa, United Kingdom and Western Europe.

Internet Search & Selection, The Innovation Centre, 225 Marsh Wall, London E14 9FW, England. *Tel*: (0171) 454 1068. *Fax*: (0171) 454 1084.
Category: Recruitment agency.
Recruitment specialty: IT/computing most skills.
Locations: Europe and United Kingdom.

Intertech Computer Consultants Ltd, Chester House, Harlands Road, Haywards Heath, West Sussex RH16 1TD, England. *Tel*: (01444) 450405. *Fax*: (01444) 457 1123.
Category: Recruitment agency.
Recruitment specialty: IT/computing permanent and contract personnel in most skills such as IBM mainframe, UNIX, ICL/DEC/AS400, ORACLE/ INGRES/SYBASE/INFORMIX, networking, communications, PC support and development, client server, OO, GVI, GSM, analysis, management and consultancy roles.
Locations: Canada, Europe, United Kingdom and United States.

IPS Accountancy Recruitment, Lloyd's Avenue House, 6 Lloyd's Avenue, London EC3N 3ES, England. *Tel*: (0171) 481 8111. *Fax*: (0171) 481 0994.
Category: Recruitment agency.
Recruitment specialty: Management and technical personnel most levels mostly for the insurance and financial services industries.
Locations: Europe and United Kingdom.

IPS Contract Management, Lloyd's Avenue House, 6 Lloyd's Avenue, London EC3N 3ES, England. *Tel*: (0171) 481 8111. *Fax*: (0171) 481 0994.
Category: Recruitment agency.
Recruitment specialty: Management and technical contract personnel in most specialty areas within the financial services industry.
Locations: Africa, Asia, Australia, Canada, Europe, Far East, Ireland, Middle East, Near East, New Zealand, South America, United Kingdom and United States.

IPS Financial Services, Lloyd's Avenue House, 6 Lloyd's Avenue, London EC3N 3ES, England. *Tel*: (0171) 481 8111. *Fax*: (0171) 481 0994.
Category: Recruitment agency.
Recruitment specialty: Management and technical personnel in most specialty areas within the financial services industry.
Locations: Africa, Asia, Australia, Canada, Europe, Far East, Ireland, Middle East, Near East, New Zealand, South America, United Kingdom and United States.

IPS Group Ltd, Lloyd's Avenue House, 6 Lloyd's Avenue, London EC3N 3ES, England. *Tel*: (0171) 481 8111. *Fax*: (0171) 481 0994.
Category: Recruitment agency.
Recruitment specialty: Management and technical personnel in most specialty areas within the insurance industry.
Locations: Africa, Asia, Australia, Canada, Europe, Far East, Ireland, Middle East, Near East, New Zealand, South America, United Kingdom and United States.

IPS Legal Recruitment, Lloyd's Avenue House, 6 Lloyd's Avenue, London EC3N 3ES, England. *Tel*: (0171) 481 8111. *Fax*: (0171) 481 0994.
Category: Recruitment agency.
Recruitment specialty: Legal personnel senior and junior levels predominantly for the insurance and financial services industries.
Locations: Europe and United Kingdom.

IPS Secretarial Recruitment, Lloyd's Avenue House, 6 Lloyd's Avenue, London EC3N 3ES, England. *Tel*: (0171) 481 8111. *Fax*: (0171) 481 0994.
Category: Recruitment agency.
Recruitment specialty: Secretarial and administrative support personnel for the insurance and financial services industries.

Locations: Europe and United Kingdom.

Irish Recruitment Consultants Ltd, 11 Ely Place, Dublin 2, Republic of Ireland. *Tel*: 00 353 1 661 0644. *Fax*: 00 353 1 661 0648.
Category: Recruitment agency.
Recruitment specialty: Most management and support levels in sales and marketing, computing, accountancy, manufacturing and secretarial etc.
Locations: Canada, Middle East, United Kingdom and United States.

Jacob Partnership, The, AW House, Chaul End Lane, Luton, Bedfordshire LU4 8EG, England. *Tel*: (01582) 566789. *Fax*: (01582) 560033.
Category: Recruitment agency.
Recruitment specialty: Engineering and technical support personnel for the construction, automotive, HVAC, validation, IT/computing, technical sales industries and specialist areas. Contract and permanent assignments, mechanical, electrical, electronic, design, project engineers and technicians.
Locations: Europe, Ireland, Middle East and United Kingdom.

Jacob Partnership, The, Spring Bridge Mews, Ealing, London W5 2AB, England. *Tel*: (0181) 566 5998. *Fax*: (0181) 566 5933.
Category: Recruitment agency.
Recruitment specialty: Engineering and technical support personnel for the construction, automotive, HVAC, validation, IT/computing, technical sales industries and specialist areas. Contract and permanent assignments, mechanical, electrical, electronics, design, project engineers and technicians.
Locations: Europe, Ireland, Middle East and United Kingdom.

Janet White Agency, 67 Jackson Avenue, Leeds, West Yorkshire LS8 1NS, England. *Tel*: (0113) 266 6507. *Fax*: (0113) 268 3077.
Category: Recruitment agency.
Recruitment specialty: Nannies, au pairs, child and family care.
Locations: Canada, Europe, United Kingdom and United States.
Additional information: Janet White Agency participates in the au pair in America programme. Candidates must be between 18 and 26 years of age, possess a full driving licence and have childcare work experience.

John Prodger Recruitment (JPR), 95 Victoria Street, St Albans, Hertfordshire AL1 3TJ, England. *Tel*: (01727) 841101. *Fax*: (01727) 838277.
Category: Recruitment agency.
Recruitment specialty: Senior technical personnel for IT/computing, telecommunications and electronics for the defence industry.
Locations: Canada, Europe, United Kingdom and United States.

John Richards Associates, 130 High Street, Newport, Shropshire TF10 7BH, England. (01952) 825247 (6 lines). *Fax*: (01952) 825249.
Category: Recruitment agency.

Recruitment specialty: Senior executive and management personnel for the sales and marketing and export specialty areas of building products and materials. Sales directors, executives, managers, export and product managers etc.

Locations: Europe, Middle East and United Kingdom.

Jonathan Lee Technical Recruitment, The Maltings, Mount Road, Stourbridge, West Midlands DY8 1HZ, England. *Tel*: (01384) 397555. *Fax*: (01384) 379396.

Category: Recruitment agency.

Recruitment specialty: Senior executive, management, technical and graduate trainee personnel for the aerospace, rail, domestic appliance, light engineering, capital goods and equipment, electronics and process industries.

Locations: Australia, Canada, Europe, New Zealand, United Kingdom and United States.

Additional information: Jonathan Lee Technical Recruitment also handle advertised and headhunt assignments.

Kestrel Consulting, BTC Bessemer Drive, Stevenage, Hertfordshire SG1 2DX, England. *Tel*: (01438) 310155. *Fax*: (01438) 310131.

Category: Recruitment agency.

Recruitment specialty: Most levels for the SAP computer system, project managers to system users etc.

Locations: Asia, Australia, Canada, Europe, Far East, New Zealand, United Kingdom and United States.

Keystone Recruitment Consultants, Head Office, Keystone House, 272/276 Pentonville Road, London N1 9JY, England. *Tel*: (0171) 278 3400/(0171) 837 6444. *Fax*: (0171) 278 2558/7299.

Category: Recruitment agency.

Recruitment specialty: Senior executive, management and technical personnel for the hotel and catering industry. Permanent and temporary basis for non-senior secretarial, printing and hotel and catering staff.

Locations: Africa, Asia, Europe, Far East, Ireland, Middle East and United Kingdom.

Keystone Recruitment Consultants, 107 Muswell Hill, London N10 3HS, England. *Tel*: (0181) 883 8322. *Fax*: (0181) 883 4268.

Category: Recruitment agency.

Recruitment specialty: Senior executive, management and technical personnel for the hotel and catering industry. Permanent and temporary basis for non-senior secretarial, printing and hotel and catering staff.

Locations: Africa, Asia, Europe, Far East, Ireland, Middle East and United Kingdom.

Keystone Recruitment Consultants, 176 Liverpool Street, Bishopsgate, London EC2 M4NQ, England. *Tel*: (0171) 283 5914. *Fax*: (0171) 283 7780.
Category: Recruitment agency.
Recruitment specialty: Senior executive, management and technical personnel for the hotel and catering industry. Permanent and temporary basis for non-senior secretarial, printing and hotel and catering staff.
Locations: Africa, Asia, Europe, Far East, Ireland, Middle East and United Kingdom.

Keystone Recruitment Consultants, 219 Oxford Street, London W1R 1AH, England. *Tel*: (0171) 434 1301. *Fax*: (0171) 494 3762.
Category: Recruitment agency.
Recruitment specialty: Senior executive, management and technical personnel for the hotel and catering industry. Permanent and temporary basis for non-senior secretarial, printing and hotel and catering staff.
Locations: Africa, Asia, Europe, Far East, Ireland, Middle East and United Kingdom.

KirchGruppe, Betastrasse 1, D-85774 Unterfohring, Germany. Tel: 00 49 8 999560.
Category: Employer.
Recruitment specialty: Technical personnel for television and film production.
Location: Europe.

KPMG Management Consultants, 37 Albyn Place, Aberdeen AB9 1JE, Scotland. *Tel*: (01224) 591000. *Fax*: (01224) 590909.
Category: Employer.
Recruitment specialty: Graduate training to chartered accountant with the Institute of Chartered Accountants of Scotland.
Location: United Kingdom.

Kuwait Oil Company, 26/28 Gt Portland Street, London W1N 5AD, England. *Tel*: (0171) 436 1990. *Fax*: (0171) 436 4992.
Category: Employer.
Recruitment specialty: Senior management and technical personnel for the oil and gas industry, onshore engineering and information technology facilities.
Location: Middle East.
Additional information: Candidates are expected to have 6 years' relevant industry experience and possess a recognised university degree.

Lawton Ware Recruitment Services, Shamrock Quay, William Street, Southampton, Hampshire SO14 5QL, England. *Tel*: (01703) 639133.
Category: Recruitment agency.
Recruitment specialty: Project managers, engineers and technical personnel for the mining industry.
Location: Africa.

Leading Edge Consulting, Chesham House, 150 Regent Street, London W1R 5FA. England. *Tel*: (01273) 326337. *Fax*: (01273) 821271.
Category: Recruitment agency.
Recruitment specialty: Senior information technology (IT) personnel. Permanent appointments in most sectors.
Locations: Asia, Australia, Canada, Europe, Far East, New Zealand. United Kingdom and United States.

Lisega GmbH, Industriegebeit Hochkamp, 27393 Zeven, Postfach 1357, Germany. *Tel*: 00 49 04281 7130.
Category: Employer.
Recruitment specialty: Manufacturing production, quality control etc.
Location: Europe.
Additional information: This company manufacture conceptual structured pipe supports and export their products worldwide. They occasionally recruit for technical personnel in the United Kingdom and recently for a project export engineer. Forward CVs to the personnel department at the above address.

LJB & Company, The Maples, 144 Liverpool Road, London N1 1LA. England. *Tel*: (0171) 609 7769. *Fax*: (0171) 607 7378.
Category: Recruitment agency.
Recruitment specialty: Senior management and technical personnel for the construction, building services and IT/computing industries. Site engineers and agents, project managers, quantity surveyors, CAD operators, HVAC design engineers, electrical design engineers, project enginers, M&E supervisors etc. Also cable and telecommunications specialists, software engineers etc.
Locations: Europe, Far East and United Kingdom.

LKRC, Evelyn House, 62 Oxford Street, London W1N 9LB, England. *Tel*: (0171) 323 2323. *Fax*: (0171) 323 4563.
Category: Recruitment agency.
Recruitment specialty: Senior management, technical and administrative support for information technology (IT), banking and management consultancy industries and specialty areas. Skilled personnel in IT/computing, investment banking, management consultants, graduates, secretarial, administrative etc.
Location: United Kingdom.

Lucy Locketts Nanny Agency, Hillview Farm, Flecknoe, Near Rugby, Warwickshire CV23 8AU, England. *Tel*: (01788) 891626/891363. *Fax*: (01788) 891626.
Category: Recruitment agency.
Recruitment specialty: Nannies, mother's helps, housekeepers, butlers, gardeners, cooks, chauffeurs.
Locations: Europe and United Kingdom.
Additional information: Permanent and temporary opportunities available. The

agency provides a full back-up for those on overseas assignments.

MacGregor Energy Services, In-Spec House, Wellheads Drive, Dyce, Aberdeen AB2 OGQ, Scotland. *Tel*: (01224) 724 265. *Fax*: (01224) 725 549/(01224) 772 168.
Category: Recruitment agency.
Recruitment specialty: Engineers and technical support personnel for the oil and gas, petrochemical, civil, marine, power and nuclear industries. Also safety, inspection and drilling personnel.
Locations: Africa, Asia, Europe, Far East, Middle East and United Kingdom.

Mactech Inspection Ltd, 23 Claremont Road, Whitley Bay, Tyne & Wear NE26 3TN, England. *Tel*: (0191) 252 1762. *Fax*: (0191) 252 1117.
Category: Recruitment agency.
Recruitment specialty: Engineers and technical personnel within the engineering industry predominantly inspection skills, NDT, welding inspection, quality assurance and control. Engineers in most disciplines, technicians and trades.
Locations: Africa, Europe, Far East, Middle East, Near East and South America.

Management Match International, 90/92 Great Portland Street, London W1N SP3, England. *Tel*: (0171) 323 3635. *Fax*: (0171) 323 5380.
Category: Recruitment agency.
Recruitment specialty: Marketing executives, all levels.
Locations: Europe, Middle East and United Kingdom.

Mandeville Resources, 8 Lake End Court, Taplow Road, Taplow, Buckinghamshire SL6 OJQ, England. *Tel*: (01628) 669345. *Fax*: (01628) 669398.
Category: Recruitment agency.
Recruitment specialty: Most management levels for the retail and general engineering industries, including technical, business to business, HVAC sales and telesales.
Location: United Kingdom.

Marchfield Engineering (Resources) Ltd, Globe House, Welsh Row, Nantwich, Cheshire CW5 5EW, England. *Tel*: (01270) 611323. *Fax*: (01270) 611324.
Category: Recruitment agency.
Recruitment specialty: Senior to junior design, engineering, commissioning and construction personnel. Skills in 3D CAD, PDS, ACAO, PDMS etc.
Locations: Africa, Asia, Australia, Canada, Europe (Scandinavia), Far East, Ireland, Middle East, Near East, New Zealand, South America, United Kingdom and United States.

Martin Jarvie Underwood & Hall, 3rd Floor, 85 The Terrace, Wellington, New Zealand.

Category: Employer.
Recruitment specialty: Most accountancy specialist areas, including auditing, taxation, accountancy, business services, insolvency and corporate advisory services.
Location: New Zealand.

Matchtech Engineering Ltd, 1590 Parkway, Solent Business Park, Fareham, Hampshire PO15 7AG, England. *Tel*: (01489) 575111/572720. *Fax*: (01489) 575883.
Category: Recruitment agency.
Recruitment specialty: Engineers and other technical personnel within the petrochemical, shipbuilding and nuclear industries for civil engineering projects, offshore etc.
Locations: Canada, Europe, Ireland, Middle East, United Kingdom and United States.

McCann Erickson Recruitment, Haddon House, 2/4 Fitzroy Street, London W1P 5AD, England.
Other offices: 6 in the United Kingdom.
Category: Recruitment agency.
Recruitment specialty: Executive, management and technical in most sectors.
Locations: United Kingdom and worldwide.

McGregor Boyall Associates, 114 Middlesex Street, London E1 7JH, England. *Tel*: (0171) 247 7444. *Fax*: (0171) 297 7975.
Category: Recruitment agency.
Recruitment specialty: IT/computing permanent and contract placements in financial markets and contract only placements in sales, trading and researched financial markets. Also IT vendor placements in management, sales, marketing and technical areas, non-financial and end user markets.
Locations: Canada, Europe, United Kingdom, United States and worldwide.

McMillan Montague Ltd, 2nd Floor, 4 City Road, Finsbury Square, London EC1Y 2AA, England. Tel: (0171) 588 8118. *Fax*: (0171) 638 7646.
Category: Recruitment agency.
Recruitment specialty: Senior executives and management levels up to managing director and sales and technical directors, senior sales and support executives, within IT and computing vendors and integrators. Vertical markets include: finance, banking, EIS ROBMS, FM and systems integration, DIP workflow, BPR etc.
Locations: Africa, Australia, Canada, Europe, Far East, New Zealand, United Kingdom and United States.

Meridian Technical Recruitment, Omega House, Broadway, Letchworth, Hertfordshire SG6 3PQ, England. *Tel*: (01462) 481499. *Fax*: (01462) 481500.

Category: Recruitment agency.
Recruitment specialty: Engineers and technical personnel, graduates to senior managers.
Location: United Kingdom.
Additional information: Salaries range from £15,000–£35,000.

Merz & McLellan Ltd, Amber Court, William Armstrong Drive, Newcastle-upon-Tyne, Tyne & Wear, NE4 7YQ, England. *Tel*: (0191) 226 1899. *Fax*: (0191) 226 1104.
Category: Recruitment agency and employer.
Recruitment specialty: Senior engineering and technical support personnel for the power generation, distribution and transmission engineering industries. Also design and site construction, commissioning sectors.
Locations: Africa, Asia, Far East, Middle East and United Kingdom.

Middleton Jeffers Recruitment Ltd, 15 Devonshire Row, London EC2M 4RQ, England. *Tel*: (0171) 377 6777. *Fax*: (0171) 377 5079.
Category: Recruitment agency.
Recruitment specialty: Permanent and temporary assignments in secretarial, administrative and languages.
Location: United Kingdom.

Middleton Jeffers Recruitment Ltd, 49 Conduit Street, London W1R 5FB, England. *Tel*: (0171) 287 2044. *Fax*: (0171) 287 3717.
Category: Recruitment agency.
Recruitment specialty: Permanent and temporary assignments in secretarial, administrative and languages.
Location: United Kingdom.

Montreal Associates (Systems) Ltd, City Gate House, 399/425 Eastern Avenue, Gants Hill, Ilford, Essex I92 6LR, England. *Tel*: (0181) 518 2211. *Fax*: (0181) 518 3898.
Category: Recruitment agency.
Recruitment specialty: IT/computing skills and specialist areas include: management and technical personnel working on open systems, mainframe and SAP consultants, incorporating most other programming languages, operating systems, databases, hardware manufacturers and applications. Serving client industries such as: banking, insurance, petrochemical, retail, government utilities, project management and software engineering.
Locations: Asia, Australia, Canada, Europe, Far East, Ireland, Middle East, Near East, New Zealand, South America, United Kingdom and United States.

Moore Control & Engineering Plc, Crofton House, Crofton Road, Portrack, Stockton, Cleveland TS18 2QZ, England. *Tel*: (01642) 678678. *Fax*: (01642) 603333.

Category: Recruitment agency.
Recruitment specialty: Senior engineers and other technical personnel within the petrochemical, oil and gas, chemical, power generation, retail and steel production industries. Mechanical, civil, structural, design, installation, inspection, commissioning engineers and technicians.
Locations: Canada, Europe, Far East, Near East, South America, United Kingdom and United States.

Morgan Bryant Personnel Ltd, 8 The Causeway, Teddington, Middlesex TW11 OHE, England. *Tel*: (0181) 255 6246/6247. *Fax*: (0181) 255 6248.
Category: Recruitment agency.
Recruitment specialty: A wide band of levels, specialist areas and sectors, including: commercial, public and private, healthcare, heavy civil engineering, construction, power, utilities, iron and steel processing, marine, maintenance and repair. Skilled personnel include: dentists and technicians, physicians and nursing staff in the health sector (to management and supervisory levels); engineers in management and operational personnel including project/contract managers; civil engineers and quantity surveyors; as well as personnel for the power generation industry; mechanical/ electrical/instrumentation and control engineers; chief and senior water distribution managers and directors; bridge and road engineers and financial controllers etc.
Locations: Canada, Middle East and United Kingdom.

Morgan & Day (Europe) Ltd, The Old Coach House, 5a Holywell Hill, St Albans, Hertfordshire AL1 1EU, England. *Tel*: (01727) 836266. *Fax*: (01727) 837989.
Category: Recruitment agency.
Recruitment specialty: Engineers, trainers and other senior technical and support personnel for the oil and gas, petrochemical, heavy industrial, food processing and pharmaceutical industries and specialty areas.
Locations: Africa, Europe, Far East, Middle East and United Kingdom.

Morgan Stanley, 25 Cabot Square, London E14 42A, England. *Tel*: (0171) 513 8000. *Fax*: (0171) 425 8990.
Other offices: 8 overseas.
Category: Employer.
Recruitment specialty: Banking, management and technical personnel.
Locations: Europe and United Kingdom.

Motor Trade Selection, Sheen Lane House, 254 Upper Richmond Road West, London SW14 8AG, England. *Tel*: (0181) 392 1818. *Fax*: (0181) 876 4631.
Category: Recruitment agency.
Recruitment specialty: Senior executive to middle management levels, especially sales roles in the retail motor industry.
Locations: Africa, Asia, Europe, Far East, Middle East and United Kingdom.

Additional information: Motor Trade Selection publish annual salary surveys for the industry.

Mott MacDonald Ltd, St Anne House, 20/26 Wellesley Road, Croydon, Surrey CR9 2UL, England. *Tel*: (0181) 686 5041/(0127) 336 5000/(0122) 346 0600. *Fax*: (0181) 681 5706/(0127) 336 5100/(0122) 346 1007.
Other offices: 5 in the United Kingdom.
Category: Engineering consultancy and employer.
Recruitment specialty: Most levels of civil, mechanical, electrical, structural and environmental engineers, from experienced chartered engineers to recent graduates.
Locations: Africa, Asia, Australia, Europe, Far East, Middle East, Near East, New Zealand and United Kingdom.
Additional information: Average annual salary level £40,000.

Moxon Dolphin Kerby International, 178/202 Great Portland Street, London W1N 6JJ, England. *Fax*: (0171) 636 5592.
Category: Recruitment agency.
Recruitment specialty: Petrochemical engineering most skills in instrumentation, processing etc.
Location: Middle East.

MPI Ltd, 109 High Street, Newport Pagnell, Buckinghamshire MK16 8EN, England. *Tel*: (01908) 617999. *Fax*: (01908) 617177.
Category: Recruitment agency.
Recruitment specialty: Specialist personnel for the electronics, telecommunications and engineering industries, designers, draughting technicians, planners, production personnel, installers etc. All employees work to strict quality and safety management standards and systems, such as BS EN ISO 9002.
Locations: Africa, Asia, Australia, Canada, Europe, Far East, Ireland, Middle East, Near East, New Zealand, United Kingdom and United States.

MPI Personnel Inc, 194 Ridge Drive, San Antonio, Texas 78228-3754, United States.
Category: Recruitment agency.
Recruitment specialty: Specialist personnel for the electronics, telecommunications and engineering industries, designers, draughting technicians, planners, production personnel, installers etc.
Locations: Africa, Asia, Australia, Canada, Europe, Far East, Ireland, Middle East, Near East, New Zealand, United Kingdom and United States.

MPI Ltd, 56 The Boulevard, Crawley, West Sussex RH10 1XH, England. *Tel*: (01293) 561070. *Fax*: (01293) 520694.
Category: Recruitment agency.
Recruitment specialty: Specialist personnel for the electronics, telecommunications and engineering industries, designers, draughting technicians, planners,

production personnel, installers etc. All employees work to strict quality and safety management standards and systems such as BS EN ISO 9002.

Locations: Africa, Asia, Australia, Canada, Europe, Far East, Ireland, Middle East, Near East, New Zealand, United Kingdom and United States.

MPI Ltd, c/o British Aerospeace, Aviation Services, Building O7L (1st Floor), Filton, Avon BS99 7AR, England. *Tel*: (01179) 363800. *Fax*: (01179) 363888.

Category: Recruitment agency.

Recruitment specialty: Specialist personnel for the electronics, telecommunications and engineering industries, designers, draughting technicians, planners, production personnel, installers etc. All employees work to strict quality and safety management standards and systems, such as BS EN ISO 9002.

Locations: Africa, Asia, Australia, Canada, Europe, Far East, Ireland, Middle East, Near East, New Zealand, United Kingdon and United States.

MPI Aviation Ltd, c/o British Aerospeace, Aviation Services, Building O7L (1st Floor), Filton, Avon BS99 7AR, England. *Tel*: (01179) 363800. *Fax*: (01179) 363888.

Category: Recruitment agency.

Recruitment specialty: Most levels of personnel and skills associated with the aviation industry. Designers, draughting technicians, airframe fitters, aircraft electricians, licensed engineers, machine shop technicians etc. All employees work to strict quality and safety management standards and systems, such as BS EN ISO 9002.

Locations: Africa, Asia, Australia, Canada, Europe, Far East, Ireland, Middle East, Near East, New Zealand, United Kingdon and United States.

MPI Ltd, International House, Tamworth Road, Hertford, Hertfordshire SG13 7DQ, England. *Tel*: (01992) 501111. *Fax*: (01992) 583384.

Category: Recruitment agency.

Recruitment specialty: Specialist personnel for the electronics, telecommunications and engineering industries, designers, draughting technicians, planners, production personnel, installers etc. All employees work to strict quality and safety management standards and systems, such as BS EN ISO 9002.

Locations: Africa, Asia, Australia, Canada, Europe, Far East, Ireland, Middle East, Near East, New Zealand, United Kingdon and United States.

MPI Aviation Ltd, International House, Tamworth Road, Hertford, Hertfordshire SG13 7DQ, England. *Tel*: (01992) 501111. *Fax*: (01992) 583384.

Category: Recruitment agency.

Recruitment specialty: Most levels of personnel and skills associated with the aviation industry. Designers, draughting technicians, airframe fitters, aircraft electricians, licensed engineers, machine shop technicians etc. All employees work to strict quality and safety management standards and systems, such as BS EN ISO 9002.

Locations: Africa, Asia, Australia, Canada, Europe, Far East, Ireland, Middle East, Near East, New Zealand, United Kingdon and United States.

MPI Ltd, Suite 1, Syer House, Stafford Court, Telford, Shropshire TF3 3BD, England. *Tel*: (01952) 290863. *Fax*: (01952) 290864.
Category: Recruitment agency.
Recruitment specialty: Specialist personnel for the electronics, telecommunications and engineering industries, designers, draughting technicians, planners, production personnel, installers etc. All employees work to strict quality and safety management standards and systems such as BS EN ISO 9002.
Locations: Africa, Asia, Australia, Canada, Europe, Far East, Ireland, Middle East, Near East, New Zealand, United Kingdom and United States.

MPI Aviation Ltd, Suite 1, Syer House, Stafford Court, Telford, Shropshire TF3 3BD, England. *Tel*: (01952) 290863. *Fax*: (01952) 290864.
Category: Recruitment agency.
Recruitment specialty: Most levels of personnel and skills associated with the aviation industry. Designers, draughting technicians, airframe fitters, aircraft electricians, licensed engineers, machine shop technicians etc. All employees work to strict quality and safety management standards and systems, such as BS EN ISO 9002.
Locations: Africa, Asia, Australia, Canada, Europe, Far East, Ireland, Middle East, Near East, New Zealand, United Kingdon and United States.

MPI Ltd, The Airport, Newmarket Road, Cambridge, Cambridgeshire CB5 8RX, England. *Tel*: (01233) 373840. *Fax*: (01233) 373846.
Category: Recruitment agency.
Recruitment specialty: Specialist personnel for the electronics, telecommunications and engineering industries, designers, draughting technicians, planners, production personnel, installers etc. All employees work to strict quality and safety management standards and systems, such as BS EN ISO 9002.
Locations: Africa, Asia, Australia, Canada, Europe, Far East, Ireland, Middle East, Near East, New Zealand, United Kingdon and United States.

MPI Aviation Ltd, The Airport, Newmarket Road, Cambridge, Cambridgeshire CB5 8RX, England. *Tel*: (01233) 373840. *Fax*: (01233) 373746.
Category: Recruitment agency.
Recruitment specialty: Most levels of personnel and skills associated with the aviation industry. Designers, draughting technicians, airframe fitters, aircraft electricians, licensed engineers, machine shop technicians etc. All employees work to strict quality and safety management standards and systems, such as BS EN ISO 9002.
Locations: Africa, Asia, Australia, Canada, Europe, Far East, Ireland, Middle East, Near East, New Zealand, United Kingdon and United States.

MRK Consulting, 1 School Lane, Bagshot, Surrey GU19 5BP, England. *Tel*: (01276) 476866. *Fax*: (01276) 479666.

Category: Recruitment agency.

Recruitment speciality: Senior executive, management, engineers and other technical personnel for the IT/computing industry. Focusing mainly on IBM hardware, open systems, client server, computer networks LAN and WAN, multi-vendor environment, digital, HP, SUN microsystems etc. in the computer industry and customer service sectors. Skills include: operational analysts, business analysts, programmers, application planners, rapid application development, DPMs, IS managers, operations/project/service management, quality, PC and open system engineers, communications broker sales, hardware and software sales, training, digital, installations, de-installations, PCMs, UNIX network, CNEs, ATM, IBM systems, databases, visual basic, SDK, C, C++, ORACLE, INGRES, SYBASE, IEF, SAP, RPG 400s, AS400s, designers, testers and development engineers etc. Assignments available on a permanent and contract basis.

Locations: Africa, Asia, Australia, Canada, Europe, Far East, Ireland, Middle East, Near East, New Zealand, South America, United Kingdom and United States.

Additional information: MRK Consulting provide consultancy services for the information technology (IT) industry, including IT service market research, multi-vendor service support, market analysis, strategic research and specialist projects.

Multicom UK Ltd, The Coach House, rear of 32 Evesham Road, Cheltenham, Gloucestershire GL52 2AB, England. *Tel*: (01242) 261275. *Fax*: (01242) 261971.

Category: Recruitment agency.

Recruitment specialty: Technical computing personnel, programmers, authors for high technology projects, in-house etc.

Locations: Northern Europe including Scandinavia and United Kingdom.

Additional information: Multicom UK Ltd offer a full technical publications service, including technical translations and media transfer facilities.

Multilingual Services Ltd, 22 Charing Cross Road, London WC2 OHR, England. *Tel*: (0171) 836 3794. *Fax*: (0171) 836 4093.

Category: Recruitment agency.

Recruitment specialty: Secretarial.

Locations: Europe and United Kingdom.

Nanny Service, The, 9 Paddington Street, London W1D 3LA, England. *Tel*: (0171) 935 3518. *Fax*: (0171) 224 0305.

Category: Recruitment agency.

Recruitment specialty: Nannies with appropriate experience.

Locations: Australia, Europe, New Zealand and United Kingdom.

NES Overseas Ltd, 11 Ambassador Place, Stockport Road, Altrincham, Cheshire WA15 8DB. *Tel*: (0161) 929 1313. *Fax*: (0161) 926 9867.
Category: Recruitment agency.
Recruitment specialty: Senior engineering and technical personnel for the oil and gas, petrochemical, power, water, telecommunications, information technology (IT), and general construction industries. Most skills in design, construction, commissioning, operations etc.
Locations: Africa, Asia, Australia, Canada, Europe, Far East, Ireland, Middle East, Near East, New Zealand, South America and United States.

Network Overseas, 34 Mortimer Street, London W1N 8JR, England. *Tel*: (0171) 580 5151. *Fax*: (0171) 580 6242.
Category: Recruitment agency.
Recruitment specialty: Most management and technical levels in engineering, within the petrochemical, construction, oil and gas, operations and maintenance industries. Also in specialist healthcare areas such as: medical consultants, nursing staff, laboratory technicians and hospital administrators.
Location: Middle East.

Network Recruitment, Kennett House, 108/110 London Road, Headington, Oxfordshire OX3 9AW, England. *Tel*: (01865) 742822. *Fax*: (01865) 741777.
Category: Recruitment agency.
Recruitment specialty: Most levels and sectors including: commercial, technical, industrial, sales and marketing and print.
Location: Europe.

Nicholas Associates Ltd, Reginald Arthur House, Percy Street, Rotherham, South Yorkshire S65 1ED, England. *Tel*: (01709) 360900. *Fax*: (01709) 370037.
Category: Recruitment agency.
Recruitment specialty: Managerial and technical personnel predominantly for the construction industry on a permanent and contract basis.
Locations: Europe, Far East, Ireland, Middle East, Near East and United Kingdom.

NRC Recruitment Specialist, 23 Ely Place, Dublin 2, Republic of Ireland. *Tel*: 00 353 1 676 8644. *Fax*: 00 353 1 676 8662.
Category: Recruitment agency and management consultancy.
Recruitment specialty: Senior executive, management and technical levels in accountancy, food, materials/logistics/procurement, printing and packaging, engineering, technical engineers, agriculture, electronics, manufacturing, quality assurance, warehousing, human resources, administration/clerical, and secretarial (PAs, WP operators etc.).
Locations: Canada, Europe, Ireland and United States.

Additional information: NRC provides additional services in management consulting and career guidance.

O'Connell Associates, 25 Harley Place, London W1N 1HB, England. *Tel*: (0171) 436 1188. *Fax*: (0171) 436 6151.
Category: Recruitment agency.
Recruitment specialty: Senior executive, management and technical personnel in the financial services sector.
Locations: Africa, Asia, Caribbean, Europe, Far East, Indian Ocean, Ireland, Middle East, Near East, South Pacific and United Kingdom.

Offshore Design Ltd, Buchanan House, 63 Summer Street, Aberdeen AB1 1SJ, Scotland. *Tel*: (01224) 628000. *Fax*: (01244) 643325.
Category: Recruitment agency.
Recruitment specialty: Engineers and other technical personnel for the oil and gas industry, operations, process, maintenance and most engineering specialty areas. Technical authors, hypermedia specialists etc.
Locations: Canada, Far East, Middle East, United Kingdom and United States.

Onstream Ltd, 583 Bath Road, Longford, near Heathrow, Middlesex UB7 0EH, England. *Tel*: (01753) 680077. *Fax*: (01753) 689194.
Category: Recruitment agency and engineering consultancy.
Recruitment specialty: Engineering and technical personnel for the oil and gas, petrochemical and civil engineering industries.
Locations: Africa, Asia, Europe, Far East, Middle East and United Kingdom.

Oriel Search Ltd, Oriel Lodge, Dunmow Hill, Fleet, Hampshire GU13 9AN, England. *Tel*: (01257) 811 438. *Fax*: (01257) 811 040.
Category: Recruitment agency.
Recruitment specialty: Senior executive and management levels, dealers etc for the financial information markets.
Locations: Canada, Europe, Ireland, United Kingdom and United States.

ORS Recruitment International, International House, 32 Greendale Drive, Middlewich, Cheshire CW10 OPH, England. *Tel*: (01606) 834002. *Fax*: (01606) 835007.
Category: Recruitment agency.
Recruitment specialty: Engineering and technical personnel for the oil and gas, petrochemical, refineries, offshore, civil construction, architectural consultants, structural designers, operations and maintenance industries and specialist areas. Also Teachers of English as Foreign Language (TEFL), apprentice instructors for most trades, consulting and design engineers.
Locations: Far East and Middle East.

Overseas Development Administration (ODA), Abercrombie House, Eaglesham Road, East Kilbride, Glasgow G75 8EA, Scotland. *Tel*: (01355) 843109.
Category: Employer.
Recruitment specialty: Most management and technical personnel working in a diverse range of specialist areas.
Locations: Worldwide.
Additional information: The ODA is funded by the British Government Aid Programme and provides a wide range of technical personnel throughout the world in over 160 countries. Duration of assignments can vary up to three years renewable.

Paradigm Associates, Bishops Court, 17a The Broadway, Old Hatfield, Hertfordshire AL9 5MA, England. *Tel*: (01707) 266363. *Fax*: (01707) 266464.
Category: Recruitment agency.
Recruitment specialty: Senior executive, management, technical and support levels, in datacommunications, telecommunications, sales and marketing, pre-sales and post-sales support and network design. Also field engineers, trainers, human resource specialists etc.
Locations: Africa, Asia, Canada, Europe, Ireland, Middle East, United Kingdom and United States.

Parc Apollo Technical Services, 2A Rose Street, Aberdeen AB1 1UA, Scotland. *Tel*: (01224) 649 649. *Fax*: (01224) 640 111.
Category: Recruitment agency.
Recruitment specialty: Engineering personnel for the petrochemical, oil and gas, water treatment and power generation industries.
Locations: Europe, Far East, Ireland, Middle East, Near East and United Kingdom.

Parc Aviation Ltd, St Johns Court, Swords Road, Santry, Dublin 9, Republic of Ireland. *Tel*: 00 353 1 842 9933. *Fax*: 00 353 1 3284/6442/9389.
Category: Recruitment agency.
Recruitment specialty: Executive, technical and support personnel on a permanent and contract basis, most skills such as: pilots, technicians, support, flight crews etc. within the aviation industry.
Locations: Asia, Australia, Canada, Europe, Far East, Ireland, Middle East, Near East, New Zealand, South America, United Kingdom and United States.
Additional information: Parc Aviation operates in over 30 countries worldwide and provides human resource services to the aviation industry from its three main operating divisions, Flight Crew Leasing, Technical and Maintenance Manpower Leasing and Aviation Consultancy. It is part of the PARC group, providing other services to their clients in PARC Healthcare International and PARC Technical Services, active in over 30 countries. Consultancy services include: infrastructure development, legal advisory,

psychometric testing, operational training, quality assurance/safety compliance with JAA regulations etc.

Parc Workforce, St Johns Court, Swords Road, Santry, Dublin 9, Republic of Ireland. *Tel*: 00 353 1 842 9933. *Fax*: 00 353 1 842 3284/6642/9389.

Category: Recruitment agency.

Recruitment specialty: Senior management, technical and support personnel in specialist industries such as: manufacturing, telecommunications, aviation, healthcare, IT/computing, construction design management. Also in the petrochemical industry, most engineering and technical disciplines including designers, technicians, CAD operators, surveyors etc.

Locations: Asia, Australia, Canada, Europe, Far East, Ireland, Middle East, Near East, New Zealand, South America, United Kingdom and United States.

Partners In Recruitment, St John's Innovation Park, Cowley Road, Cambridge, Cambridgeshire CB4 4WS, England. *Tel*: (01223) 328935.

Category: Recruitment agency.

Recruitment specialty: Management, technical and administrative support personnel for the packaging industry, materials, machinery, manufacturing and technology. Most levels of personnel, middle management, accountancy, administrative support etc.

Locations: Asia, Europe, Middle East and United Kingdom.

Partners In Recruitment, Suites 1 & 2, Meadow Lane Business Park, St Ives, Cambridgeshire PE17 4LG, England. *Tel*: (01480) 493344. *Fax*: (01480) 493343.

Category: Recruitment agency.

Recruitment specialty: Management, technical and administrative support personnel for the packaging industry, materials, machinery, manufacturing and technology. Most levels of personnel, middle management, accountancy, administrative support etc.

Locations: Asia, Europe, Middle East and United Kingdom.

Peter Glaser & Associates, Bramble Hill, Bramble Lane, Christchurch, Dorset BH23 5NB. *Tel*: (01425) 276622. *Fax*: (01425) 278278.

Category: Recruitment agency.

Recruitment specialty: Senior executive, management and technical personnel for the construction, water, waste, environmental, highways, pharmaceutical and petrochemical industries.

Locations: Africa, Asia, Europe, Far East, Ireland, Middle East, Near East, South America and United Kingdom.

Additional information: Peter Glaser & Associates offer clients advice, planning and execution of resourcing assignments, including confidential search, advertising, register search and the supply of temporary specialist personnel.

Peter Stoner & Associates, 73 Pavilion Gardens, Staines, Middlesex TW18 1LT, England. *Tel/Fax*: (01784) 457787.
Category: Recruitment agency.
Recruitment specialty: Director to site engineer levels in the construction industry as quantity surveyors, engineers, site managers, project managers, contract managers etc.
Locations: Africa, Asia, Europe, Far East, Middle East and United Kingdom.

Petrolic Consultants Ltd, 174 High Street, Guildford, Surrey GU1 3HW, England. *Tel*: (01483) 302133. *Fax*: (01483) 579891.
Category: Recruitment agency.
Recruitment specialty: Technical and support personnel for the petrochemical, oil and gas, water, food, pharmaceutical and process plant industries.
Locations: Ireland, United Kingdom and worldwide.

PGL Young Adventure Ltd, Alton Court, Penyard Lane, Ross-on-Wye, Hereford & Worcester HR9 5NR, England. *Tel*: (01989) 767833. *Fax*: (01989) 765451.
Category: Employer.
Recruitment specialty: Temporary seasonal (March to September) assignments at children's activity holiday centres. Activity instructors, group leaders, catering and domestic staff.
Locations: Europe and United Kingdom.
Additional information: All assignments are residential and full training will be given.

PIA Ltd, Blagrave House, Blagrave Street, Reading, Berkshire RG1 1PW, England. *Tel*: (01734) 600660. *Fax*: (01734) 600666.
Category: Recruitment agency.
Recruitment specialty: Technical and support personnel with the oil and gas, pharmaceutical, water, food and biotechnology industries.
Location: United Kingdom.

Pipco Ltd, St Giles House, 11 Quay Street, Bristol, Avon BS1 2JL, England. *Tel*: (01179) 294490. *Fax*: (01179) 294470.
Category: Recruitment agency.
Recruitment specialty: Engineering and support personnel for the construction industry, building, mechanical, electrical engineers and technicians, project staff, trades and general labour.
Locations: Africa, Asia, Canada, Central Europe, Eastern Europe (including Mongolia and Russia), Far East, Ireland, Middle East, United Kingdom and United States.

Premmit Associates Ltd, 33 Eccleston Square, London SW1V 1PH, England. *Tel*: (0171) 834 7253. *Fax*: (0171) 834 3544.
Category: Recruitment agency.

Recruitment specialty: Executive, management and technical personnel for the IT/computing, hardware and software engineering, electronics, defence, aerospace, pharmaceutical and biotech industries. Also general sales and marketing, human resources, finance etc.

Locations: Canada, Europe, Middle East, Near East, United Kingdom and United States.

Prime Recruitment Contracts, 105a East Street, Southampton, Hampshire SO14 3HH, England. *Tel*: (01703) 631415.*Fax*: (01703) 631568.

Category: Recruitment agency.

Recruitment specialty: Management, engineering and technical personnel for the oil and gas, shipbuilding and marine, aerospace, rail, IT/computing, civil and structural engineering and building services. Engineers and technical support staff in electrical, mechanical, software, marine etc.

Locations: Europe, Far East, Middle East and United Kingdom.

Additional information: Speculative candidate enquiries are not required.

Problems Unlimited Agency, 86 Alexandra Road, Windsor, Berkshire SL4 1HN, England. *Tel*: (01753) 830101. *Fax*: (01753) 831194.

Category: Recruitment agency.

Recruitment specialty: Au pairs and mother's helps.

Locations: Europe and United Kingdom

Additional information: Au pairs – age groups 18 to 27 years, conversational English language skills a minimum requirement, childcare experience is advantageous and familiarity with simple household tasks. Mother's helps – age 20 years minimum, childcare experience is essential and the ability to take responsibility of child/children and the home in the absence of the employer. A mature attitude is essential and a good level of conversational English. All candidates must provide excellent references and a medical certificate.

Professional & Engineering Consultants Ltd, Riverside House, 1/5 High Street, London Corner, Hertfordshire AL2 1LE, England. *Tel*: (01727) 824444/ (01634) 261773. *Fax*: (01727) 824390.

Category: Recruitment agency.

Recruitment specialty: Management and engineering personnel for the oil and gas, petrochemical, information technology (IT), pharmaceuticals, manufacturing, civil and architectural engineering industries. Engineer designers, project managers etc.

Locations: Africa, Asia, Europe, Far East, Ireland, Middle East and United Kingdom.

Professional Management Resources Ltd, PO Box 23, Wadhurst, East Sussex TN5 6XL, England. *Tel*: (01892) 784226. *Fax*: (01892) 784228.

Category: Recruitment agency.

Recruitment specialty: Senior engineering, technical and support personnel for the civil engineering, construction, oil and gas, petrochemical, power, utilities, water, telecommunications and IT/computing industries including training etc.

Locations: Africa, Asia, Europe, Far East, Ireland, Middle East, Near East and United Kingdom.

Progressive Computer Recruitment, 266/276 Upper Richmond Road, London SW15 6TQ, England. *Tel*: (0181) 957 1700. *Fax*: (0181) 957 1777.

Category: Recruitment agency.

Recruitment specialty: General recruitment, most levels and technical areas.

Locations: Asia, Australia, Canada, Europe, Far East, Ireland, Middle East, New Zealand, United Kingdom and United States.

Project Management Professional Services Ltd, PMP House, Gardner Road, Maidenhead, Berkshire SL6 7RJ, England. *Tel*: (01628) 75444. *Fax*: (01628) 26203.

Category: Recruitment agency.

Recruitment specialty: Project management most levels of personnel and skilled areas such as: planning, system and project engineers, project managers, cost controllers and estimators and document controllers etc.

Location: United Kingdom.

Project Resourcing, 26A High Street, Hounslow, Middlesex TW3 1NW, England. *Tel*: (0181) 572 7363. *Fax*: (0181) 570 4365.

Category: Recruitment agency.

Recruitment specialty: Senior management, engineers and technical personnel for the construction industry.

Locations: Africa, Asia, Europe, Far East, Middle East and Near East.

Quarry Dougall Group, 37/41 Bedford Row, London WC1R 4JH, England. *Tel*: (0171) 405 6062. *Fax*: (0171) 831 6394.

Other offices: 6 overseas.

Category: Recruitment agency.

Recruitment specialty: Specialist legal personnel in both private practice and commerce and industry, from newly qualified solicitors to partners and teams.

Locations: Asia, Australia, Canada, Europe, Far East, Ireland, New Zealand, United Kingdom and United States.

Additional information: Quarry Dougall is staffed fully by qualified lawyers who are able to combine their previous practical legal skills with extensive experience in recruitment and further professional training including the MBA and IPD qualifications. Special Project Lawyer, a sister company, uses consultants with extensive experience of the short term contract market to provide a professional service to clients seeking fixed-term cover. Other specialist divisions within the group advise a high profile client base on advertising, outplacement counselling and career management.

Quarry Dougall Retail Sales & Marketing, 37/41 Bedford Row, London WC1R 4JH, England. *Tel*: (0171) 405 6062. *Fax*: (0171) 831 6394.
Other offices: 6 overseas.
Category: Recruitment agency.
Recruitment specialty: Senior board level executives to middle management levels of personnel, buyers, merchandisers, general marketing managers, account directors etc, specifically for the retail, sales and marketing specialist areas.
Locations: Asia, Australia, Canada, Europe, Far East, Ireland, New Zealand, United Kingdom and United States.
Additional information: Salaries range from £15,000–£150,000.

Rada Recruitment Communications Ltd, 195 Euston Road, London NW1 1BN, England. *Tel*: (0171) 388 8564. *Fax*: (0171) 388 3102.
Category: Recruitment agency.
Recruitment specialty: Senior executive, management and graduate trainees.
Location: United Kingdom.
Additional information: Rada Recruitment is a recruitment advertising agency with experience in creative strategy, planning, media research and buying, response management and graduate recruitment. Speculative candidate enquiries are not required.

Randstad Inter Engineering Ltd, Builder House, Mayors Road, Altrincham, Cheshire WA15 9RP, England. *Tel*: (0161) 929 1882. *Fax*: (0161) 929 1836.
Category: Recruitment agency.
Recruitment specialty: Engineering and technical personnel within the construction and design industries. A wide band of skills and levels, project managers through to site engineers etc.
Locations: Europe, Far East, Middle East and United Kingdom.

Ranger Oil Ltd, Ranger House, Walnut Tree Close, Guildford, Surrey GU1 4US, England.
Category: Employer.
Recruitment specialty: Oil processing and production personnel, production, drilling and reservoir engineers etc.
Locations: Africa, Canada and United Kingdom.

Raymond Laurence Ltd, 29 High Street, Pinner, Middlesex HA5 5PH, England. *Tel*: (0181) 866 5678/1155. *Fax*: (0181) 866 6678.
Category: Recruitment agency.
Recruitment specialty: Technical sales and marketing personnel in most sectors, such as: sales directors, executives and managers, marketing executives and assistants, account executives and managers and technical sales engineers.
Locations: Europe, Middle East and United Kingdom.

Reason International Ltd, Heath Lane, Woburn Sands, Bedfordshire MK17 8TN, England. *Tel*: (01908) 282201. *Fax*: (01908) 287051.
Category: Recruitment agency.
Recruitment specialty: Management and technical personnel, project managers, system designers, software specialists, consultants etc. Skills in: software, hardware, systems and products, datacommunications and telecommunications, open systems, embedded systems, Windows, database, UNIX, NT, pre and post sales.
Locations: Europe, Far East and United Kingdom.

Recruitment Holdings Ltd, The Cedars, Church Road, Ashford, Kent TN23 1RQ, England. *Tel*: (01233) 638476/638471/639071. *Fax*: (01233) 645702.
Category: Recruitment agency.
Recruitment specialty: Management, engineers and other technical and IT/computing personnel for the oil and gas, process, construction, building services, water and power generation industries. Specialists in construction safety, on/off shore and engineering support.
Locations: Africa, Asia, Europe, Far East, Middle East and United Kingdom.

Reed Overseas, 448/450 Midsummer Boulevard, Milton Keynes, Bedfordshire MK9 2EA, England. *Tel*: (01908) 694524. *Fax*: (01908) 694803.
Category: Recruitment agency.
Recruitment specialty: Management and technical support personnel for most sectors.
Locations: Africa, Asia, Australia, Canada, Europe, Far East, Middle East, Near East, New Zealand, South America, United Kingdom and United States.

Regency Nannies, 50 Hans Crescent, London SW1X ONA, England. *Tel*: (0171) 225 1055. *Fax*: (0171) 584 7265.
Category: Recruitment agency.
Recruitment specialty: Trained nannies, NNEB etc. for permanent and short term assignments.
Locations: Europe, Far East, Middle East and United Kingdom.

Relational Designers Ltd, Owen House, Heathside Crescent, Woking, Surrey GU22 7AG, England. *Tel*: (01483) 776623/888999. *Fax*: (01483) 776653/888998.
Category: Recruitment agency.
Recruitment specialty: IT/computing specialist personnel, relational database consultants especially skilled in ORACLE and its tools.
Locations: Asia, Australia, Canada, Ireland, New Zealand, United Kingdom and United States.

Resources International Plc, 31 Bedford Square, London WC1 3EG, England. *Tel*: (0171) 314 4200. *Fax*: (0171) 323 3094.

Category: Recruitment agency.

Recruitment specialty: Contract IT/computing personnel most levels and skills.

Locations: Asia, Australia, Canada, Europe, Far East, Ireland, Middle East, Near East, United Kingdom and United States.

Additional information: Resources International Plc provides a fully comprehensive recruitment service: planning, designing and conducting advertising campaigns, outplacement staff, career counselling, search & selection of IT, corporate and general management personnel.

Roevin Management Services Ltd, 43 Dee Street, Aberdeen AB1 2DY, Scotland. *Tel*: (01224) 572852. *Fax*: (01224) 571983.

Other offices: 10 in the United Kingdom.

Category: Recruitment agency.

Recruitment specialty: General and specialised skills in most sectors.

Locatioins: Africa, Asia, Canada, Europe, Far East, Ireland, Middle East, Near East, South America, United Kingdom and United States.

Rosta Engineering Co Ltd, 87A Castle Street, Edgeley, Stockport, Cheshire SK3 9AR, England. *Tel*: (0161) 477 2111. *Fax*: (0161) 480 4599.

Category: Recruitment agency.

Recruitment specialty: Most levels of management, technical and administrative personnel on a permanent and contract basis, involved in specialty areas and industries such as: the design and construction of buildings, structural design, process and chemical engineering, petrochemical, water treatment and waste projects. Also design work for the automotive industry and transportation.

Locations: Asia, Canada, Europe, Far East, Middle East, United Kingdom and United States.

Rowan Resources, Rowan House, Crown Business Park, Tredegar, Gwent NP2 4EF, Wales. *Tel*: (01495) 308621. *Fax*: (01495) 308609.

Category: Recruitment agency.

Recruitment specialty: Specialists in areas of engineering and senior management.

Locations: Africa, Asia, Far East, Middle East, Near East and United Kingdom.

Roxby Engineering International Ltd, Roxby House, Station Road, Sidcup, Kent DA15 7EJ, England. *Tel*: (0181) 300 3393. *Fax*: (0181) 300 4400.

Category: Employer.

Recruitment specialty: Engineering and other technical personnel for the petrochemical, oil and gas industries.

Locations: Far East, Middle East and United Kingdom.

Rugby Design & Engineering Services Ltd, 1 Riverside House, Wickford, Essex SS11 8BB, England. *Tel*: (01268) 561020. *Fax*: (01268) 571483.

Category: Recruitment agency.

Recruitment specialty: Senior management, engineers and other technical personnel in the automotive, electrical and mechanical engineering, building services and information technology (IT) industries on permament, contract and temporary basis.

Locations: Europe and United Kingdom.

Sales Placement Ltd, 5 Herbert Place, Dublin 2, Republic of Ireland. *Tel*: 00 353 1 668 5144. *Fax*: 00 353 1 676 3710.

Category: Recruitment agency.

Recruitment specialty: Senior executive, management, technical and trainee personnel within the sales and marketing, contract, FMCG, healthcare and pharmaceutical specialist areas and industries.

Locations: Africa, Canada, Europe, Ireland, Middle East, United Kingdom and United States.

Sales Placement Ltd, 9 Lower Crescent, Belfast BT7 1NR, Northern Ireland.

Category: Recruitment agency.

Recruitment specialty: Senior executive, management, technical and trainee personnel within the sales and marketing, contract, FMCG, healthcare and pharmaceutical specialist areas and industries.

Locations: Africa, Canada, Europe, Ireland, Middle East, United Kingdom and United States.

Sales Solutions, The, 227 High Street, Epping, Essex CM16 4BP, England. *Tel*: (01992) 561711. *Fax*: (01992) 561811.

Category: Recruitment agency.

Recruitment specialty: Sales executives for the information technology (IT) industry.

Locations: Europe, United Kingdom and United States.

Santos Engineering Services Ltd, 19 Clanwilliam Street, Dublin 2, Republic of Ireland. *Tel*: 00 353 1 661 9911. *Fax*: 00 353 1 661 2310.

Category: Recruitment agency.

Recruitment specialty: Engineering and other technical personnel within the petrochemical, oil and gas, power generation, cement production, building services, civil engineering, construction and design specialist areas and industries.

Locations: Asia, Australia, Canada, Europe, Far East, Ireland, Middle East, Near East, New Zealand, South America, United Kingdom and United States.

Saxoncourt Recruitment, 59 South Molton Street, London W14 1HH, England. *Tel*: (0171) 491 1919. *Fax*: (0171) 499 9374.

Category: Recruitment agency.

Recruitment specialty: English language teachers for language schools.

Locations: Asia, Europe, Far East, Middle East, Near East, South America and United Kingdom.

Additional information: Candidates must hold a degree and recognised TEFL qualification.

SBS Ltd, Centre Point, 103 New Oxford Street, London WC1A 1DY, England. *Tel*: (0171) 240 7575. *Fax*: (0171) 240 7580.

Category: Recruitment agency.

Recruitment specialty: Senior management, engineers and technical personnel within the IT/computing industry. Specialist skills include: SYBASE, ORACLE, IBM hardware, INGRES, PC development and support, networking and SAP.

Locations: Eastern Europe, United Kingdom and Western Europe,

Scientific Staff Consultants, 50 Lincolns Inn Fields, London WC2A 3PF, England. *Tel*: (0171) 242 4266. *Fax*: (0171) 404 4148.

Category: Recruitment agency.

Recruitment specialty: Management and sales and marketing personnel within the medical and healthcare specialist areas, field, regional and national sales management and product and marketing management technical specialists. Also export representatives and management assignments.

Location: United Kingdom.

Additional information: Candidates are expected to have prior industry experience. Export positions, although based in the United Kingdom, cover countries worldwide.

Scorex (UK) Ltd, Arndale House, Charles Street, Bradford, West Yorkshire BD1 1EJ, England. *Tel*: (01274) 762800. *Fax*: (01274) 762801.

Category: Employer.

Recruitment specialty: Graduates with numerate, computing, business analysis skills, client empathy and good presentation.

Location: United Kingdom.

Additional information: Scorex (UK) Ltd is a major supplier of credit scanning systems to banks, building societies, finance houses etc. throughout the United Kingdom. Candidates from a mathematical and/or statistical background are preferred.

Scot Contracts Company Ltd, 11 Summer Street, Aberdeen AB1 1SB, Scotland. *Tel*: (01224) 643 623. *Fax*: (01224) 642 589.

Category: Recruitment agency.

Recruitment specialty: Engineering and technical personnel for the petrochemical (non-oil) industry, electronics engineers, safety officers, quality assurance/controllers, technical support, draughting technicians, buyers, accountants, labourers etc.

Locations: Africa, Asia, Europe and United Kingdom.

Seaforth Maritime Ltd, Seaforth Centre, Waterloo Quay, Aberdeen AB2 1BS, Scotland. *Tel*: (01224) 573 401. *Fax*: (01224) 575 946.
Category: Recruitment agency.
Recruitment specialty: Specialist engineering and technical personnel for marine, logistics and general engineering.
Locations: Africa, Europe and United Kingdom.

Sector Personnel, 12 Well Court, London EC4M 9DN, England. *Tel*: (0171) 489 0165. *Fax*: (0171) 236 2824.
Category: Recruitment agency.
Recruitment specialty: IT/computing permanent and contract management and technical personnel for the banking and finance services.
Locations: Canada, United Kingdom and United States.

Selected Options Ltd, South Bank Technopark, 90 London Road, London SE1 6LN, England. *Tel*: (0171) 922 8818. *Fax*: (0171) 922 8838.
Category: Recruitment agency.
Recruitment specialty: IT/computing most levels and skills.
Locations: Africa, Australia, Canada, Europe, Ireland, New Zealand, United Kingdom and United States.

Sheila Burgess International, 4 Cromwell Place, London SW7 2JS, England. *Tel*: (0171) 584 6446. *Fax*: (0171) 584 1824.
Category: Recruitment agency.
Recruitment specialty: Bilingual secretaries and personal assistants.
Locations: Europe (Belgium, France and Germany).
Additional information: French language qualifications at degree level and with secretarial training, touch typing 45 words per minute minimum and word processing skills. All clients of Sheila Burgess International are international companies working in English and French languages and generally with a US management style.

Sherry Sherratt Technical Recruitment Ltd, PO Box 4529, London SW18 3XD, England. *Tel*: (0181) 875 1895. *Fax*: (0181) 875 1894. .
Category: Recruitment agency.
Recruitment specialty: Healthcare and engineering industries, medical and nursing staff in most specialties, medical physicists etc., civil engineers, quantity surveyors, structural/mechanical and electrical engineers, accountants etc.
Locations: Asia, Europe, Far East, Middle East, Near East and South America.

Sherwood Engineering Recruitment, Sherwood House, Aldwarne Road, Parkgate, Rotherham, South Yorkshire S62 6BU, England. *Tel/Fax*: (01709) 710800.
Category: Recruitment agency.
Recruitment specialty: Senior management, engineering and technical personnel

for the engineering and construction industries. Project directors and managers, foremen/supervisors and other technical staff.

Locations: Africa, Asia, Canada, Europe, Far East, Ireland, Middle East, Near East, South America, United Kingdom and United States.

Silicon Valley Group, Consultants House, 60 High Street, Sandhurst, Surrey GU17 8DY, England. *Tel*: (01252) 877778, *Fax*: (01252) 875737.

Category: Recruitment agency.

Recruitment specialty: Management and technical personnel within the IT/ computing industry, specialising in ATC, ILS/reliability, information technology (IT), communications, quality assurance and networking. Skills include: project managers, analyst programmers, draughting technicians, technical authors and software, systems, electronics, test and mechanical engineers etc.

Locations: Canada, Europe, Far East, Ireland, Middle East, United Kingdom and United States.

Additioinal information: Silicon Valley Group is a recruitment consultancy and software house.

Southwest Computer Resources, 14/16 St Thomas Street, Bristol, Avon BS1 6JT, England. *Tel*: (0117) 987 6655. *Fax*: (0117) 987 7701.

Category: Recruitment agency.

Recruitment specialty: IT/computing industry, most levels from management to trainees. Most skills hardware and software including specialists with experience in ABM AS400s and RPG400s etc.

Locations: Canada, Europe, Middle East, United Kingdom and United States.

Sperry Sun Drilling Services, (Recruiting Office), Tangen 16, 4070 Randaberg, Norway. *Fax*: 00 47 5 141 0002.

Category: Employer.

Recruitment specialty: Professional/technical personnel with directional drilling and measurement service experience including MWD, drilling and completion engineers.

Locations: Norway and worldwide.

Additional information: Suitably qualified and experienced candidates are welcome to forward their detailed CVs.

Spitfire Selection, Norfolk House, 196 Old Bedford Road, Luton, Bedfordshire LU2 7HW, England. *Tel*: (01582) 37023. *Fax*: (01582) 455587.

Category: Recruitment agency.

Recruitment specialty: Senior executive and management levels, mainly in information technology (IT) and sales management and teams.

Locations: Canada, Europe, Ireland, United Kingdom and United States.

Additional information: Spitfire Selection is a client orientated only recruitment organisation, working exclusively on a retained search and selection assignment basis. Speculative candidate enquiries are not required.

Staffaire Ltd, 3 St Mary's Courtyard, Ware, Hertfordshire SG12 9EG, England. *Tel*: (01920) 460461. *Fax*: (01920) 464684.
Category: Recruitment agency.
Recruitment specialty: Most levels and skills in the aviation maintenance, construction and building services industries.
Locations: Africa, Canada, Ireland, United Kingdom and United States.

Staffwise Technical, Staffwise Business Centre, Portsmouth Road, Cosham, Hampshire PO6 2SL, England. *Tel*: (01705) 383423. *Fax*: (01705) 201845.
Category: Recruitment agency.
Recruitment specialty: Management personnel in the construction, information technology (IT), oil and gas, petrochemical, manufacturing industries and structural design, logistics, electrical and instrumentation specialist areas.
Locations: Asia, Europe, Far East, Middle East, Near East and United Kingdom.

Staniforth Endsor & Partners Ltd, 3 The Courtyard, Ashley Road, Hale, Altrincham, Cheshire WN4 3NG, England. *Tel*: (0161) 929 1481. *Fax*: (0161) 929 8098.
Category: Recruitment agency.
Recruitment specialty: Senior executive to middle management levels of personnel for most sectors.
Locations: Canada, Europe, Ireland, United Kingdom and United States.

Steele Dixon & Associates, Home Farm Barn, Thrupp Lane, Radley, Abingdon, Oxfordshire OX14 3NG, England. *Tel*: (01235) 536440. *Fax*: (01235) 536448.
Category: Recruitment agency.
Recruitment specialty: Senior management and most other levels of personnel including scientific and technical, within the automotive, engineering, sales and marketing, services, telecommunications and networking industries.
Locations: Africa, Asia, Europe, Far East, Ireland, Middle East, Near East and United Kingdom.

STM Recruitment International, 91 Mitchell Street, Glasgow G1 3LF, Scotland. *Tel*: (0141) 221 7757. *Fax*: (0141) 226 5597.
Category: Recruitment agency.
Recruitment specialty: Most engineering and technical personnel in mechanical and electrical engineering, telecommunications, electronics, IT/computing, marine engineering and construction industries.
Locations: Europe, South America and United Kingdom.

Strategic Resources European Recruitment Consultants Ltd, Union Buildings, 15 Union Street, Aberdeen AB11 5BU, Scotland. *Tel*: (01224) 583123. *Fax*: (01224) 583122.
Category: Recruitment agency.
Recruitment specialty: Management and technical personnel within the oil and

gas industry in most specialist areas, engineering, commercial etc.
Location: United Kingdom.

Strongfield Aviation Ltd, 62 Marylebone High Street, London W1M 3AF. *Tel*: (0171) 224 1200. *Fax*: (0171) 224 0031.
Other offices: 2 in the United Kingdom and 11 overseas including 7 representative offices.
Category: Recruitment agency.
Recruitment specialty: Maintenance and support personnel for the aviation industry, flight crew, cabin staff and maintenance engineers and technicians.
Locations: Asia, Canada, Europe, Far East, Ireland, Middle East, Near East, South America, United Kingdom and United States.

Strongfield Engineering Ltd, 62 Marylebone High Street, London W1M 3AF. *Tel*: (0171) 224 1200. *Fax*: (0171) 224 0031.
Other offices: 2 in the United Kingdom and 11 overseas including 7 representative offices.
Category: Recruitment agency.
Recruitment consultancy: Senior engineering and technical personnel within the aerospace, electronics, space, telecommunications, automotive, power, rail, civil and computing industries.
Locations: Asia, Canada, Europe, Far East, Ireland, Middle East, Near East, South America, United Kingdom and United States.

Strongfield International Plc, 62 Marylebone High Street, London W1M 3AF. *Tel*: (0171) 224 1200. *Fax*: (0171) 224 0031.
Other offices: 2 in the United Kingdom and 11 overseas including 7 representative offices.
Category: Recruitment agency.
Recruitment consultancy: Senior engineering and technical personnel within the aerospace, electronics, space, telecommunications, automotive, power, rail, civil and computing industries. Also maintenance and support personnel for the aviation industry, flight crew, cabin staff and maintenance engineers and technicians.
Locations: Asia, Canada, Europe, Far East, Ireland, Middle East, Near East, South America, United Kingdom and United States.

Swan Recruitment, 118 Victory House, Somers Road North, Portsmouth, Hampshire PO1 1PJ, England. *Tel*: (01705) 838784. *Fax*: (01705) 838790.
Category: Recruitment agency.
Recruitment specialty: Senior engineers, designers and technical personnel, within the oil and gas, petrochemical, pharmaceutical process, construction, design and commissioning industries.
Locations: Africa, Far East, Middle East and United Kingdom.

TA Engineering Services Ltd, Badentoy Avenue, Portlethen, Aberdeen AB12 4YB, Scotland. *Tel*: (01224) 780790. *Fax*: (01224) 783078.
Category: Recruitment agency.
Recruitment specialty: Management and technical personnel, senior engineers, consultants, specialist technicians and trades etc. in most engineering based industries.
Locations: Asia, Europe, Far East, Ireland, Middle East and United Kingdom.
Additional information: TA Engineering offer specialist consultancy services to their clients in reliability maintenance, criticality studies etc.

Tangent International, Shelduck House, 10/11 Woodbrook Crescent, Billericay, Essex CM12 OEQ, England. *Tel*: (01277) 630055. *Fax*: (01277) 633133.
Category: Recruitment agency.
Recruitment specialty: Most levels of personnel for the IT/computing industry on a permanent and contract basis. Skills in software engineering, real time software engineering, cellular and mobile communications etc.
Locations: Africa, Asia, Australia, Canada, Europe, Far East, Ireland, Middle East, Near East, New Zealand, Scandinavia, South America, United Kingdom and United States.
Additional information: Tangent International offer professional advice and guidance to contractors seeking assignments overseas.

Tate International, Southbank House, Black Prince Road, London SE1 7SJ, England. *Tel*: (0171) 793 0406. *Fax*: (0171) 587 0988.
Category: Recruitment agency.
Recruitment specialty: English language teachers, TEFL qualified, for private schools and childcare personnel.
Location: Europe (Italy).

TDM Europe Ltd, Hunter House, Biggin Hill Airport, Biggin Hill, Kent TN16 3BN, England. *Tel*: (0195) 957 0707. *Fax*: (0195) 957 0606.
Category: Recruitment agency.
Recruitment specialty: Senior engineers and other technical personnel for the aerospace and telecommunications industries, CNC programmers, software engineers, designers, project engineers, R/F designers, network planners etc.
Locations: Asia, Australia, Canada, Europe, Far East, Ireland, Middle East, New Zealand, United Kingdom and United States.

TDM Technical Services, 107 Delaware Avenue, Suite 500, Buffalo, New York, NY 14202, United States.
Category: Recruitment agency.
Recruitment specialty: Senior engineers and other technical personnel for the aerospace and telecommunications industries, CNC programmers, software engineers, designers, project engineers, R/F designers, network planners etc.
Locations: Asia, Australia, Canada, Europe, Far East, Middle East, New Zealand and United States.

TDM Technical Services, 3 Church Street, Suite 300, Toronto, Ontario, Canada. *Tel*: 00 416 777 007. *Fax*: 00 416 777 1117.
Category: Recruitment agency.
Recruitment specialty: Senior engineers and other technical personnel for the aerospace and telecommunications industries, CNC programmers, software engineers, designers, project engineers, R/F designers, network planners etc.
Locations: Asia, Australia, Canada, Europe, Far East, Middle East, New Zealand and United States.

TDM Technical Services, JL Griya Raya Utara #20, Bandung, Indonesia. *Tel*: 00 011 62 2221 2952. *Fax*: 00 011 62 2221 2952.
Category: Recruitment agency.
Recruitment specialty: Senior engineers and other technical personnel for the aerospace and telecommunications industries, CNC programmers, software engineers, designers, project engineers, R/F designers, network planners etc.
Locations: Asia, Australia, Far East and New Zealand.

Team One Recruitment, 30 Station Road, Redhill, Surrey RH1 1PD, England. *Tel*: (01737) 768696. *Fax*: (01737) 767838.
Category: Recruitment agency.
Recruitment specialty: Engineers and technical personnel for the aviation industry.
Location: Europe.

Technicon, 34 Coldharbour Lane, Harpenden, Hertfordshire AL5 4UN, England. *Tel*: (01582) 764422. *Fax*: (01582) 764777.
Category: Recruitment agency.
Recruitment specialty: Engineering design and styling personnel for the automotive industry, vehicles only.
Locations: Africa, Australia, Canada, Europe, New Zealand, South America, United Kingdom and United States.

Technostaff, Mel House, 31 South Terrace, Cork, Republic of Ireland. *Tel*: 00 353 21 312777. *Fax*: 00 353 21 965381.
Category: Recruitment agency.
Recruitment specialty: Engineering and technical support personnel for the manufacturing, construction and service industries. Most areas of engineering, electronics and computing etc.
Locations: Europe, Far East, Ireland and Middle East.

TEK Personnel Consultants Ltd, Bells Square, Trippet Lane, Sheffield, South Yorkshire S1 2FY, England. *Tel*: (0114) 276 1699. *Fax*: (0114) 272 7929.
Category: Recruitment agency.
Recruitment specialty: Most skills, levels and sectors especially the manufacturing industry.
Locations: Europe and United Kingdom.

Teknica UK Ltd, Holborn Tower, 137 High Holborn, London WC1V 6PW, England.
Category: Employer.
Recruitment specialty: Management and technical personnel for the oil engineering industry. Project and contract assignments for senior engineers and designers, draughting technicians skilled in autoCAD, onshore projects.
Locations: Africa (Libya) and United Kingdom.
Additional information: Most engineers degree qualified with at least 10 years' industry experience, single status contracts on a rotational basis are 10 weeks on and 3 weeks off.

TFPL, 17/18 Britton Street, London EC1M 5NQ, England. *Tel*: (0171) 251 5522. *Fax*: (0171) 251 8318.
Other offices: 1 overseas.
Category: Recruitment agency.
Recruitment specialty: Personnel for the information industry, librarians, information managers, researchers, sales and marketing. Specialist industry areas include: database providers, Internet specialists, online searchers, library software specialists etc. Most roles and skills within the information industry in its broadest sense.
Locations: Canada, Europe, United Kingdom and United States.

Theaker Monro & Newman, Regency Court, 62/66 Deansgate, Manchester. Greater Manchester M3 2EN, England. *Tel*: (0161) 832 0033.
Other offices: 4 in the United Kingdom and 60 overseas.
Category: Executive search agency.
Recruitment specialty: Senior executive and management personnel for most levels and sectors.
Locations: United Kingdom and worldwide.

Thomas Mining Associates, PO Box 2023, Bournemouth, Dorset BH4 8YR, England. *Tel*: (01202) 751 658. *Fax*: (01202) 764 448.
Category: Recruitment agency.
Recruitment specialty: Engineering and technical personnel for the mining, quarrying and extractive industries, including most services and associated functions. Placements cover a wide band of levels and skills, ranging from main board to technical workforce. Geologists, mining engineers, metallurgists, mechanical/electrical/civil/construction engineers, accountancy and most administrative functions.
Locations: Africa, Asia, Australia, Canada, Europe, Far East, Ireland, Middle East, Near East, New Zealand, Russia, South America, United Kingdom and United States.

Thompson & Morgan (UK) Ltd, Poplar Lane, Ipswich, Suffolk IP8 3BU, England. *Tel*: (01473) 688588. *Fax*: (01473) 680199.
Category: Employer.

Recruitment speciality: Management and generalist personnel for international seed distributors. Skills in: warehouse duties, data input (VDU), customer care, home workers etc.
Locations: Australia, Canada, Europe, New Zealand, United Kingdom and United States.

Thomson Support Services Ltd, Roentgen Road, Basingstoke, Hampshire RG24 8NG, England. *Tel*: (01256) 331010. *Fax*: (01256) 331011.
Category: Recruitment agency.
Recruitment speciality: Engineers for the electronics industry, software and hardware, design engineers, project managers (research and development), ILS/LSA engineers, quality, proposals/bid engineers, sales and marketing, systems design engineers, maintenance and installation.
Locations: Asia, Europe, Far East, Middle East and United Kingdom.

Total Technology (Northern) Ltd, 110/115 Corn Exchange Buildings, Cathedral Street, Manchester, Greater Manchester M4 3BN, England. *Tel*: (0161) 832 1675. *Fax*: (0161) 832 1681.
Category: Recruitment agency.
Recruitment speciality: Management, specialist technical and support personnel on a contract basis, within the power generation, process plant, petrochemical, oil and gas, construction and building services industries.
Locations: Asia, Europe, Far East, Middle East and United Kingdom.

Trafalgar Personnel Ltd, Townfield House, 27/29 Townfield Street, Chelmsford, Essex CM1 1QL, England. *Tel*: (01245) 496111. *Fax*: (01245) 344615.
Category: Recruitment agency.
Recruitment specialty: Senior executive, management and technical support personnel for the building and civil engineering industries. Permanent and contract assignments for consulting engineers, developers, architects and all associated mechanical and electrical contractors and consultants. Specialists for the design and construction of major projects mostly for overseas assignments.
Locations: Africa, Asia, Europe, Far East, Middle East and Near East.

TRG European, 21 Lovat Lane, London EC3R 8EB, England. *Tel*: (0171) 283 6794/(0171) 236 2661. *Fax*: (0171) 929 5706/(0171) 621 0286.
Category: Recruitment agency.
Recruitment specialty: Sales personnel, telephonists, engineers, communications support, technical support, network controllers etc.
Locations: Asia, Europe, Far East, Middle East, Near East, South America and United Kingdom.

Turner Facilities Management Ltd, 21 Gatwick Metro Centre, Balcombe Road, Horley, Surrey RH6 9GA, England.
Category: Employer.

Recruitment specialty: Buildings and facilities maintenance engineers and support staff.

Locations: United Kingdom and overseas.

United Medical Enterprises Ltd, Guy's Hospital, 20 Newcomen Street, London SE1 1YR, England. *Tel*: (0171) 387 1898. *Fax*: (0171) 378 0706.

Other offices: 1 in Ireland.

Category: Recruitment agency.

Recruitment specialty: Medical and nursing specialists, paramedical and ancillary support staff including catering, facility engineers, electrical and mechanical engineers and technical support personnel.

Locations: Australia, Middle East, New Zealand and United Kingdom

Vicky Mann & Associates, 39 Bedford Square, London WC1B 3EG, England. *Tel*: (0171) 436 4243. *Fax*: (0171) 436 0211.

Other offices: 1 in the United Kingdom and 3 overseas.

Category: Executive search agency.

Recruitment specialty: Senior executive and management personnel predominantly in public relations, corporate communications, investor relations and public affairs etc.

Locations: Asia, Europe, Far East and United Kingdom.

VIP International, 17 Charing Cross Road, London WC2H OEP, England. *Tel*: (0171) 930 0541. *Fax*: (0171) 930 2860.

Category: Recruitment agency.

Recruitment specialty: Management and support personnel for the hospitality industry.

Locations: Africa, Asia, Australia, Europe, Far East, Ireland, Middle East, Near East, New Zealand, South America and United Kingdom.

VIP International, Chefs International Culinary Division, 17 Charing Cross Road, London WC2H OEP, England. *Tel*: (0171) 930 0541. *Fax*: (0171) 930 2860.

Category: Recruitment agency.

Recruitment specialty: Chefs and other culinary personnel.

Locations: Africa, Asia, Australia, Europe, Far East, Ireland, Middle East, Near East, New Zealand, South America and United Kingdom.

VIP International, Chefs UK Culinary Division, 17 Charing Cross Road, London WC2H OEP, England. *Tel*: (0171) 930 0541. *Fax*: (0171) 930 2860.

Category: Recruitment agency.

Recruitment specialty: Chefs and other culinary personnel.

Locations: Ireland and United Kingdom.

VIP International, Cruise Line & Shipping Division, 17 Charing Cross Road, London WC2H OEP, England. *Tel*: (0171) 930 0541. *Fax*: (0171) 930 2860.

Category: Recruitment agency.

Recruitment specialty: Management and technical support personnel within the cruise and shipping industry.

Locations: Africa, Asia, Australia, Europe, Far East, Ireland, Middle East, Near East, New Zealand, South America and United Kingdom.

VIP International, Executive & Management (Overseas) Division, 17 Charing Cross Road, London WC2H OEP, England. *Tel*: (0171) 930 0541. *Fax*: (0171) 930 2860.

Category: Recruitment agency.

Recruitment specialty: Senior executive, management and technical personnel for most sectors.

Locations: Africa, Asia, Australia, Europe, Far East, Ireland, Middle East, Near East, New Zealand, South America and United Kingdom.

VIP International, Leisure Overseas & UK Division, 17 Charing Cross Road, London WC2H OEP, England. *Tel*: (0171) 930 0541. *Fax*: (0171) 930 2860.

Category: Recruitment agency.

Recruitment specialty: Leisure industry most skills and levels of personnel.

Locations: Africa, Asia, Australia, Europe, Far East, Ireland, Middle East, Near East, New Zealand, South America, and United Kingdom.

Waggett & Company, 4 Clifford Street, London W1X 1RB, England. *Tel*: (0171) 494 2551. Fax: (0171) 439 0222.

Category: Employer.

Recruitment specialty: Manufacturers of pressure vessels and specialist steel structures for the oil, gas, chemical and mining sectors.

Location: Asia.

Additional information: Occasionally require business development personnel to work overseas.

Wallace Hind Associates, 5 Duncan Close, Moulton Park, Northampton, Northamptonshire NN3 6WL, England. *Tel*: (01604) 671176. *Fax*: (01604) 642733.

Category: Recruitment agency.

Recruitment specialty: Senior and other levels of sales personnel in most industries including a specialist interest in engineering, packaging, print, export, chemical and general industrial and commercial sectors and markets.

Location: United Kingdom.

Additional information: Export positions, although based in the United Kingdom, cover countries worldwide.

Westbourne Design Services Ltd, Guardian House, Enoch Lane, Lockwood Scar, Huddersfield, West Yorkshire HD4 6BL, England. *Tel*: (01484) 435800. *Fax*: (01484) 435802.

Category: Recruitment agency.

Recruitment specialty: Technical personnel for the mechanical process and civil engineering industries, hands-on skilled areas such as site supervisors and inspectors.

Locations: Africa, Asia, Europe, Far East, Ireland, Middle East, Near East and United Kingdom.

Wey Personnel, 1 High Street, Godalming, Surrey GU7 1AZ, England. *Tel*: (01483) 414222. *Fax*: (01483) 425437.

Category: Recruitment agency.

Recruitment specialty: Senior engineers, technical and support personnel for the power generation, energy and chemical industries. Also most general office and administrative staff for the United Kingdom.

Locations: Africa, Asia, Europe, Far East, Middle East and United Kingdom.

Windows Resourcing Ltd, Shirley Lodge, 470 London Road, Slough, Berkshire SL3 8QY, England. *Tel*: (01753) 710439. *Fax*: (01753) 540873.

Category: Recruitment agency.

Recruitment specialty: Senior management, technical and support personnel for the IT/computing industry, training, support and development roles, project management, for permanent and contract assignments. Skills include: PC environments, WINDOWS, UNIX, ORACLE, LOTUS etc.

Locations: Europe, Ireland and United Kingdom.

WIR Management, 1/3 Mill Street, Maidstone, Kent ME15 6XW, England. *Tel*: (01622) 662226. *Fax*: (01622) 662069.

Category: Recruitment agency.

Recruitment specialty: Medical specialists, nursing staff, paramedical and support personnel, including medical facility engineers.

Locations: Africa and Middle East.

Workforce International Ltd, 100 Wellington Street, Leeds, West Yorkshire LS1 4LT, England. *Tel*: (01532) 433555. *Fax*: (01532) 457555.

Category: Recruitment agency.

Recruitment specialty: Management, engineering and other technical personnel for the engineering and construction industries. Trades, welders, electricians, fitters etc. and technical specialists such as: CAD operators, general engineers, surveyors etc.

Locations: Asia, Europe, Far East, Middle East and United Kingdom.

Workforce International Ltd, 51 Waterloo Road, Wolverhampton, West Midlands WV1 4QJ, England. *Tel*: (01902) 22224. *Fax*: (01902) 21895.

Category: Recruitment agency.

Recruitment specialty: Management, engineering and other technical personnel for the engineering and construction industries. Trades, welders, electricians, fitters etc. and technical specialists such as: CAD operators, general engineers, surveyors etc.

Locations: Asia, Europe, Far East, Middle East and United Kingdom.

Workforce International Ltd, Spring Court, Spring Road, Hale, Cheshire WA14 2UQ, England. *Tel*: (0161) 929 7007. *Fax*: (0161) 929 7514.
Category: Recruitment agency.
Recruitment specialty: Management, engineering and other technical personnel for the engineering and construction industries. Trades, welders, electricians, fitters etc. and technical specialists such as: CAD operators, general engineers, surveyors etc.
Locations: Asia, Europe, Far East, Middle East and United Kingdom.

World Crews, 52 York Place, Bournemouth, Dorset BH7 6JN, England. *Tel/Fax*: (01202) 431520.
Category: Recruitment agency.
Recruitment specialty: Crews for private and chartered yachts including: skippers, engineers, chefs, cooks, hostesses, sailing school instructors, deckhands and boat minders.
Locations: Australia, Canada, Caribbean, Europe, Far East, Ireland, Mediterranean, New Zealand, United Kingdom and United States.

World ORT Union, ORT House, 126 Albert Street, London NW1 7NE, England. *Tel*: (0171) 446 8500. *Fax*: (0171) 446 8653.
Category: NGO.
Recruitment specialty: Management, technical and support personnel with overseas teaching, training, project management experience in training, project management experience in agriculture, computer education, mother and childcare, small business development, women in development and most technical and vocational training.
Locations: Africa, Asia, Eastern Europe and South America.
Additional information: The World ORT Union implements technical assistance projects in developing countries.

Wray Partnership, The, 150 Regent Street, London W1R 5FA, England. *Tel*: (0171) 734 9571. *Fax*: (0171) 494 3634.
Category: Recruitment agency.
Recruitment specialty: Senior management and technical personnel within the IT/computing industry, in banking, financial services and insurance and retail specialist areas for permanent and contract assignments.
Locations: Far East and United Kingdom.

Wright Matsui Association Japan, 8/16 Mirokuji, 3 Chome, Fujisawa-Shi, Kanagawa, 251 Japan. *Tel/Fax*: 00 81 466 28 0023.
Category: Recruitment agency.
Recruitment specialty: Management personnel for the construction industry in most specialty areas, civil engineering, building, building services, quantity surveying etc. for consulting engineers, international contractors and

professional quantity surveying firms.

Locations: Africa, Asia, Europe, Far East, Middle East, Near East and South America.

WS Recruitment, Cottrell House, High Street, Angmering, West Sussex BN16 4AE, England. *Tel*: (01903) 786199. *Fax*: (01903) 787616.

Category: Recruitment agency.

Recruitment specialty: Senior management and technical personnel for the oil and gas, petrochemical industries. Specialty areas include: design, construction, production, drilling safety etc.

Locations: Africa, Far East, Middle East and South America.

Wynnwith Engineering Co Ltd, Aviation Division, Commercial House, Chapel Street, Woking, Surrey GU21 1BY, England. *Tel*: (01483) 748201. *Fax*: (01483) 772222.

Category: Recruitment agency.

Recruitment specialty: Management, technical and support personnel for the aviation industry.

Locations: Asia, Caribbean, Europe, Middle East and United Kingdom.

Wynnwith Engineering Co Ltd, Electrical and Building Services Division, Commercial House, Chapel Street, Woking, Surrey GU21 1BY, England. *Tel*: (01483) 748202. *Fax*: (01483) 772222.

Category: Recruitment agency.

Recruitment specialty: Management, technical and support personnel for the building, electrical, mechanical and petrochemical industries and specialist areas.

Locations: Asia, Caribbean, Europe, Middle East and United Kingdom.

Wynnwith Engineering Co Ltd, IT & Telecommunications Division, Commercial House, Chapel Street, Woking, Surrey GU21 1BY, England. *Tel*: (01483) 748203. *Fax*: (01483) 772222.

Category: Recruitment agency.

Recruitment specialty: Management, technical and support personnel for the IT/computing industry, telecommunications etc.

Locations: Asia, Caribbean, Europe, Middle East and United Kingdom.

Appendix
Firms and Offices by Recruitment Specialty

This appendix lists firms and offices by recruitment specialty. Look in it for your preferred field(s) of work, and then locate the relevant firms either in the list of consultancy services (pages 15–105) or in the list of agencies and employers (pages 107–182). Note that some firms appear in both lists.

Account executives, Crone Corkill
  Raymond Laurence
Accountancy, Ahnkwon & Seihwa
  Arthur Morris
  ASA International
  Barchester Royce
  Beament Leslie Thomas
  Bouresli Auditing Office
  Campbell Birch Executive
    Recruitment
  Chuo Audit Corporation
  Colombo Fiduciaria
  CONTAX Gesellschaft
  Denge Denetim Yeminli Mali
    Musavirlik Anonim Sirketi
  Douglas Llambias
  Dr Helmut Fischer & Dr Bertram
    Fischer
  Dr W Meili & Partner AG
  Dr W Schlage & Company
  Drake International
  Dutton International
  Ellis Employment
  Firstaff Personnel Consultants
  FM Recruitment
  FSS Group
  Goh Tan & Company
  Goldsmith Fox PKF
  Grafton Recruitment
  Harel Drouin & Associes
  Hellinger Hahnemann Schulte-Gross
    & Partner
  Hill & Company
  Hoggett Bowers
  Hunters Search & Selection

HZ Praha sro
Industrie-und Verkehrstreuhand
International Auditing
Irish Recruitment Consultants
KPMG Management Consultants
Martin Jarvie Underwood & Hall
MCD
Morris Brankin & Company
NRC Recruitment Specialist
Pannell Kerr Forster
Partners In Recruitment
PKF Consulting
PKF Euroconsult GmbH
PKF Hellas
Price Waterhouse
Ross Melville PKF
Scot Contracts Company
Sherry Sherratt Technical
  Recruitment
Smythe Ratcliffe
T. N. Soong & Company
Thomas Le C. Kuen & Company
Thomas Mining Associates
Tilintarkastajien Oy-Ernst & Young
Activity instructors, PGL Young
  Adventure
Actuarial, Christopher Murray
  Towers Perrin
Administrators, Crone Corkill
Advertising, Bilinguagroup
  Harrison Jones Associates
Aeronautical Engineering, Haztek
  Executive Search
Aerospace, Aeroquip EID
  Alan Davis & Associates

Beechwood Recruitment
Butler International
CDI International
Commissioning & Technical Services
ESDU International
Hoggett Bowers
Horton International
Hunterskil Howard
ISIS Consultants
JED Consultants
Jonathan Lee Technical Recruitment
Premmit Associates
Prime Recruitment Contracts
Strongfield Engineering
Strongfield International
TDM Europe
TDM Technical Services
Varley Walker
Agriculture, Cargill Technical Services
Christopher Murray
NRC Recruitment Specialist
World ORT Union
Aircraft personnel, Butler International
CTS International
MPI Aviation
Architecture, DJ Mills Management
Eden Brown Recruitment
Euro Elite Consultants
ORS Recruitment
Professional & Engineering
Consultants
Trafalgar Personnel
Asset and liability management, NPA
Management Services
Au pairs, Au Pair In America
Avalon Au Pairs
Bees Knees Agency
Euro Pair Agency
Janet White Agency
Problems Unlimited Agency
Auditing, Arthur Andersen
CONTAX Gesellschaft
Pannell Kerr Forster
Automation, JED Consultants
Automotive, Aeroquip EID
Beechwood Recruitment
CCL Recruitment International
CDI International
GPW Search & Selection
Hawtal Whiting Holdings
Horton International
Jacob Partnership

Mascotech Engineering Europe
Rosta Engineering
Rugby Design & Engineering Services
Steel Dixon & Associates
Strongfield Engineering
Strongfield International
Technicon
Varley Walker
Aviation, Capital Group
Grafton Recruitment
MPI Aviation
Parc Aviation
Parc Workforce
Staffaire
Strongfield Aviation
Strongfield International
Team One Recruitment
Wynnwith Engineering
Avionics, Datel Staff Contracting
Banking, Alexander Mann Associates
Amanda Barrington Appointments
Aston Zoraster
Bilinguagroup
Douglas Llambias
ERAS
Executive Choice
Humana International Group
Hunters Search & Selection
LKRC
Management Search International
Morgan Stanley
NPA Management Services
Right International
Wray Partnership
Bilingual, Bilinguagroup
Boyce Agency
Crone Corkill
Drake International
Sheila Burgess International
Bioscience, Euromedica
Biotech, PIA
Premmit Associates
Boat minders, World Crews
Bridge and road engineering, Boyden
Executive Search & Selection
Brown & Root
Euro Elite Consultants
Morgan Bryant Personnel
Building industry, AIL International
Anders Glaser Willis
Daulton Construction Personnel
DJ Mills Management

Hill McGlynn
LJB & Company
Network Recruitment
Pipco
Prime Recruitment Contracts
Recruitment Holdings
Rugby Design & Engineering Services
Santos Engineering Services
Staffaire
Total Technology (Northern)
Trafalgar Personnel
Wright Matsui Association Japan
Wynnwith Engineering
Business services, CONTAX
   Intercai Mondiale
   PKF
   Wetherby
Buyers, Career Management
   International
   Eden Brown Recruitment
   Quarry Dougall Retail Sales &
     Marketing
   Scot Contracts Company
Cabin staff, Strongfield Aviation
   Strongfield International
Cable TV, Anthony Benjamin
   International
   Bull Thompson International
   Butler International
CAD designers, Mascotech Engineering
   Europe
Capital goods, Jonathan Lee Technical
   Recruitment
Catalogues, DM Management
   Consultants
Catering, DH Associates
   Grafton Recruitment
   PGL Young Adventure
   United Medical Enterprises
   VIP International
   World Crews
Cement, Santos Engineering Services
Change management, James Lambert
   Consulting
Chemical engineering, ESDU
   International
   FHELP Marketing
   Haztek Executive Search
   Rosta Engineering
   Waggett & Company
   Wallace Hind Associates
   Wey Personnel

Chemical industry, Cappo International
   Carlcrest
   CSL Recruitment
   European Project Consultants
   Griffon Management
   ISIS Consultants
   Management Search International
   Moore Control & Engineering
   Morgan Bainbridge
   O'Loughlin Partnership
   Penspen
   Varley Walker
Civil engineering, Acer Consultants
   Anders Glaser Wills
   Ashbrittle
   Beechwood Recruitment
   BePos
   Boyden Executive Search & Selection
   Brunel Recruitment
   Butler International
   Campbell Birch Executive Recruitment
   Daulton Construction Personnel
   DJ Mills Management
   Dutton International
   Eden Brown Recruitment
   Engineering Resource Management
   Global Reflex Corporation
   Heads Employment
   Hunter Personnel Contracts
   Ling Recruitment International
   MacGregor Energy Services
   Matchtech Engineering
   Moore Control & Engineering
   Morgan Bryant Personnel
   Mott MacDonald
   Onstream
   ORS Recruitment International
   Peter Glaser & Associates
   Prime Recruitment Contracts
   Professional & Engineering
     Consultants
   Professional Management Resources
   Santos Engineering Services
   Shanahan Engineering
   Sherry Sherratt Technical Recruitment
   Strongfield Engineering
   Strongfield International
   Thomas Mining Associates
   Trafalgar Personnel
   Westbourne Design Services
   Wright Matsui Association Japan
Client server, James Lambert Consulting

Commercial, ADA/Austin Knight
  Campbell Birch Executive
    Recruitment
  Humana International Group
  Hunters Search & Selection
  Network Recruitment
  Reclamebureau Timmermans
  Reynell
Commissioning, Heads Employment
  Marchfield Engineering
  Merz & McLellan
  Moore Control & Engineering
  NES Overseas
  Shanahan Engineering
  Swan Recruitment
  UK Inspection
Communications, Circuit Resources
  Goodman Graham & Associates
  ISIS Consultants
Companions, Bees Knees Agency
Compensation reward, Hewitt Associates
Computing consultants, Renaissance
  Solutions
Construction, ABB Higrade Resources
  Alasdair Graham Associates
  Ashbrittle
  Barchester Royce
  Boyden Executive Search & Selection
  Campbell Birch Executive
    Recruitment
  Career Management International
  Commissioning & Technical Services
  Contracts Consultancy
  CSL Recruitment
  Daulton Construction Personnel
  DJ Mills Management
  Eden Brown Recruitment
  Engineering Resource Management
  Eskal Strategic Resources
  European Project Consultants
  Global Reflex Corporation
  Grafton Recruitment
  Harrison Jones Associates
  Heads Employment
  Heston (Middle East)
  Horton International
  ISIS Consultants
  Jacob Partnership
  Ling Recruitment International
  LJB & Company
  Management Search International
  Marchfield Engineering

  Merz & McLellan
  Morgan Bryant Personnel
  NES Overseas
  Network Overseas
  Nicholas Associates
  ORS Recruitment International
  Parc Workforce
  Peter Glaser & Associates
  Peter Stoner & Associates
  Pipco
  Professional Management Resources
  Project Resourcing
  Randstad Inter Engineering
  Recruitment Holdings
  Santos Engineering Services
  Sherwood Engineering Recruitment
  Staffaire
  Staffwise Technical
  STM Recruitment International
  Swan Recruitment
  Technostaff
  Thomas Mining Associates
  Torres & Partners
  Total Technology (Northern)
  UK Inspection
  Varley Walker
  Workforce International
  Wright Matsui Association Japan
Consultants, Hutchinson's Recruitment
  Trafalgar Personnel
  Wright Matsui Association Japan
Consumer electronics, Hunterskil Howard
  Kilvington Saville & Partners
Contract catering, Dutton International
Contract management, Morgan Bryant
  Personnel
  Peter Stoner & Associates
Cooks, World Crews
Corporate advisory services, Pannell Kerr
  Forster
Corporate communications, AAD
  Executive Selection
  Vicky Mann & Associates
Cosmetic industry, O'Loughlin
  Partnership
Cost analysis, Mascotech Engineering
  Europe
Cost and planning engineering, Contracts
  Consultancy
Cost control, Project Management
  Professional Services
Cotton industry, Cargill Technical

Services
Credit control, Firstaff Personnel
    Consultants
Cruise lines, VIP International
Cryogenics, European Project
    Consultants
Customer service, Crone Corkill
    Intercai Mondiale
    Thompson & Morgan
Customs and duties, Beament Leslie
    Thomas
Data warehousing, James Lambert
    Consulting
Datacommunications, Hamilton Parker
    Associates
    Paradigm Associates
    Weltec
Dealing room systems, Executive Choice
Deck hands, World Crews
Defence industry, Commissioning &
    Technical Services
    Hoggett Bowers
    Hunters Search & Selection
    ISIS Consultants
    John Prodger Recruitment
    Premmit Associates
Derivatives sales, NPA Management
    Services
Desalination, CSL Recruitment
Design and construction engineering,
    Rosta Engineering
    Trafalgar Personnel
Design engineering, Aker Oil & Gas
    Technology
    Aquinas
    Brunel Recruitment
    Campbell Birch Executive
        Recruitment
    Career Management International
    Eden Brown Recruitment
    Euro Elite Consultants
    Fasttrack Recruitment
    Hamilton Parker Associates
    Intereurope Recruitment
    Marchfield Engineering
    Merz & McLellan
    MPI
    MPI Personnel
    NES Overseas
    PHDS Engineering Group
    Randstad Inter Engineering
    Swan Recruitment

TDM Europe
TDM Technical Services
Teknica UK
Thomson Support Services
UK Inspection
Design management, Parc Workforce
Designer engineering, Parc Workforce
    Professional & Engineering
    Consultants
Desk top publishing (DTP), Harriet
    Gabb Recruitment
Distribution, Aston Zoraster
    BJD Logistics
    Bull Thompson International
    Campbell Birch Executive
        Recruitment
    Merz & McLellan
    Varley Walker
Domestic, Lucy Locketts Nanny Agency
Drainage, Euro Elite Consultants
Draughting technicians, Intereurope
    Recruitment
Drilling engineers, Ranger Oil
Drinks industry, Keith Townrow &
    Partners
Economics, Cargill Technical Services
    Intercai Mondiale
Editorial, Maine Tucker Recruitment
    Consultants
    Staniforth Endsor & Partners
Education, Varley Walker
Electrical contractors, Trafalgar Personnel
Electrical engineering, BePos
    Boyden Executive Search & Selection
    Cappo International
    DBM International
    DJ Mills Management
    Dutton International
    Firstaff Personnel Consultants
    Global Reflex Corporation
    Heads Employment
    Hunter Personnel Contracts
    Jacob Partnership
    JED Consultants
    Ling Recruitment International
    Management Search International
    Mascotech Engineering Europe
    Morgan Bryant Personnel
    Mott MacDonald
    Pipco
    Prime Recruitment Contracts
    Rugby Design & Engineering Services

Shanahan Engineering
Sherry Sherratt Technical Recruitment
Staffwise Technical
STM Recruitment International
Thomas Mining Associates
United Medical Enterprises
Varley Walker
Wynnwith Engineering
Electricity generation, Horton
    International
Electronic engineering, Beechwood
    Recruitment
Butler International
Cliveden Technical Recruitment
Datel Staff Contracting
ISIS Consultants
Jacob Partnership
John Prodger Recruitment
Jonathan Lee Technical Recruitment
Merc Partners
MPI
MPI Personnel
NRC Recruitment Specialist
Scot Contracts Company
STM Recruitment International
Strongfield Engineering
Strongfield International
Technostaff
Thomson Support Services
Varley Walker
Electronics industry, Alan Davis &
    Associates
Premmit Associates
Randall Massey Consultants
Energy, ABB Higrade Resources
ISIS Consultants
JED Consultants
Macmillan Davies Consultants
Wey Personnel
Engineering consultants, Hunter
    Personnel Contracts
Engineering curtain walling, Barchester
    Royce
Engineering design, ABB Higrade
    Resources
Human Engineering
Jacob Partnership
Ling Recruitment International
ORS Recruitment International
Technicon
Wetherby
Engineering drilling, Sperry Sun Drilling

    Services
Engineering, Head Hunt International
Engineering – highways, Peter Glaser &
    Associates
Engineering – installation, Moore Control
    & Engineering
Engineering – maintenance, Turner
    Facilities Management
Engineering – process, Offshore Design
Engineering – refining, ORS Recruitment
    International
Engineering – sales, Human Engineering
Engineering – tunnelling, Hunter
    Personnel   Contracts
Entertainment, Bull Thompson
    International
Environmental, Acer Consultants
INTEC UK
ISIS Consultants
Mott MacDonald
Peter Glaser & Associates
Executive, Adderley Featherstone
Kanoo Group
Export industry, John Richards
    Associates
Scientific Staff Consultants
Wallace Hind Associates
Extractive engineering, Thomas Mining
    Associates
Facilities, Metzger Recruitment
    Consultants
SSR Group Services
United Medical Enterprises
Film, Amanda Barrington Appointments
KirchGruppe
Finance, Aston Zoraster
Barnett Consulting Services
Bull Thompson International
Capita Recruitment Services
Douglas Llambias
FM Recruitment
FSS Europe
FSS Group
Management Search International
Premmit Associates
Torres & Partners
Wetherby
Financial analysts, Campbell Birch
    Executive Recruitment
Financial, Anglo Arabian Services
Antal International
ARA International

Charity People
Christopher Murray
Firstaff Personnel Consultants
Firth & Associates
Hoggett Bowers
Liebrecht Persona Iwerbung
Reclamebureau Timmermans
Reynell
Financial control, Morgan Bryant
   Personnel
Financial dealers, Oriel Search
Financial planning, Intercai Mondiale
Financial services, AAD Executive
   Selection
Accord Group Tyzack
ADA/Austin Knight
Adamson & Partners
Alexander Mann Associates
ASA International
Austin Knight
Consult
Ellis Employment
ERAS
FSS Financial Selection Services
Goodman Graham & Associates
Head Hunt International
Hillman Saunders
Horton International
IPS Accountancy Recruitment
IPS Contract Management
IPS Financial Services
Macmillan Davies Consultants
Merc Partners
Morgan Bainbridge
O'Connell Associates
Right International
Wray Partnership
Flight crew, Parc Aviation
Strongfield Aviation
Strongfield International
FMCG, Accord Group Tyzack
Aston Zoraster
Bull Thompson International
Human Engineering
Macmillan Davies Consultants
Management Search International
Morgan Bainbridge
Portman Price
Torres & Partners
Food industry, Aston Zoraster
Cargill Technical Services
Carlcrest

Foodjobs
Griffon Management
Helix Recruitment
Keith Townrow & Partners
McCourt Newton Consulting Group
Morgan & Day
NRC Recruitment Specialist
Petrolic Consultants
PIA
Foreign exchange, NPA Management
   Services
Fund raising, Charity People
General administrative, LKRC
   Middleton Jeffers Recruitment
General business sectors, Humana
   International Group
General commercial, Austin Knight
   Bull Thompson International
General engineering, AAD Executive
   Selection
Anglo Arabian Services
Barnett Consulting Services
Bull Thompson International
Capital Group
Castlebay
Chiyoda International
Christopher Murray
Cliveden Technical Recruitment
Commissioning & Technical Services
Contracts Consultancy
Dawood Consultants
Fastec
Fasttrack Recruitment
Foodjobs
GPW Search & Selection
Harrison Jones Associates
Hartley Services
Heston (Middle East)
Human Engineering
Hunter Personnel Contracts
INTEC UK
Interacto Services
Intereurope Recruitment
Macmillan Davies Consultants
Mandeville Resources
Mascotech Engineering Europe
Meridian Technical Recruitment
MPI
MSL International
NRC Recruitment Specialist
Offshore Design
Paradigm Associates

Peter Stoner & Associates
Roevin Management Services
Rowan Resources
Seaforth Maritime
Sherry Sherratt Technical Recruitment
Sherwood Engineering Recruitment
SSR Group Services
TA Engineering Services
Torres & Partners
Wallace Hind Associates
Weltec
Workforce International
General executive and management,
    Ashton Penny Partnership
Barry Latchford Associates
Bartwell International
Boyden Executive Search & Selection
DHA Resourcing Solutions
DRAX Dearman Associates
Federal Resources Europe
Finlayson Wagner & Black
Herst Austin Rowley
Hoskyns Consulting
Howgate Sable & Partners
Marque Executive Resourcing
Morgan & Banks
Motor Trade Selection
Nicholson International
PA Consulting Group
Phil Vignoles Associates
REL Consultancy Group
Spiers Ayres Townshend
Staniforth Endsor & Partners
Theaker Monro & Newman
VIP International
General executive and technical,
    Andromedia
General executive, management and
    technical, Cognos International
CTC Consulting
Dickens Hazell & Associates
Digby Morgan Consulting
Eurosearch Associates
Grafton Recruitment
Hanover Fox International
Hunter Staff Consultants
Hutchinson's Recruitment
IMMC
InterExec Career Management
Job Maeglerne
Knight Chapman
KPMG Management Consulting

McCann Erickson Recruitment
Millar Associates
Montaner & Asociados
Norma Consulting
Paradigm Associates
Robert Walters Associates
Simpson Crowden Consultants
Vantage Management Consultants
General industrial, Austin Knight
CB Linnell
Grafton Recruitment
Liebrecht Persona Iwerbung GmbH
General management, AAD Executive
    Selection
ABB Higrade Resources
Anglo Arabian Services
Douglas Llambias
Firth & Associates
Hamilton Parker Associates
Kramer Westfield
Rowan Resources
General management and technical,
    Axone Consultants
Cannon Persona International
    Recruitment
Conker
CRC Direct
Emigration Consultancy Services
European Human Resource
    Consultants
INTEC UK
IPS Group
Premier International Consultants
Progressive Computer Recruitment
Reed Overseas
General project management, World ORT
    Union
General secretarial, Firstaff Personnel
    Consultants
LKRC
Maine Tucker Recruitment
    Consultants
Middleton Jeffers Recruitment
General technical, Hartley Services
Geologists, Thomas Mining Associates
Geotechnical, Euro Elite Consultants
Hill McGlynn
Graduates, Acer Consultants
Executive Recruitment Services
KPMG Management Consultants
LKRC
Maine Tucker Recruitment

Consultants
Meridian Technical Recruitment
Mott MacDonald
Rada Recruitment Communications
Scorex (UK)
Graphic design, Staniforth Endsor &
    Partners
Group leaders, PGL Young Adventure
Health & safety, Aker Oil & Gas
    Technology (UK)
    Haztek Executive Search
    INTEC UK
    Scot Contracts Company
    SSR Group Services
Healthcare, Action Health
    Adamson & Partners
    Angel International Recruitment
    ARA International
    Bull Thompson International
    Career International Recruitment
    Ellis Employment
    Euromedica
    Executive Facilities (Maidenhead)
    Fairstaff Agency
    FHELP Marketing
    Grafton Recruitment
    Healthcall Euromed
    Merc Partners
    Morgan Bainbridge
    Morgan Bryant Personnel
    Network Overseas
    Parc Workforce
    Portman Price
    Scientific Staff Consultants
    Sherry Sherratt Technical Recruitment
    United Medical Enterprises
    WIR Management
High tech, Alan Davis & Associates
    Contracts Consultancy
Hospitality industry, Berkeley Scott Group
    Ellis Employment
    Hospitality Group Worldwide
    VIP International
Hotels and catering, Action Recruitment
    Bull Thompson International
    FM Recruitment
    Keystone Recruitment Consultants
Housekeepers, Bees Knees Agency
Human resources, AAD Executive
    Selection
    Campbell Birch Executive
        Recruitment

Cole Henry Associates
Consult
Crone Corkill
Harrison Jones Associates
Hewitt Associates
Nichols Consultancy
NRC Recruitment Specialist
Paradigm Associates
Premmit Associates
SAS Executive Recruitment
Wetherby
Hygiene, Foodjobs
Hypermedia, Offshore Design
Import and export, Bilinguagroup
Industrial catering, Drake International
Industrial electronics, Hunterskil Howard
Industrial engineering, Morgan & Day
    (Europe)
    Network Recruitment
Industrial executive and technical, ADA/
    Austin Knight
Industrial sector, Reclamebureau
    Timmermans
    Reynell
Information industry, TFPL
Information technology, AAD Executive
    Selection
    ABB Higrade Resources
    Accord Group Tyzack
    Alan Davis & Associates
    Anthony Benjamin & Associates
    ARA International
    Campbell Birch Executive
        Recruitment
    CDI International
    DM Management Consultants
    Dutton International
    ERAS
    Hoggett Bowers
    Hunters Search & Selection
    Kuwait Oil Company
    NES Overseas
    Spitfire Selection
    Staffwise Technical
    Torres & Partners
    Varley Walker
    Wetherby
Insolvency, CONTAX Gesellschaft
    Pannell Kerr Forster
Inspection, INTEC UK
    Mactech Inspection
    Moore Control & Engineering

UK Inspection
Weltec
Installation, UK Inspection
Instrumentation, Cappo International
Dutton International
Global Reflex Corporation
Heads Employment
Morgan Bryant
Shanahan Engineering
Staffwise Technical
Insurance, Christopher Murray
Hillman Saunders
Hunters Search & Selection
Insurance Personnel Services
IPS Accountancy Recruitment
IPS Group
Right International
Wray Partnership
Interim management, Campbell Birch
    Executive Recruitment
Capita Recruitment Services
PA Consulting Group
Internet, TFPL
Interpreters, Bilinguagroup
Boyce Agency
Investment banking, LKRC
Investor relations, Vicky Mann &
    Associates
Iron and steel processing, Morgan Bryant
Personnel
IT/Computing industry, Acetech Personnel
Alba International
AMS Management Systems
Aston Zoraster
Audiobyte Business Consultants
Austin Harrison Worldwide
Barchester Royce
Beechwood Recruitment
Bull Thompson International
Capita Recruitment Services
Certes Computing
Charity People
Circuit Resources
Cliveden Technical Recruitment
CMG
Comms People
Computec International Resources
Computer People International
Computer People South
Computer Team Group
Computer Resource Centre
Compuvac

CTA International Search & Selection
Dalroth & Partners
Dart Resourcing Group
Datel Staff Consulting
Dawood Consultants
DBM International
DP Group
DS Group
EAE Manpower
Eagling Computer Services
Earl Associates
EC Consultants
Elan Communications
Ellis Employment
ESDU International
Eurolink Group
Eurosoft Services
Executive Facilities (Maidenhead)
Executive Recruitment Services
First (1st) Future
Firstaff Personnel Consultants
Footprint Computer
Gatton Consulting Group
Goodman Graham & Associates
Grafton Recruitment
Hamilton Parker Associates
Hanover Matrix
Hawtal Whiting Holdings
Head Hunt International
Horton International
Human Engineering
Hunters Search & Selection
Hunterskil Howard
IBNIX
Information Management Resources
Ingineur Software Solutions
Intereurope Recruitment
Intermanagement Group
Internet Search & Selection
Intertech Computer Consultants
Irish Recruitment Consultants
ISIS Consultants
Jacob Partnership
James Baker Associates
John Prodger Recruitment
Kestrel Consulting
Kilvington Saville & Partners
Kramer Westfield
Leading Edge Consulting
LJB & Company
LKRC
Logica United Kingdom

Macmillan Davies Consultants
McGregor Boyall Associates
Merc Partners
Montreal Associates
Morgan Bainbridge
MRK Consulting
Multicom UK
Nucleus Associates
Parallel International
Parc Workforce
Portman Price
Premmit Associates
Prime Recruitment Contracts
Pro Fit Computer Recruitment
Professional & Engineering
 Consultants
Professional Management Resources
Recruitment Holdings
Relational Designers
Resources International
Right International
Rugby Design & Engineering Services
SBS
Sector Personnel
Selected Options
Silicon Valley Group
Southwest Computer Resources
STM Recruitment International
Strongfield Engineering
Strongfield International
Tangent International
TDM Europe
TDM Technical Services
Technostaff
Thomson Support Services
TRG European
Triage
Windows Resourcing
Wray Partnership
Wynnwith Engineering
Laboratory, Foodjobs
Land and hydrographic surveying, Career
 Management International
Languages, Middleton Jeffers Recruitment
Legal, ASA International
 Beament Leslie Thomas
 Bilinguagroup
 Campbell Birch Executive
 Recruitment
 Christopher Murray
 Dutton International
 Ellis Employment

Executive Recruitment Services
Hillman Saunders
Hughes Castell
IPS Legal Recruitment
Management Search International
Quarry Dougall Group
Reynell Legal Recruitment
Leisure industry, Bull Thompson
 International
 FM Recruitment
 Portman Price
 VIP International
Librarians, TFPL
Library software, TFPL
Life and general insurance, Towers Perrin
Light engineering, Jonathan Lee
 Technical Recruitment
Linguistics, Head Hunt International
Livestock, Cargill Technical Services
Logistics, Aston Zoraster
 BJD Logistics
 DH Associates
 Firstaff Personnel Consultants
 NRC Recruitment Specialist
 Seaforth Maritime
 Staffwise Technical
 Wetherby
Maintenance, DH Associates
 DJ Mills Management
 Morgan Bryant
 Network Overseas
 Offshore Design
 Shanahan Engineering
 Strongfield Aviation
 Strongfield International
Management and technical, Overseas
 Development Administration
Management consultancy, BFC
 Consultancy Services
 Hunters Search & Selection
 LKRC
 Pannell Kerr Forster Associates
 Portman Price
Manufacturing industry, AAD Executive
 Selection
 Accord Group Tyzack
 Aston Zoraster
 Butler International
 Career Management International
 CDI International
 Christopher Murray
 DBM International

Firstaff Personnel Consultants
Firth & Associates
Hawtal Whiting Holdings
Irish Recruitment Consultants
ISIS Consultants
Lisega
Macmillan Davies Consultants
McCourt Newton Consulting Group
NRC Recruitment Specialist
Parc Workforce
Partners in Recruitment
PHDS Engineering Group
Professional & Engineering
    Consultants
Staffwise Technical
Technostaff
TEK Personnel Consultants
Torres & Partners
Wetherby
Manufacturing – medical, Helix
    Recruitment
Manufacturing – oil and gas, Waggett
    &   Company
Manufacturing – plastics and packaging,
    Conrad Taylor Marketing
Manufacturing – scientific equipment,
    Helix Recruitment
Marine and coastal design, Euro Elite
    Consultants
Marine, Alasdair Graham Associates
Marine and port operations, CSL
    Recruitment
Marine engineering, Butler International
    MacGregor Energy Services
    Morgan Bryant Personnel
    Prime Recruitment Contracts
    Seaforth Maritime
    STM Recruitment International
    World Crews
Marketing, Anglo Arabian Services
    Astles Partnership
    Cargill Technical Services
    Charity People
    Connect Medical Recruitment
    Crone Corkill
    DM Management Consultants
    Ellis Employment
    Ennismore Partnership
    First (1st) Future
    Focus Executive
    Foodjobs
    Intercai Mondiale

Kramer Westfield
Metzger Recruitment Consultants
Michael J Stevens Human Resource
    Consultancy
Portman Price
Premmit Associates
Quarry Dougall Retail Sales &
    Marketing
SAS Executive Recruitment
Materials, Hill McGlynn
    NRC Recruitment Specialist
    O'Loughlin Partnership
    Partners In Recruitment
Mathematical sciences, ESDU
    International
Mechanical engineering, BePos
    Boyden Executive Search & Selection
    Campbell Birch Executive
        Recruitment
    Cappo International
    DBM International
    DJ Mills Management
    Dutton International
    ESDU International
    Firstaff Personnel Consultants
    Global Reflex Corporation
    Heads Employment
    Hunter Personnel Contracts
    Jacob Partnership
    JED Consultants
    Management Search International
    Moore Control & Engineering
    Morgan Bryant Personnel
    Mott MacDonald
    Pipco
    Prime Recruitment Contracts
    Rugby Design & Engineering Services
    Shanahan Engineering
    Sherry Sherratt Technical Recruitment
    STM Recruitment International
    Thomas Mining Associates
    Trafalgar Personnel
    United Medical Enterprises
    Varley Walker
Media, Accord Group Tyzack
    Amanda Barrington Appointments
    Goodman Graham & Associates
    Rada Recruitment Communications
Medical devices, O'Loughlin Partnership
Merchandisers, Quarry Dougall Retail
        Sales & Marketing
Merchant banking, Hunters Search &

Selection
Metallurgists, Thomas Mining Associates
Microbiology, Foodjobs
Military equipment, Datel Staff
    Contracting
Mining, Hunter Personnel Contracts
    Thomas Mining Associates
    Waggett & Company
Monolingual secretarial, Euro Secretaries
Mother and childcare, World ORT Union
Mother's help, Problems Unlimited
    Agency
Motor industry, Christopher Murray
Multi media industry, Dart Resourcing
    Group
Multilingual secretarial, Euro Secretaries
Nannies, Bees Knees Agency
    Janet White Agency
    Lucy Locketts Nanny Agency
    Nanny Service
    Regency Nannies
Natural resources development, Cargill
    Technical Services
Not For Profit sector, Charity People
Nuclear industry, Carlcrest
    Commissioning & Technical Services
    McGregor Energy Services
    Matchtech Engineering
Occupational health, Drake International
Office management, Maine Tucker
    Recruitment Consultants
Oil & gas, ABB Higrade Resources
    Abu Dhabi Gas Liquefaction
    Aker Oil & Gas Technology
    Alasdair Graham Associates
    Alba
    Aquinas
    ARA
    Beechwood Recruitment
    Camco Drilling
    Cappo International
    Career Management
    Carlcrest
    Castlebay
    CLEAS
    Contracts Consultancy
    CSL
    CST
    EM Engineering
    Eskal Strategic Resources
    European Project Consultancy
    Global Reflex Corporation

Harrison Jones Associates
Heston (Middle East)
Hoggett Bowers
Horton International
JED Consultants
Kuwait Oil Company
MacGregor Energy Services
Management Search International
Moore Control & Engineering
Morgan & Day (Europe)
NES Overseas
Network Overseas
Offshore Design
Onstream
ORS Recruitment International
Parc Apollo Technical Services
Penspen
Petrolic Consultants
PIA
Prime Recruitment Contracts
Professional & Engineering
    Consultants
Professional Management Resources
Recruitment Holdings
Roxby Engineering International
Santos Engineering Services
Shanahan Engineering
Shaw & Hatton International
Staffwise Technical
Strategic Resources
Swan Recruitment
Total Technology
UK Inspection
WS Recruitment
Oil engineering, Teknica UK
Oil exploration, Enterprise Oil
    Jawaby Oil Service
Oil processing, Ranger Oil
Oil production, CLEAS
    Enterprise Oil
    Jawaby Oil Service
    Ranger Oil
Operations and maintenance, Offshore
    Design
    ORS Recruitment International
Packaging, Partners In Recruitment
    Pendleton Recruitment Consultants
    Varley Walker
    Wallace Hind Associates
Paper industry, Pendleton Recruitment
    Consultants
Pensions, Towers Perrin

Personal assistants, Bilinguagroup
  Harriet Gabb Recruitment
  Maine Tucker Recruitment
    Consultants
Petrochemical industry, ABB Higrade
    Resources
  Abu Dhabi Gas Liquefaction
  Alasdair Graham Associates
  Alba International (IOM)
  Aquinas
  ARA International
  Barchester Royce
  Butler International
  Camco Drilling Group
  Carlcrest
  Castlebay
  CDI International
  Chiyoda International
  Commissioning & Technical Services
  CSL Recruitment
  Dutton International
  Engineering Resource Management
  Eskal Strategic Resources
  FHELP Marketing
  Hoggett Bowers
  Ling Recruitment International
  MacGregor Energy Services
  Matchtech Engineering
  Moore Control & Engineering
  Morgan & Day (Europe)
  Moxon Dolphin Kerby International
  NES Overseas
  Network Overseas
  Onstream
  ORS Recruitment International
  Parc Apollo Technical Services
  Parc Workforce
  Peter Glaser & Associates
  Petrolic Consultants
  PHDS Engineering Group
  Professional & Engineering
    Consultants
  Professional Management Resources
  Rosta Engineering
  Roxby Engineering International
  Santos Engineering Services
  Scot Contracts
  Staffwise Technical
  Swan Recruitment
  Total Technology
  UK Inspection
  Weltec

  WS Recruitment
  Wynnwith Engineering
Petroleum processing, Aker Oil & Gas
    Technology
Pharmaceutical industry, Adamson &
    Partners
  Alan Davis & Associates
  Beechwood Recruitment
  Bull Thompson International
  Carlcrest
  CSL Recruitment
  Euromedica
  European Project Consultants
  Haztek Executive Search
  Macmillan Davies Consultants
  Morgan & Day (Europe)
  O'Loughlin Partnership
  Peter Glaser & Associates
  Petrolic Consultants
  PHDS Engineering Group
  PIA
  Premmit Associates
  Professional & Engineering
    Consultants
  Swan Recruitment
  Varley Walker
Pilots, Parc Aviation
Pipeline construction, Contracts
    Consultancy
Planning and design, Global Reflex
    Corporation
  MPI
  Project Management Professional
    Services
Plastics, McCourt Newton Consulting
    Group
  O'Loughlin Partnership
Power, Strongfield Engineering
  Strongfield International
Power generation, Alasdair Graham
    Associates
  Aquinas
  BePos
  Carlcrest
  Contracts Consultancy
  CSL Recruitment
  Dutton International
  Engineering Resource Management
  Global Reflex Corporation
  MacGregor Energy Services
  Merz & McLellan
  Moore Control & Engineering

Morgan Bryant Personnel
NES Overseas
Parc Apollo Technical Services
Professional Management Resources
Recruitment Holdings
Santos Engineering
Shanahan Engineering
Total Technology
Wey Personnel
Printing industry, Keystone Recruitment
    Consultants
Morgan Bainbridge
Network Recruitment
NRC Recruitment Specialist
Wallace Hind Associates
Privatisation, Cargill Technical Services
Process engineering, ARA International
Ashbrittle
BePos
Butler International
Cappo International
FHELP Marketing
Haztek Executive Search
Jonathan Lee Technical Recruitment
Recruitment Holdings
Swan Recruitment
TASK Contracts
Westbourne Design Services
Process plant, Petrolic Consultants
Total Technology
Procurement, Aker Oil & Gas
    Technology
Contracts Consultancy
NRC Recruitment Specialist
Product development, Foodjobs
Product management, Interacto Services
JED Consultants
John Richards Associates
Production mining, Hunter Personnel
    Contracts
Production, MPI Personnel
Programme management, Mascotech
    Engineering Europe
Project engineering, Brunel Recruitment
Eden Brown Recruitment
Jacob Partnership
Project Management Professional
    Services
TDM Europe
TDM Technical Services
Project management, Boyden Executive
    Search & Selection

Career Management International
Contracts Consultancy
Daulton Construction Personnel
Global Reflex Corporation
Heston (Middle East)
Hill McGlynn
Information Management Resources
INTEC UK
JED Consultants
Kestrel Consulting
Morgan Bryant Personnel
Peter Stoner & Associates
Professional & Engineering
    Consultants
Project Management Professional
    Services
Sherwood Engineering Recruitment
Thomson Support Services
Proofreaders, Staniforth Endsor &
    Partners
Property, Barchester Royce
Public affairs, Vicky Mann & Associates
Public relations, Crone Corkill
Vicky Mann & Associates
Public sector, Reynell
Publishing, Bilinguagroup
Purchasing, Beechwood Recruitment
Campbell Birch Executive
    Recruitment
Foodjobs
Quality assurance, BePos
DBM International
Global Reflex Corporation
Heads Employment
Mactech Inspection
NRC Recruitment Specialist
Scot Contracts Company
Wetherby
Quality consultants, INTEC UK
Quality control, Global Reflex
    Corporation
Hawtal Whiting Holdings
Heads Employment
Hunter Personnel Contracts
Lisega GmbH
Quality management, IQS International
MPI
Quantity surveying, Daulton Construction
    Personnel
Hill McGlynn
Hunter Personnel Contracts
Morgan Bryant Personnel

Peter Stoner & Associates
Sherry Sherratt Technical
  Recruitment
Wright Matsui Association Japan
Quarrying, Thomas Mining Associates
Rail, Euro Elite Consultants
  Jonathan Lee Technical Recruitment
  Prime Recruitment Contracts
  Strongfield Engineering
  Strongfield International
Railway design engineering, Haztek
  Executive Search
Railways, Acer Consultants
  Alasdair Graham Associates
  Butler International
Receptionists, Maine Tucker Recruitment
  Consultants
Refining, FHELP Marketing
Registered nurses, Cambridge Collection
Reliability engineering, Haztek Executive
  Search
Reliability specialists, Human
  Engineering
Research & development, AAD Executive
  Selection
  Beechwood Recruitment
  Hamilton Parker Associates
  Thomson Support Services
Response management, Rada
  Recruitment Communications
Retail, Aston Zoraster
  Bull Thompson International
  Cole Henry
  DH Associates
  Harrison Jones Associates
  Management Search International
  Moore Control & Engineering
  Morgan Bainbridge
  Motor Trade Selection
  Portman Price
  Quarry Dougall Retail Sales &
  Marketing
  Wray Partnership
Risk assessment, Haztek Executive
  Search
  NPA Management Services
Risk management, Arthur Andersen
Roads, Euro Elite Consultants
Rural development, Cargill Technical
  Services
Safety management, Heads Employment
Sailing schools, World Crews

Sales, Anglo Arabian Services
  Astles Partnership
  Bilinguagroup
  Career Management International
  Ellis Employment
  Ennismore Partnership
  First (1st) Future
  Focus Executive
  Hanover Matrix
  Jacob Partnership
  John Richards Associates
  Mandeville Resources
  McMillan Montague
  Metzger Recruitment Consultants
  Michael J Stevens Human Resource
  Consultancy
  NPA Management Services
  Premmit Associates
  Raymond Laurence
  Sales Recruitment Specialist
  Sales Solution
  SAS Executive Recruitment
  Spitfire Selection
  TRG European
Sales and marketing, AAD
  Accord Group Tyzack
  Barnett Consulting
  Beechwood Recruitment
  Campbell Birch Executive
  Recruitment
  Christopher Murray
  Circuit Resources
  Drake International
  Earl Associates
  Executive Choice
  Firstaff Personnel Consultants
  Firth & Associates
  FSS Europe
  Hamilton Parker Associates
  HB Associates
  Head Hunt International
  Helix Recruitment
  Irish Recruitment Consultants
  John Richards Associates
  Network Recruitment
  Nichols Consultancy
  Paradigm Associates
  Quarry Dougall Retail Sales
  Marketing
  Raymond Laurence
  Sales Placement
  Scientific Staff Consultants

SSR Group Services
Steele Dixon & Associates
TFPL
Thomson Support Services
TSA
Torres & Partners
Wetherby
Sales and support, McMillan Montague
Seasonal work, PGL Young Adventure
Secretarial, ASA International
  Bees Knees Agency
  Harriet Gabb Recruitment
  IPS Secretarial Recruitment
  Multilingual Services
Securities, NPA Management Services
Security, SSR Group Services
Seed distribution, Thompson & Morgan
Service industries, Technostaff
Shipbuilding, Matchtech Engineering
  Prime Recruitment Contracts
Shipping, VIP International
Site inspectors, Westbourne Design
  Services
Site management, Peter Stoner &
  Associates
Site supervisors, Westbourne Design
  Services
Skippers, World Crews
Small business development, World ORT
  Union
Space, Strongfield Engineering
  Stats Support Services
  Staniforth Endsor & Partners
Steel production, Moore Control &
  Engineering
Structural design, ORS Recruitment
  International
  Staffwise Technical
Structural engineering, BePos
  Eden Brown Recruitment
  ESDU International
  Heads Employment
  Hunter Personnel Contracts
  Moore Control & Engineering
  Mott MacDonald
  Prime Recruitment Contracts
  Rosta Engineering
  Sherry Sherratt Technical Recruitment
Styling, Hawtal Whiting Holdings
Subsea petroleum drilling, Aker Oil &
  Gas Technology
Surveying, Parc Workforce

System migration, James Lambert
  Consulting
Taxation, Beament Leslie Thomas
  CONTAX Gesellschaft
  Pannell Kerr Forster
Teachers, Inlingua
  International House
  ORS Recruitment International
  Saxoncourt Recruitment
  Tate International
  World ORT Union
Technical and management, Overseas
  Development Administration (ODA)
Technical authors, Campbell Birch
  Executive Recruitment
  Intereurope Recruitment
  Offshore Design
  Staniforth Endsor & Partners
Technical illustrators, Intereurope
  Recruitment
  ORS Recruitment International
Technical sales, Foodjobs
Technical training, Staniforth Endsor &
  Partners
Telecommunications, Accord Group
  Tyzack
  Alan Davis & Associates
  Aston Zoraster
  Beechwood Recruitment
  Bull Thompson International
  Butler International
  Career Management International
  CSL Recruitment
  Datel Staff Contracting
  DBM International
  European Project Consultants
  Hamilton Parker Associates
  Hanover Matrix
  Horton International
  Hunterskil Howard
  Intercai Mondiale
  John Prodger Recruitment
  Kilvington Saville & Partners
  Kramer Westfield
  Macmillan Davies Consultants
  Management Search International
  Merc Partners
  MPI
  MPI Personnel
  NES Overseas
  Paradigm Associates
  Park Workforce

Professional Management Resources
Right International
SAS Executive Recruitment
Steele Dixon & Associates
STM Recruitment International
Strongfield Engineering
Strongfield International
TDM Europe
TDM Technical Services
Torres & Partners
TSA Human Resources
Wynnwith Engineering
Telesales, Mandeville Resources
Sales Recruitment Specialist
Television production, KirchGruppe
Test and development engineering,
     Mascotech Engineering Europe
Timing and release analysts, Mascotech
     Engineering Europe
Trade marks and patents, Adamson &
     Partners
Trading, NPA Management Services
Traffic and transportation, Euro Elite
     Consultants
Training, Campbell Birch Executive
     Recruitment
     IQS International
     Nichols Consultancy
Translators, Bilinguagroup
     Boyce Agency
Transmission engineering, Merz &
     McLellan
Transportation, ABB Higrade Resources
     Aston Zoraster
     BJD Logistics
     Campbell Birch Executive
        Recruitment
     European Project Consultants
     Hawtal Whiting Holdings
     ISIS Consultants
     Rosta Engineering
Travel and expeditions, Encounter
     Overland Expeditions
Treasury, NPA Management Services
Trilingual secretaries, Crone Corkill
TV secretarial, Amanda Barrington

Appointments
Utilities, Butler International
     EM Engineering
     Engineering Resource Management
     Horton International
     ISIS Consultants
     Macmillan Davies Consultants
     Morgan Bryant Personnel
     Professional Management Resources
Validation, Jacob Partnership
Voice/data communication, Anthony
     Benjamin International
Voluntary work, International Voluntary
     Service
Warehousing, Campbell Birch Executive
     Recruitment
     Foodjobs
     NRC Recruitment Specialist
     Thompson & Morgan
Waste disposal, Peter Glaser & Associates
     Rosta Engineering
Water, Acer Consultants
     Alasdair Graham Associates
     Carlcrest
     Commissioning & Technical Services
     EM Engineering
     Global Reflex Corporation
     Horton International
     NES Overseas
     Penspen
     Peter Glaser & Associates
     Petrolic Consultants
     PIA
     Professional Management Resources
     Recruitment Holdings
Water supply, Euro Elite Consultants
Water treatment, CSL Recruitment
     Euro Elite Consultants
     Ling Recruitment International
     Parc Apollo Technical Services
     Rosta Engineering
Wholesale and distribution, Cole Henry
     Associates
Word processing, Maine Tucker
     Recruitment Consultants
Yacht crews, World Crews

HOW TO EMIGRATE
Your complete guide to a successful future overseas

Roger Jones

Would you like to pack your bags, and make a completely new life for yourself overseas? According to a recent poll, thousands of people would, dreaming of a better lifestyle, new horizons and a more rewarding future. But how do you actually go about it? Which countries should you consider, and what visas and permits will you need? In practical steps, this book will set you on the right path, with essential advice and information on weighing up your prospects, choosing the right location, coping with immigration, the actual move, housing, employment and settling in successfully to your new life overseas. Written by a leading writer of books on living and working overseas. 'Very practical and entertaining – I would recommend it.' *Phoenix/ Association of Graduate Careers Advisory Services.*

176pp. illus. 1 85703 101 6.

HOW TO FIND TEMPORARY WORK ABROAD
A world of opportunities for everyone

Nick Vandome

Would you like the chance to work abroad – perhaps to expand your horizons, finance an extended holiday, or use some 'time between'? Whatever your aims and interests, this practical book has something for you. It explains where to find the opportunities suited to your own particular interests, how to apply and be selected, how to manage money, passports, permits, insurance and accommodation, and how to get the most out of your experience overseas. Whether you plan to stay abroad for a couple of weeks or most of the year, this is the book for you, packed with valuable employment advice and contacts. Nick Vandome is a young freelance writer who has spent a year abroad on three occasions, in France, Australia, Africa and Asia. His articles have appeared in *The Guardian, The Scotsman, The Daily Telegraph* and elsewhere. He is also author of *How to Get a Job in Australia* in this series.

160pp. illus. 1 85703 109 1.

OBTAINING VISAS AND WORK PERMITS
How and where to obtain the services of immigration lawyers and consultants worldwide

Roger Jones

Today more people than ever are keen to put down roots in foreign countries on either a temporary or long-term basis. But many need advice on how to surmount the many legal obstacles to taking up residence in a foreign land. This unique guide and directory by the author of *How to Emigrate* lists experts in immigration law and procedures who can guide you through the pitfalls and help you obtain the necessary visas. Whether you are planning to settle abroad or have already made the move and now wish to make your residence permanent, their assistance could be crucial in effecting a successful outcome. The entries in the book have been carefully compiled as a result of detailed questionnairing, and provide a valuable new resource for all visa applicants and professional advisers. Roger Jones is a leading writer and broadcaster on international employment matters who has 12 years' experience of living and working overseas.

144pp. illus. 1 85703 414 7.

HOW TO TRAVEL ROUND THE WORLD
Your practical guide to the experience of a lifetime

Nick Vandome

Fed up with the situation back home? Want to have some fun, adventure and excitement? Then this is the book for you. Written by a travel writer with extensive first-hand knowledge, this book explains how to prepare for a real globetrotting adventure, how to plan your itinerary, how to organise passports, visa permits and other international paperwork, how to plan your means of travel, kitting yourself out, planning for health and safety on the move, learning to live with different languages and cultures, earning as you go, trouble shooting, and more. The book is complete with a gazetteer of international travel information, case studies, contacts for travel, health and work, further reading, and index. Go for it – and give yourself the experience of a lifetime.

224pp. illus. 1 85703 121 0.

HOW TO GET A JOB ABROAD
A handbook of opportunities and contacts

Roger Jones

Now in a fourth fully revised edition, this top-selling title is essential for everyone planning to spend a period abroad. It contains a big reference section of medium and long-term job opportunities and possibilities, arranged by region and country of the world, and by profession/occupation. There are more than 100 pages of specific contacts and leads, giving literally hundreds of updated addresses and much hard-to-find information. There is a classified guide to overseas recruitment agencies, and even a multi-lingual guide to writing application letters. 'A fine book for anyone considering even a temporary overseas job.' *The Evening Star.* 'A highly informative and well researched book ... containing lots of hard information and a first class reference section ... A superb buy.' *The Escape Committee Newsletter.* 'A valuable addition to any careers library.' *Phoenix (Association of Graduate Careers Advisory Services).* 'An excellent addition to any careers library ... Compact and realistic ... There is a wide range of reference addresses covering employment agencies, specialist newspapers, a comprehensive booklist and helpful addresses ... All readers, whether careers officers, young adults or more mature adults, will find use for this book.' *Newscheck/ Careers Services Bulletin.* Roger Jones has himself worked abroad for many years and is a specialist writer on expatriate and employment matters.

272pp. illus. 1 85703 182 2. 4th edition.

HOW TO TEACH ABROAD
Your guide to opportunities worldwide

Roger Jones

This is a fully revised and re-set second edition, updated to reflect the many changes in the international teaching scene. 'An excellent book ... An exhaustive and practical coverage of the possibilities and practicalities of teaching overseas.' *The Escape Committee Newsletter.* 'An invaluable asset for anyone contemplating teaching abroad. Offers a great deal of very practical advice.' *Education.* 'A comprehensive guide – well set out and user friendly ... This is a useful, relatively cheap addition to any careers library, that I can recommend.' *Phoenix/Association of Graduate Careers Advisory Services.* Roger Jones has himself worked abroad in Austria, Cambodia, Thailand, Turkey and the Middle East. He is also author of *How to Get a Job Abroad* in this series.

192pp. illus. 1 85703 108 3. 2nd edition.

WORKING ON CONTRACT WORLDWIDE
How to triple your earnings by working as an independent contractor anywhere in the world

Rod Briggs

Working as a contractor in today's widening international skills market can bring enormous personal financial gain. Earnings can often be treble those of a normal staff salary. Contracting also offers a degree of personal development, professional variety and independence rarely possible in traditionally paid employment. This new book is the first to explain in practical steps how to break into the lucrative world of contracting. It explains what 'contracting' means, how to become a contractor yourself, how to cope with the professional, commercial and personal aspects of contracting – and how to maximise the opportunities it can offer. Intended originally for engineers, this book will in fact be invaluable for people in almost any profession or discipline. Rod Briggs has himself worked for over 25 years as a contractor in the UK, southern Africa, the Middle East and many countries in western Europe.

160pp. illus. 1 85703 429 5.

HOW TO SPEND A YEAR ABROAD
Taking time out from study or work

Nick Vandome

A year abroad is now a very popular option among thousands of school leavers, students, and people taking a mid-life break. This book sets out the numerous options available from making the decision to go, to working on a kibbutz, to teaching English as a foreign language, to adapting to life at home on your return. 'Should be required reading... Unlike most reference books this is one which should be read right through, and that is a pleasure as well as being very informative. It is totally comprehensive... very good value for money.' *The School Librarian.* 'Excellent.' *Careers Guidance Today.* Nick Vandome is a young freelance writer who has spent a year abroad on three occasions, in France, Australia, Africa and Asia. His articles have appeared in *The Guardian, The Scotsman, The Daily Telegraph* and elsewhere.

176pp. illus. 1 85703 070 2. 2nd edition.

FINDING A JOB IN CANADA
How and where to discover the well paid jobs and a great new lifestyle

Valerie Gerrard

Over 250,000 people a year emigrate to Canada. For many it offers a lifestyle that is uniquely appealing. Indeed, the United Nations recently declared Canada 'the best country in the world in which to live.' Living in Canada generally means finding employment there. This book outlines how to do just that. It is an up-to-date guide to the available opportunities and how to take advantage of them. It takes you step-by-step through the whole process of achiving permission to work, finding the job you want, landing that job and settling in. A graduate of the University of British Columbia, Valerie Gerrard is a Canadian with many years' experience of working in Canada, and personal experience of helping others to relocate there.

160pp. illus. 1 85703 404 X.

HOW TO GET A JOB IN AMERICA
A guide to employment opportunities and contacts

Roger Jones

Further updated and revised, this popular book helps you to turn your dream into reality by explaining the work possibilities open to non-US citizens. Drawing on the experiences of individuals, companies and recruitment agencies Roger Jones reveals the range of jobs available, the locations, pay and conditions, and how to get hired. The book includes the latest on immigration procedures following the 1990 US Immigration Act. This is an essential handbook for everyone planning to work in the US, whether on a short-term vacation assignment, on secondment or contract, or on a permanent basis. Roger Jones is a freelance author scecialising in careers and expatriate matters and has himself worked overseas. 'Essential for anyone who is thinking of working in the US.' *Going USA.* 'Outlines with some thoroughness the procedures a future immigrant or temporary resident would have to undertake... For young people considering a US exchange or summer vacation jobs is particularly worthwhile.' *Newscheck/ Careers Service Bulletin.* 'Very good value for money.' *School Librarian journal.*

224pp. illus. 1 85703 168 7. 3rd edition.

How To Books provide practical help on a large range of topics. They are available through all good bookshops or can be ordered direct from the distributors. Just tick the titles you want and complete the form on the following page.

___ Apply to an Industrial Tribunal (£7.99)
___ Applying for a Job (£7.99)
___ Applying for a United States Visa (£15.99)
___ Be a Freelance Journalist (£8.99)
___ Be a Freelance Secretary (£8.99)
___ Be a Local Councillor (£8.99)
___ Be an Effective School Governor (£9.99)
___ Become a Freelance Sales Agent (£9.99)
___ Become an Au Pair (£8.99)
___ Buy & Run a Shop (£8.99)
___ Buy & Run a Small Hotel (£8.99)
___ Cash from your Computer (£9.99)
___ Career Planning for Women (£8.99)
___ Choosing a Nursing Home (£8.99)
___ Claim State Benefits (£9.99)
___ Communicate at Work (£7.99)
___ Conduct Staff Appraisals (£7.99)
___ Conducting Effective Interviews (£8.99)
___ Copyright & Law for Writers (£8.99)
___ Counsel People at Work (£7.99)
___ Creating a Twist in the Tale (£8.99)
___ Creative Writing (£9.99)
___ Critical Thinking for Students (£8.99)
___ Do Voluntary Work Abroad (£8.99)
___ Do Your Own Advertising (£8.99)
___ Do Your Own PR (£8.99)
___ Doing Business Abroad (£9.99)
___ Emigrate (£9.99)
___ Employ & Manage Staff (£8.99)
___ Find Temporary Work Abroad (£8.99)
___ Finding a Job in Canada (£9.99)
___ Finding a Job in Computers (£8.99)
___ Finding a Job in New Zealand (£9.99)
___ Finding a Job with a Future (£8.99)
___ Finding Work Overseas (£9.99)
___ Freelance DJ-ing (£8.99)
___ Get a Job Abroad (£10.99)
___ Get a Job in America (£9.99)
___ Get a Job in Australia (£9.99)
___ Get a Job in Europe (£9.99)
___ Get a Job in France (£9.99)
___ Get a Job in Germany (£9.99)
___ Get a Job in Hotels and Catering (£8.99)
___ Get a Job in Travel & Tourism (£8.99)
___ Get into Films & TV (£8.99)
___ Get into Radio (£8.99)
___ Get That Job (£6.99)
___ Getting your First Job (£8.99)
___ Going to University (£8.99)
___ Helping your Child to Read (£8.99)
___ Investing in People (£8.99)
___ Invest in Stocks & Shares (£8.99)

___ Keep Business Accounts (£7.99)
___ Know Your Rights at Work (£8.99)
___ Know Your Rights: Teachers (£6.99)
___ Live & Work in America (£9.99)
___ Live & Work in Australia (£12.99)
___ Live & Work in Germany (£9.99)
___ Live & Work in Greece (£9.99)
___ Live & Work in Italy (£8.99)
___ Live & Work in New Zealand (£9.99)
___ Live & Work in Portugal (£9.99)
___ Live & Work in Spain (£7.99)
___ Live & Work in the Gulf (£9.99)
___ Living & Working in Britain (£8.99)
___ Living & Working in China (£9.99)
___ Living & Working in Hong Kong (£10.99)
___ Living & Working in Israel (£10.99)
___ Living & Working in Japan (£8.99)
___ Living & Working in Saudi Arabia (£12.99)
___ Living & Working in the Netherlands (£9.99)
___ Lose Weight & Keep Fit (£6.99)
___ Make a Wedding Speech (£7.99)
___ Making a Complaint (£8.99)
___ Manage a Sales Team (£8.99)
___ Manage an Office (£8.99)
___ Manage Computers at Work (£8.99)
___ Manage People at Work (£8.99)
___ Manage Your Career (£8.99)
___ Managing Budgets & Cash Flows (£9.99)
___ Managing Meetings (£8.99)
___ Managing Your Personal Finances (£8.99)
___ Market Yourself (£8.99)
___ Master Book-Keeping (£8.99)
___ Mastering Business English (£8.99)
___ Master GCSE Accounts (£8.99)
___ Master Languages (£8.99)
___ Master Public Speaking (£8.99)
___ Obtaining Visas & Work Permits (£9.99)
___ Organising Effective Training (£9.99)
___ Pass Exams Without Anxiety (£7.99)
___ Pass That Interview (£6.99)
___ Plan a Wedding (£7.99)
___ Prepare a Business Plan (£8.99)
___ Publish a Book (£9.99)
___ Publish a Newsletter (£9.99)
___ Raise Funds & Sponsorship (£7.99)
___ Rent & Buy Property in France (£9.99)
___ Rent & Buy Property in Italy (£9.99)
___ Retire Abroad (£8.99)
___ Return to Work (£7.99)
___ Run a Local Campaign (£6.99)
___ Run a Voluntary Group (£8.99)
___ Sell Your Business (£9.99)

How To Books

- Selling into Japan (£14.99)
- Setting up Home in Florida (£9.99)
- Spend a Year Abroad (£8.99)
- Start a Business from Home (£7.99)
- Start a New Career (£6.99)
- Starting to Manage (£8.99)
- Starting to Write (£8.99)
- Start Word Processing (£8.99)
- Start Your Own Business (£8.99)
- Study Abroad (£8.99)
- Study & Learn (£7.99)
- Study & Live in Britain (£7.99)
- Studying at University (£8.99)
- Studying for a Degree (£8.99)
- Successful Grandparenting (£8.99)
- Successful Mail Order Marketing (£9.99)
- Successful Single Parenting (£8.99)
- Survive at College (£4.99)
- Survive Divorce (£8.99)
- Surviving Redundancy (£8.99)
- Take Care of Your Heart (£5.99)
- Taking in Students (£8.99)
- Taking on Staff (£8.99)
- Taking Your A-Levels (£8.99)
- Teach Abroad (£8.99)
- Teach Adults (£8.99)
- Teaching Someone to Drive (£8.99)
- Travel Round the World (£8.99)
- Use a Library (£6.99)
- Use the Internet (£9.99)
- Winning Consumer Competitions (£8.99)
- Winning Presentations (£8.99)
- Work from Home (£8.99)
- Work in an Office (£7.99)
- Work in Retail (£8.99)
- Work with Dogs (£8.99)
- Working Abroad (£14.99)
- Working as a Holiday Rep (£9.99)
- Working in Japan (£10.99)
- Working in Photography (£8.99)
- Working in the Gulf (£10.99)
- Working on Contract Worldwide (£9.99)
- Working on Cruise Ships (£9.99)
- Write a CV that Works (£7.99)
- Write a Press Release (£9.99)
- Write a Report (£8.99)
- Write an Assignment (£8.99)
- Write an Essay (£7.99)
- Write & Sell Computer Software (£9.99)
- Write Business Letters (£8.99)
- Write for Publication (£8.99)
- Write for Television (£8.99)
- Write Your Dissertation (£8.99)
- Writing a Non Fiction Book (£8.99)
- Writing & Selling a Novel (£8.99)
- Writing & Selling Short Stories (£8.99)
- Writing Reviews (£8.99)
- Your Own Business in Europe (£12.99)

To: Plymbridge Distributors Ltd, Plymbridge House, Estover Road, Plymouth PL6 7PZ. Customer Services Tel: (01752) 202301. Fax: (01752) 202331.

Please send me copies of the titles I have indicated. Please add postage & packing (UK £1, Europe including Eire, £2, World £3 airmail).

☐ I enclose cheque/PO payable to Plymbridge Distributors Ltd for £

☐ Please charge to my ☐ MasterCard, ☐ Visa, ☐ AMEX card.

Account No.

Card Expiry Date ___ 19 ☎ Credit Card orders may be faxed or phoned.

Customer Name (CAPITALS) ....

Address ....

.... Postcode ....

Telephone........................... Signature ....

Every effort will be made to despatch your copy as soon as possible but to avoid possible disappointment please allow up to 21 days for despatch time (42 days if overseas). Prices and availability are subject to change without notice. CODE BPA